IMAGES
of America

CIMARRÓN AND PHILMONT

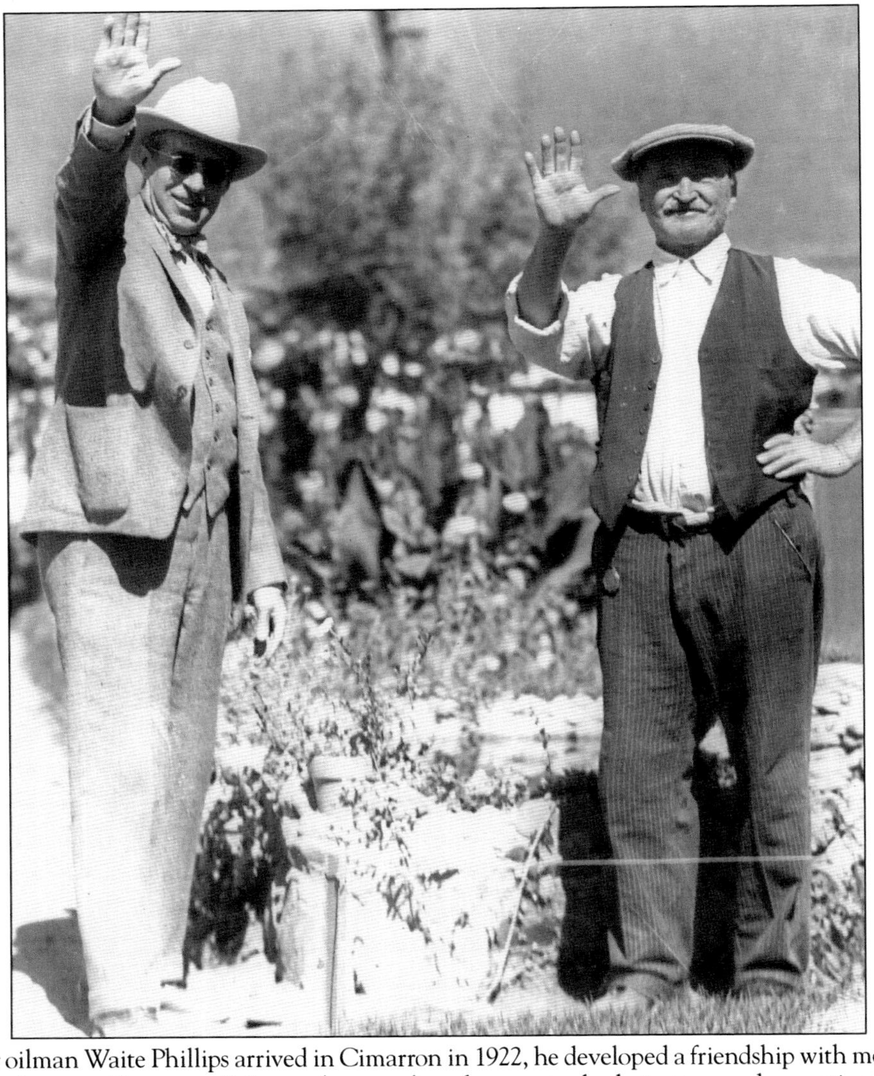

After oilman Waite Phillips arrived in Cimarron in 1922, he developed a friendship with mercantile owner Lorenzo "Lawrence" Rosso that was based on mutual admiration and an active business relationship. The Philmont Ranch contracted with Rosso's Cimarron Mercantile Company to have acres of apples harvested and marketed and to supply the ranch with farm supplies and equipment. Phillips immersed himself in local lore even as he collected historical artifacts for his spectacular Villa Philmonte. He was interested in learning as much as possible about the history of Cimarron and the Philmont lands. In an October 1935 letter to Fred Lambert, Phillips writes, "While on the ranch this summer someone told me about an old history of the Rayado Ranch and fort over there . . . I would like to have any old documents that tell the romantic history of the country and I shall hope to have the opportunity of discussing these things with you the next time I come out." In large measure, Phillips's gift of Philmont Scout Ranch has perpetuated an interest in the history of Cimarron. (Philmont Scout Ranch.)

On the Cover: Hotelier Henry Lambert (arms folded) and a curious assortment of his friends and family stand against the north facade of his St. James Hotel during a patriotic celebration around 1905. Lambert's saloon, restaurant, and 43 rooms were witnesses to at least 26 murders, most committed in "self defense," during Cimarron's wilder days. (Lambert family.)

IMAGES
of America

CIMARRÓN AND PHILMONT

Randall M. MacDonald, Gene Lamm,
and Sarah E. MacDonald

ARCADIA
PUBLISHING

ISBN 978-0-7385-9527-6

Published by Arcadia Publishing
Charleston, South Carolina

Printed in the United States of America

Library of Congress Control Number: 2011943058

For all general information, please contact Arcadia Publishing:
Telephone 843-853-2070
Fax 843-853-0044
E-mail sales@arcadiapublishing.com
For customer service and orders:
Toll-Free 1-888-313-2665

Visit us on the Internet at www.arcadiapublishing.com

To the people of New Mexico on the 100th anniversary of statehood

RMM: To Kevin Malcolm Farrell, John Herbert Thomas Farrell, and Maximilian Colby Farrell, with the hope that their New Mexico adventures will be wondrous and life-affirming.

GL: To Bill and Cathryn, for remembering.

SEM: To Alex Klausing.

Contents

Acknowledgments		6
Introduction		7
1.	Prehistory	9
2.	Maxwell's Ranche	17
3.	The Colfax County War	27
4.	The Railroad Era	41
5.	New Town	55
6.	Neighboring Communities	75
7.	Ranching	91
8.	Philmont	105
Bibliography		127

Acknowledgments

The histories of Cimarron and Philmont can scarcely be told in so slender a volume as this. Our purpose in these pages is to provide a glimpse into the lives of those who have made Cimarron a unique community and those who have hiked the trails and loved the land and people of Philmont. To the extent we have succeeded, we owe a great deal to the generosity of others.

This project would not have materialized without the invaluable assistance of those who shared materials, time, expertise, and memories. We are most appreciative of Mark Anderson, John Clark, Paul Grasse, Bryan Hayek, Nancy Klein, Shelley O'Neill, and Robin Tate Taylor of Philmont Scout Ranch; Mark Griffin, David K. Park, and Heidi Steppe of the Boy Scouts of America; Linda Davis and the CS Ranch; Andy Wahll of The Old Mill; Thayla Wright of the Arthur Johnson Memorial Library; Roger Sanchez of the Raton Museum; Anita "Annie" McDaniel of the Taos Historic Museums; Debbie Lang of Eastern New Mexico University; Daisy Njoku of the National Anthropological Archives, Smithsonian Institution; Gretchen Sammis of the Chase Ranch; Steve Boyce and Mike Hobbs of the Express UU Bar Ranch; Patricia Hewitt of the New Mexico History Museum; Daniel Kosharek of the Palace of the Governors Photo Archives; Holly Bennett and Nora Galbraith of Florida Southern College; María E. Montoya; Nancy Brown-Martinez and Mike Kelly, Center for Southwest Research, University of New Mexico; Sara Henderson White and Fred Woodward, University Press of Kansas; and Rebecca Wells, University of California Press.

We extend our gratitude to these friends, acquaintances, and colleagues who provided material assistance and encouragement: Sue Bohlen-Butler, Tracy Boyce, Brent Clark, Todd Conklin, Henry Cruz, Sandy and Larry Danna, Kathy Hoy Eltiste, Jane Garcia, Nicole Georgeff, Donald Gumaer, Lorraine Gutierrez, Vicky Harper, Steve Hentzelman, the Hickman family, Alex Klausing, Fred and Rosie Lambert, Lucille Langemann, Luann Lorence, Marge Martin, Roberta McKeegan, Liz and Craig Painter, Martin Pavletich, Emma and Lento Rosso, Mike Rosso, Randy Saunders, Ed Sitzberger, Julia Davis Stafford, Grethe Ullrich, Kathy Veit, Phil Wehman, SaraLou and Steve Wilkerson, Mariah Williamson, Eric Young, and Shari and Stephen Zimmer. As always, Arcadia Publishing has been wonderful to work with, from our initial correspondence with Jared Jackson to the cheerful guidance of Lauren Hummer, Kristie Kelly, and Catherine Hodges.

Special appreciation goes to Susan Priest MacDonald and to Constance Marsh MacDonald and Malcolm M. MacDonald.

This project has been of intense personal interest and started to take shape over 20 years ago. All three of us have served on the seasonal staff of Philmont Scout Ranch, and we have returned many times. Cimarron and Philmont hold a special place for us, just as they do for so many others, and we look forward to seeing what comes next, as the stories of both unfold.

Introduction

On a late afternoon in the summer of 1706, Gen. Juan de Ulibarrí and his 140 man–strong contingent of soldiers, settlers, and Indians approached a group of unknown natives beside a rather large but pleasant river. Ulibarrí had been charged with returning a group of Picuris Indians who had fled to Colorado a decade earlier. The general's diary for July 21 would record the first meeting between Europeans and members of the Jicarilla Apache tribe, as well as the first entry of Europeans into the Cimarron Valley. Ulibarrí named the stream the Río de Santa Maria Magdalena. Thirteen years later, in early fall, Gov. Antonio Valverde and 500 men would take a similar route to confront warring Utes and Comanches in southeastern Colorado. To the river of "La Jicarilla," Valverde gave the name *Nuestra Señora del Rosario*; the Apaches simply called it La Flecha, or "the arrow." By 1800, the river was known as the Cimarrón, Spanish for "wild" or "untamed," now usually written without the accent mark. It has been suggested that the name originated from a description of the indigenous sheep or runaway horses in the area, but a more likely explanation can be found in the geological history of the region outlined in chapter one.

The natives whom Ulibarrí and his compatriots encountered along the Cimarron Valley were not the first inhabitants to flourish here. As the last ice age waned 20,000 years ago, mammoth and mastodon crossed over the then-dry Bering Strait into Alaska in search of greener pastures. Prehistoric Siberian hunters in search of food and clothing followed these prey during their migration south along the front range of the Rockies. Evidence of these early Americans was unknown until 1908 when ranch foreman George McJunkin, the son of slaves, observed ancient bison bones eroding out of an arroyo 50 miles northeast of Cimarron. When the site was investigated in 1926, a unique, fluted arrowhead was discovered adjacent to the bones. The culture that created the 10,000-year-old artifact was named after Folsom man. A few years later, southern New Mexico produced projectiles from the slightly older culture of Clovis man. These Paleoamericans were the earliest inhabitants of the Cimarron area. Eventually, the culture of Folsom man evolved into what we recognize as the Anasazi or Ancestral Pueblo culture, whose people built the ancient pit houses and adobe structures found throughout the Southwest. They lived in the area from about 400 to 1300 and left a record of their dwellings along the Ponil Creek on the Philmont Scout Ranch. By 1400, they were replaced by the sedentary Jicarilla Apaches and Moache Utes of Ulibarrí's time and the nomadic Comanche and Cheyenne Indians of the Plains.

Following the Louisiana Purchase in 1803 and Lewis and Clark's exploration of this newly acquired land, the lure of riches beyond the Missouri River proved irresistible to many. The first to venture west across the "Great American Desert" were trapping parties sent by French, American, and British fur companies to the Rockies and the Northwest. Pelts were shipped back east along the Platte and Arkansas Rivers to Kansas or south to the Spanish border town of Taos. Some of these trappers found life easier as traders, serving as middlemen between those who hunted and those who purchased pelts. However, few merchants ventured deep into New Spain owing to severe trade restrictions with its northern neighbor—few, that is, until Missouri trader William

Becknell, 17 men, and a pack mule train left Franklin, Missouri, in September 1821 for the purpose of "trading for Horses and Mules, and catching Wild Animals of every description."

Since spring, rumors had spread that Mexicans were eager to gain their independence from Spain; were this to happen, the road to Santa Fe would be opened for trade. Mexico did declare independence, and Becknell and his party entered Santa Fe in mid-November. Their route followed the Arkansas River west to present-day La Junta, Colorado, before turning south over Raton Pass, skirting the future site of Cimarron, and bending around the Southern Rockies into Santa Fe. Upon arrival, Becknell traded the goods he had obtained along the way for Mexican wares before returning to Missouri. The following year, Becknell took a much larger party along a slightly different route that avoided the difficult climb over Raton Pass and shortened the journey by several days but crossed land more prone to Indian raids and with limited water. Both routes would be followed, with trappers using the Cimarron Canyon as a shortcut to Taos and traders traveling south on to Santa Fe. The original longer path is referred to as the Mountain Route; the shorter is known as the Cimarron Cutoff, after the Kansas town where it leaves the Arkansas River.

The history of Cimarron as a village begins with the Santa Fe Trail and threads its way through the award and sale of an enormous land grant, the discovery of gold and coal, the arrival and demise of a railroad with its lumber and cattle industries, the creation of a "New Town" adjacent to but preserving an "Old Town," the disappearance of once flourishing communities, and the breakup and consolidation of land into large ranches. Throughout all this, the populace was subjected to the Mexican-American, Civil, Indian, and Colfax County Wars. In short, the story of Cimarron mirrors that of the entire West.

Today, ranching, tourism, and the nearby Philmont Scout Ranch are mainstays of the Cimarron economy. The National Park Service Santa Fe Trail Site along Highway 64 and the Walking Tour of Old Town introduce visitors to the rich history of the area where the St. James Hotel, Old Jail, The Old Mill museum, and local cemetery are visible reminders of what once was. Each summer, over 23,000 campers visit the Philmont Scout Ranch to hike the rugged country once teeming with trappers and prospectors. Philmont's interpretive backcountry camps are based on different aspects of Cimarron history and provide a unique educational experience for the Scouts. Visitors to the ranch can tour the Philmont Museum and Seton Memorial Library, the Villa Philmonte, and the Kit Carson Museum in the Rancho Rayado Historic District for additional historical insight into Cimarron and the surrounding area. Finally, not to be missed are day trips to nearby Eagle Nest and Elizabethtown, reached by following the old rail bed through spectacular Cimarron Canyon, as well as the nearby Dawson Cemetery.

One

Prehistory

Three hundred million years ago, Earth's continental land masses collided into a single supercontinent called Pangaea. One result of this was an uplift in the interior of Pangaea called the Ancestral Rocky Mountains, located almost precisely where the Rocky Mountains are today. Presumably about the same time, a weakening of the continental crust occurred along a line stretching from southern Arizona to northeastern New Mexico known as the Jemez Lineament. By 70 million years ago, the ancient mountains had eroded and been replaced by a vast inland sea, stretching from the Gulf of Mexico to the Arctic Ocean.

Over the next five million years, the present-day Rockies were uplifted, slowly replacing the sea with a lush tropical landscape. Dinosaurs thrived in this new environment, but their time was brief. An asteroid struck the earth near the Yucatan peninsula, and the resulting ash cloud cooled the planet sufficiently to kill off the largest of these reptiles. These events have been recorded by the only known T. rex footprint as well as an iridium deposition layer resulting from the asteroid collision, both discovered in the mid-1980s just a few miles north of Cimarron.

The southernmost range of the Rocky Mountains is called the Sangre de Cristo Mountains, or "Blood of Christ," and comprises the Taos and Cimarron Ranges, separated by Moreno Valley. Initially, the valley drained south through Cieneguilla Creek, but about eight million years ago, a string of volcanoes along the weak Jemez Lineament erupted resulting in blockage of the valley. With the valley now landlocked, waters within it rose. Eventually, one of the rivers eroding the eastern flank of the Sangre de Cristos cut through a weakened rock wall, draining Moreno Valley and releasing a torrent of water like an arrow onto the Eastern Plains. After every spring thaw or thunderous summer downpour, this unruly river would deluge the surrounding countryside. This was the Cimarron: wild and untamed. The spectacular canyon that the river has carved is now a state park, popular for its camping and fishing opportunities as well as its geological formations such as the impressive Palisades Sill.

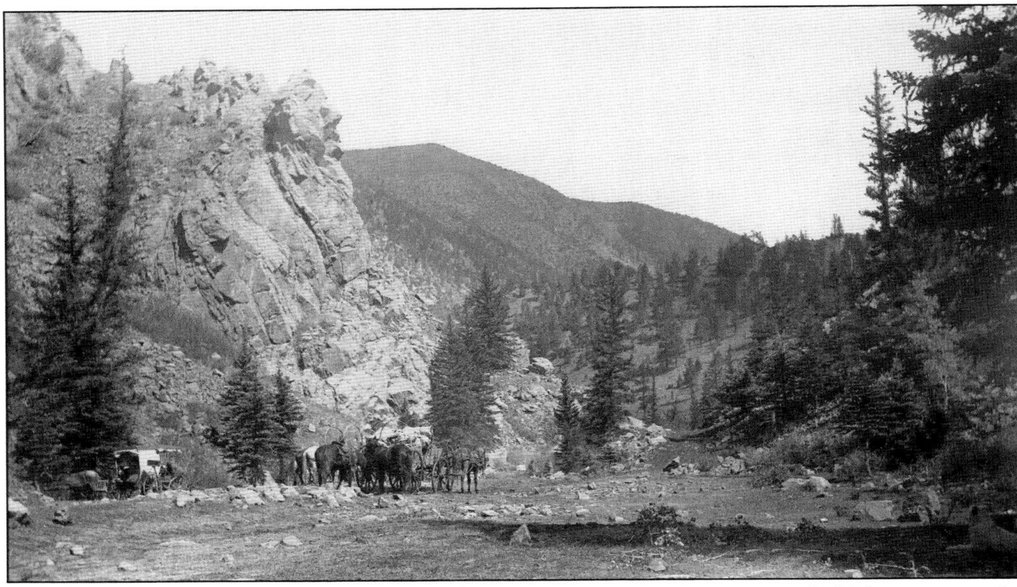

This 1904 photograph by Raton photographer Thomas Fitzsimmons entitled "Gateway to the Cimarron Cañon" shows several wagons and horse teams against an inhospitable but beautiful backdrop. Fitzsimmons produced many photographs illustrating the natural wonders of Colfax County, and a number were reproduced as postcards for Raton shops. Several feature the dog shown in the foreground at the lower right and other figures to highlight the scale of the canyon. (Authors' collection.)

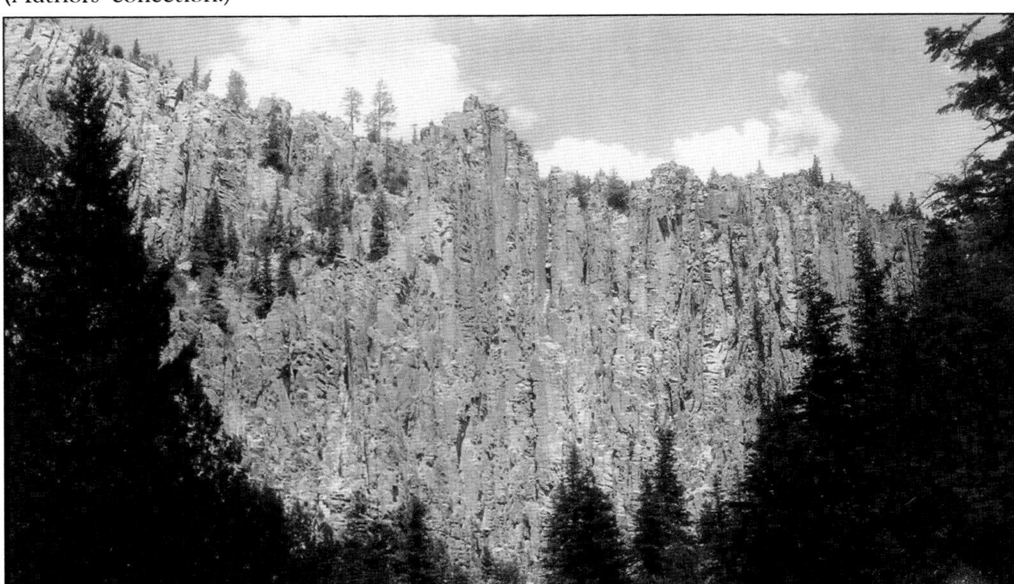

The sheer Palisades Sill—estimated to be between 26 million and 34.7 million years old—is visible on the north side of US Highway 64 in Cimarron Canyon State Park. The sill is an igneous rock body that formed from volcanic activity underground and intruded between older rock beds. Climbing the Palisades is generally prohibited, but nearby Maverick Cliff and Probe 1 Cliff are developed sandstone crags. (Authors' collection.)

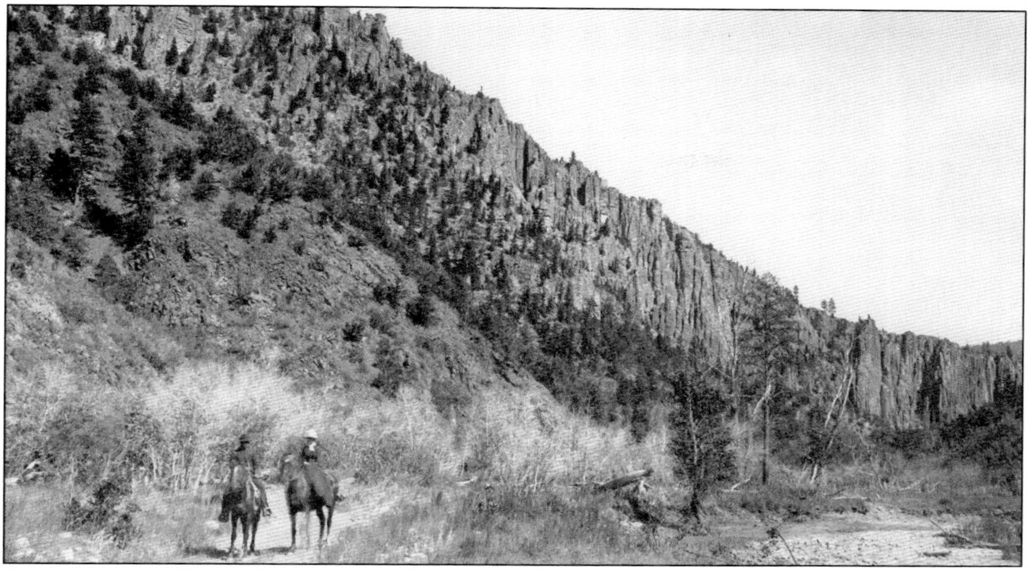

A circuitous pathway through the Cimarron Canyon was improved into the principal travel route from Cimarron westward after gold was discovered on Baldy Mountain in 1866, and the road carried stagecoach passengers to and from Springer during an 1890s mining revival. Here, a couple on horseback passes the Palisades along what became Route 33, formed a section of US Route 485 in 1927, and became part of familiar US Highway 64 in 1931, here later known as Highway of the Immortals. (The Old Mill.)

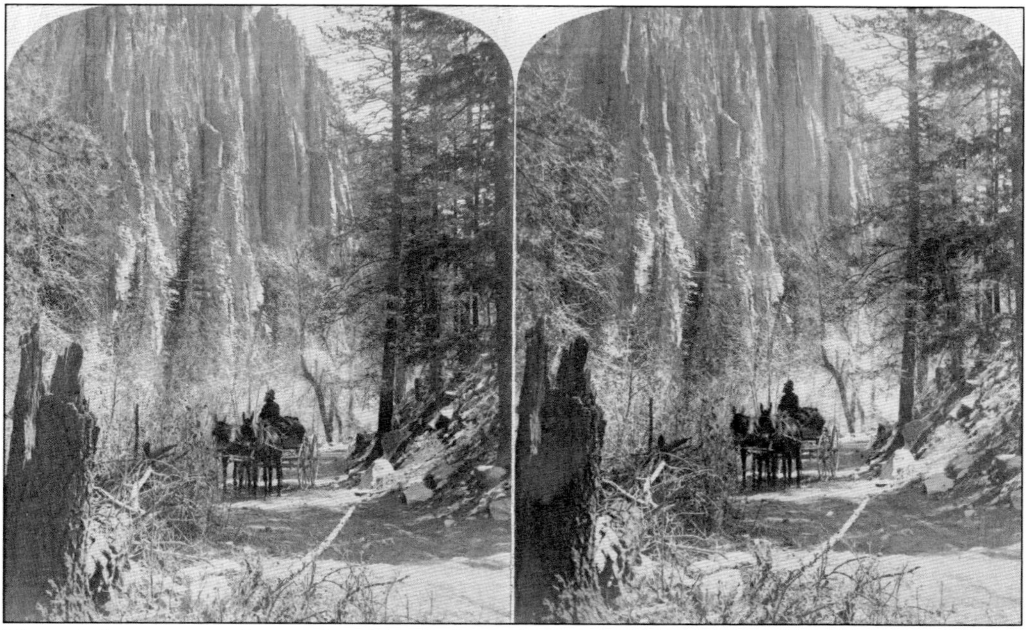

Most of the stereographs produced by acclaimed photographer Byron H. Gurnsey (1833–1880) document the natural landscape of 1870s Colorado. This undated stereograph identified as the "Cimarron Cañon" and published as part of Gurnsey's Rocky Mountain Views series is one of a small number depicting New Mexico scenes. This perspective of the Palisades is unmistakable and is familiar to drivers headed east through the canyon today. (Authors' collection.)

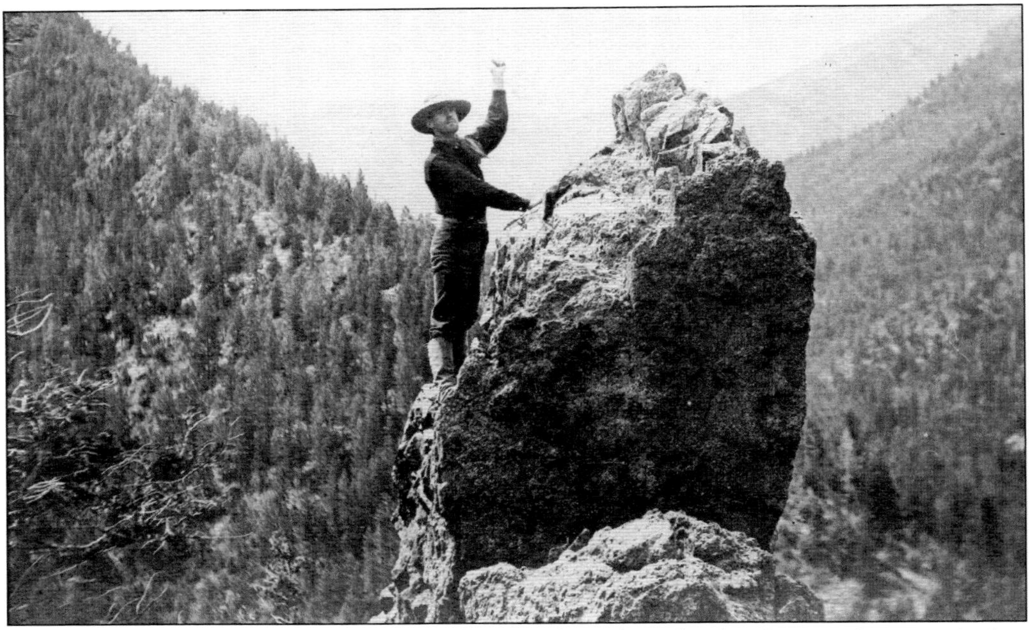

This dramatic view purports to show Mailbox Rock at the Palisades. It is not known whether this is the same protrusion known as the Devil's Mailbox atop the Palisades that is visible from the Palisades Sill roadside parking area (N 36° 32.253 W 105° 09.146). It certainly could be part of that formation, which is hundreds of feet above the canyon floor and Cimarron River. (Raton Museum.)

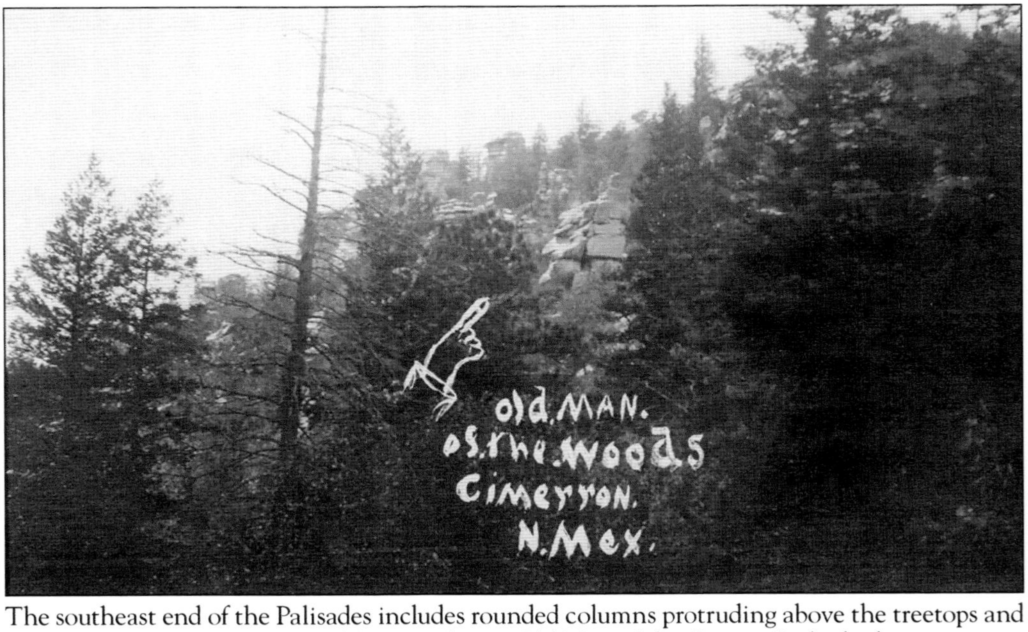

The southeast end of the Palisades includes rounded columns protruding above the treetops and a feature known as "Old Man of the Woods" or "Old Man of the Canyon," which also appears on Albertype postcards and c. 1900 stereographs. Immediately east of the Palisades, the enormous formation identified in one c. 1910–1930 postcard image as "Mother Grundy" rests precariously on a slope high above the north side of the highway. (Troutman Studio, authors' collection.)

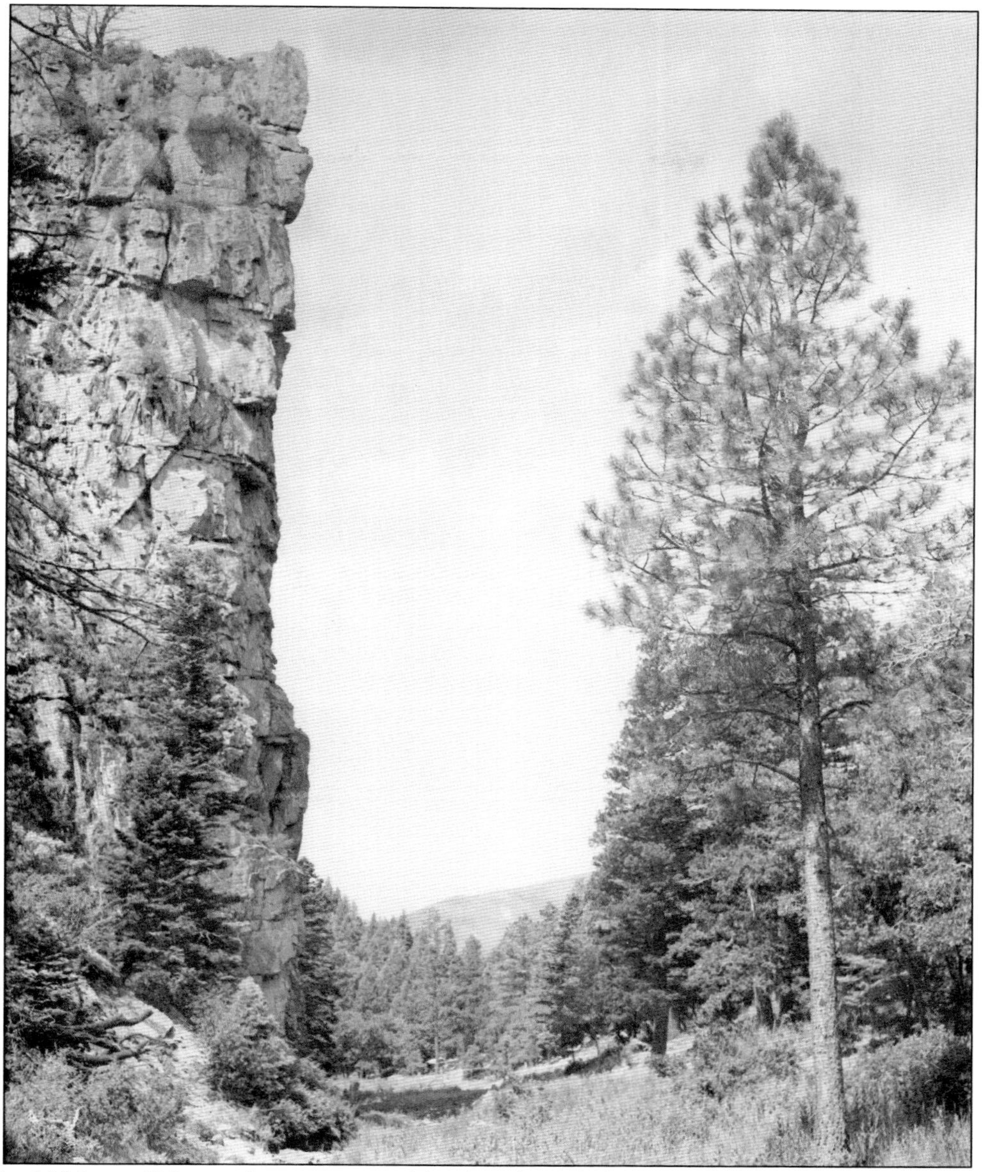

The 256-foot-tall Lovers Leap is a signal landmark of Philmont's south country. Composed of light-colored porphyritic dacite, the feature is similar geologically to Cathedral Rock and to the Palisades in Cimarron Canyon. Campfire stories tell of a forlorn Native American couple who leapt to their deaths from the precipice, eternally united, but the true origin of the name is more difficult to discern. It certainly predates Waite Phillips's ownership; this photograph is from as early as 1890 when Lovers Leap was on Francis Clutton's Urraca Ranch. One romantic tale is known to be true: John James "Jack" (1858–1947) and Gertrude Hastings Sisson Nairn (1860–1924) purchased land from George Webster Jr. a mile east of Lovers Leap in 1910. There, they built an elegant hacienda known today as Casa del Gavilan, a delightful bed-and-breakfast. Sadly, Gertrude predeceased her husband by many years. He kept her ashes on a mantel in their home, and following his death, his friends buried their ashes together near the base of Lovers Leap. (The Old Mill.)

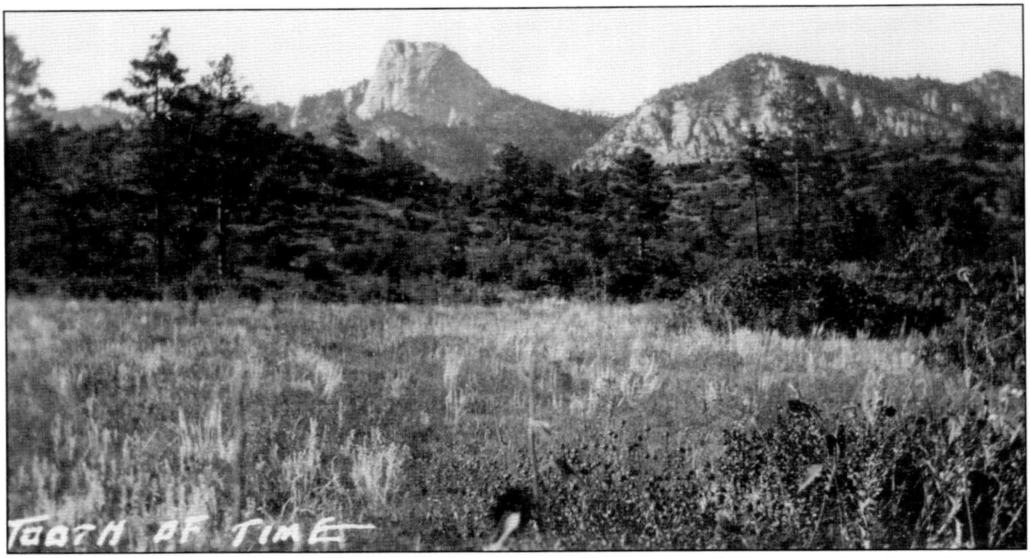

Travelers heading south along the Santa Fe Trail were seven days from Santa Fe when they saw the Tooth of Time rising above the plains. Scouts recognize it as "an igneous intrusion of dacite porphyry formed in the Tertiary period of the Cenozoic era," and its likeness is found on belt buckles and other Philmont keepsakes. This undated photograph appears to have been taken from the present-day Urraca Trail. (The Old Mill.)

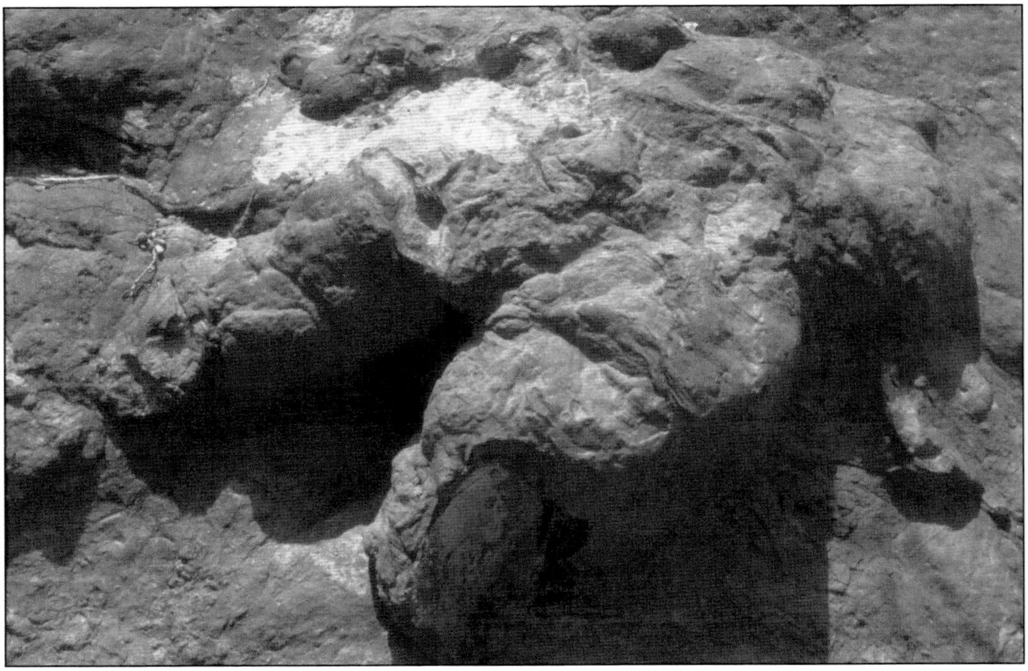

Of all the creatures which once roamed the earth, the most fascinating to young boys is that terrifying carnivore *Tyrannosaurus rex*. The only definitive footprint of this dinosaur was discovered along Ponil Creek by geologist Charles Pillmore in 1983, pressed into a muddy shallow over 65 million years ago. This site on Philmont Scout Ranch is usually visited by Scouts whose first night in the wilderness is at nearby Anasazi Camp. (The Old Mill.)

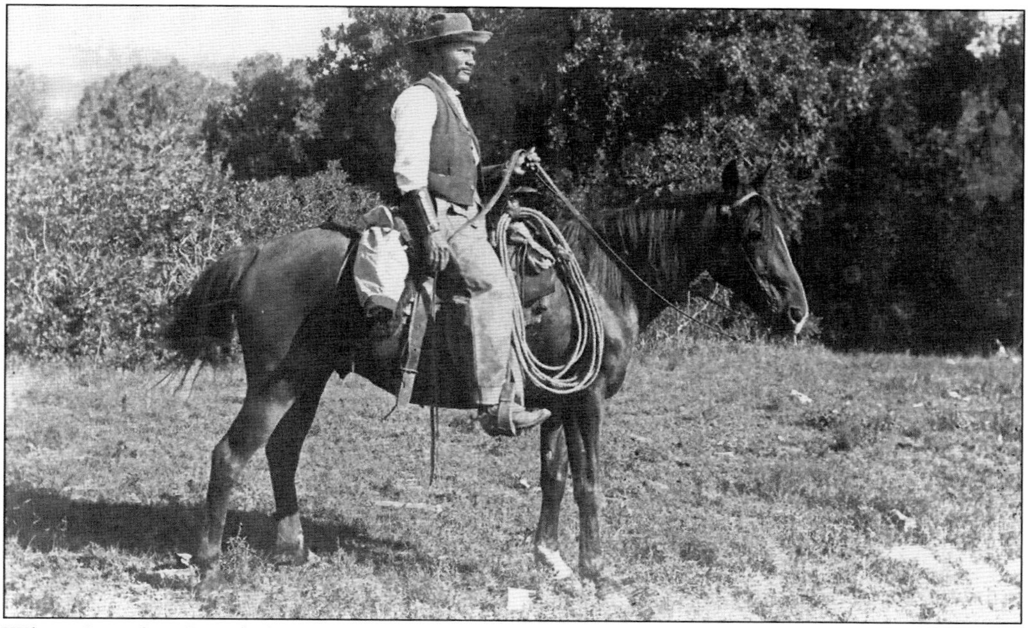

When Crowfoot Ranch foreman George McJunkin discovered extremely large bison bones near Folsom, he mentioned this to two Raton businessmen. Unfortunately, McJunkin died in 1922, just a few months before Carl Schwachheim and Fred Howarth investigated the now-famous "bone pit" where 11,000 year-old "Folsom point" artifacts were later uncovered. These discoveries gave birth to American archeology. (Eastern New Mexico University Golden Library Special Collections.)

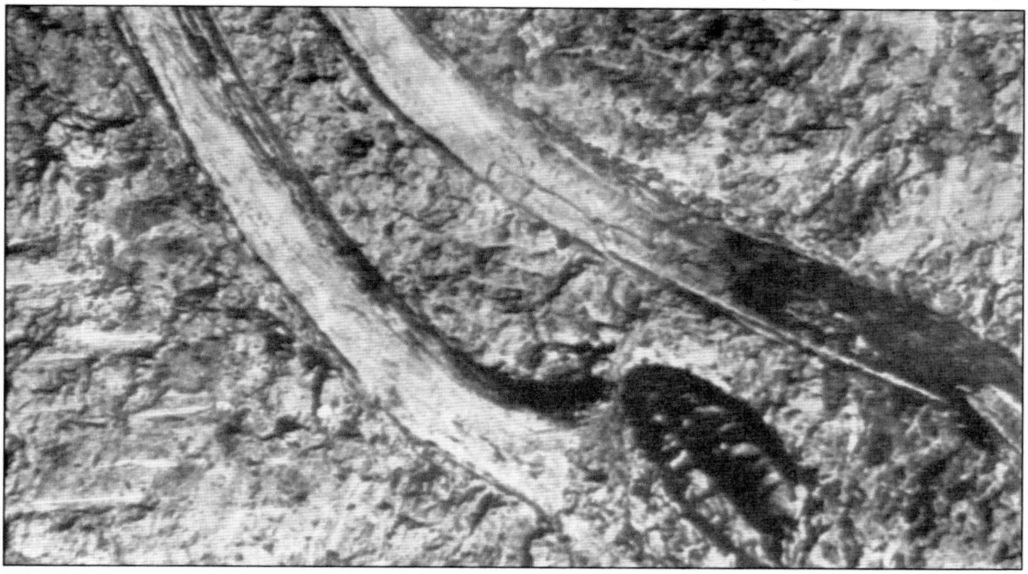

The Folsom Point was unique among ancient artifacts because of the fluting, or shallow groove, chipped lengthwise along the point (the dark object between the bones). Previous points, such as those found in France, showed no such design element. Because fluting tends to yield a broken and thus useless flake, the introduction of this technology into early American cultures is deemed important and has been called the first American invention, although its specific purpose is not yet known. (Eastern New Mexico University Golden Library Special Collections.)

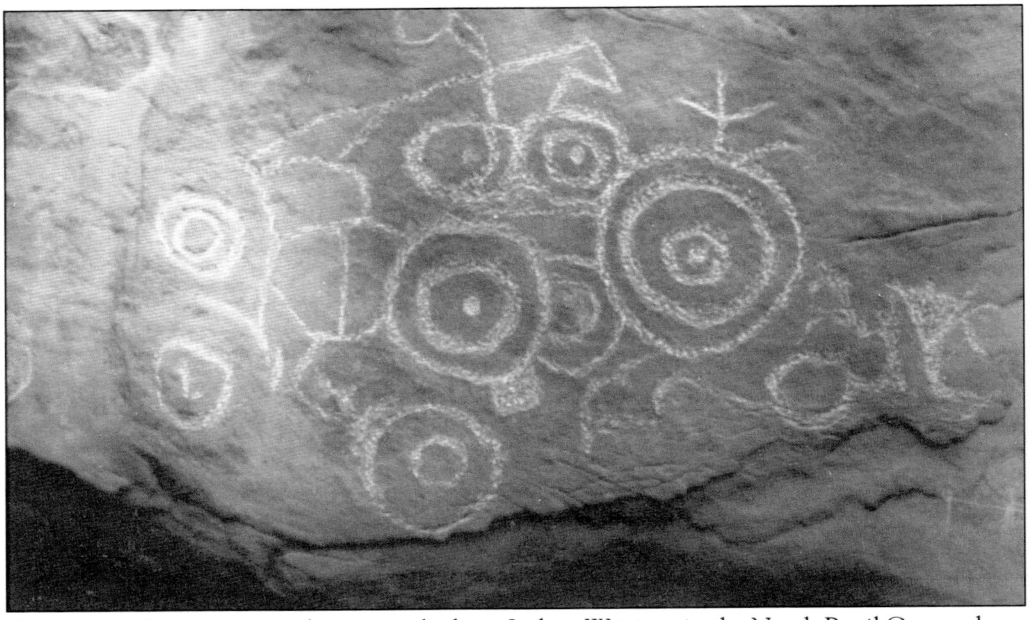

These and other Anasazi Indian petroglyphs at Indian Writings in the North Ponil Canyon have fascinated Scouts for decades since this 1939 photograph. An archaeological program was initiated at Indian Writings in 1956, and the camp once known as Scribblins has been memorialized in the "Philmont Ranger Song." The site presently includes pit house, slab house, and burial site excavations. (Philmont Scout Ranch.)

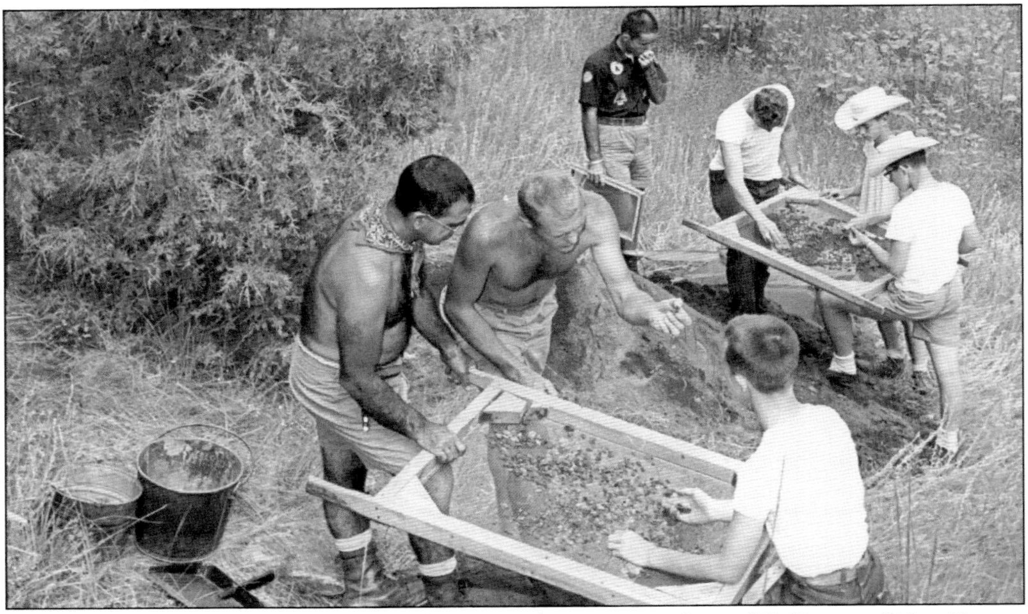

These late-1950s campers follow in the footsteps of scoutmaster Samuel D. Bogan of New Haven, Connecticut, and Philturn guide Billy Wetsel, who led six Scouts on the Philturn Archaeological Expedition in 1941. Their expedition was documented in a contemporaneous typescript journal and in the 1946 book *Let the Coyotes Howl: A Story of Philmont Scout Ranch*, both authored by Bogan. (Philmont Scout Ranch.)

Two

Maxwell's Ranche

In 1826, a 17-year-old Missouri runaway caught a wagon train to Santa Fe before wintering in Taos. He spent the next year alternating jobs as teamster, cook, or interpreter. The following year, the youth accompanied Ewing Young, who had been a member of Becknell's first expedition, on a trapping party to California. The young man's name was Christopher "Kit" Carson. Many others would venture west as Carson did and learn to survive in the vast wilderness. Some chose new paths westward—to California, Oregon, or Utah—but those would serve migrations of people, not commerce. For 60 years, until the advent of the railroad, the Santa Fe Trail guided a young nation's quest for wealth and adventure. Sometime in the early 1840s, Carson met Lucien Bonaparte Maxwell, a fellow trapper, and the two became close friends. During a stay at Carson's home in Taos, Maxwell was introduced to Luz Beaubien, the daughter of prominent businessman Charles Beaubien, and the two were soon married. Maxwell and Carson would later serve together as hunter and guide on John C. Frémont's western expeditions.

After Texas declared independence in 1836, Anglo encroachment became a serious concern for Mexican officials. To stem the tide of immigrants, Mexico, as had Spain before it, awarded land grants to individuals who would settle the land—construct permanent structures, grow crops, build towns, pacify Indians—and keep the Anglos at bay. In 1841, Beaubien and Guadalupe Miranda were awarded a grant of land east of Taos. When Beaubien's only son was killed during the Taos Revolt of 1847, the job of managing the grant fell to his son-in-law. Shortly thereafter, Maxwell and Carson moved across the mountains from Taos to settle along Rayado Creek. This site on the Santa Fe Trail offered a good source of water and provided a convenient route over to Taos. Ten years later, probably during a severe drought, Maxwell and Carson moved to a small settlement 11 miles north beside the Cimarron River. When a gristmill was built to provide flour for local settlers, soldiers, and Indians, "Maxwell's Ranche" became an important stop along the trail.

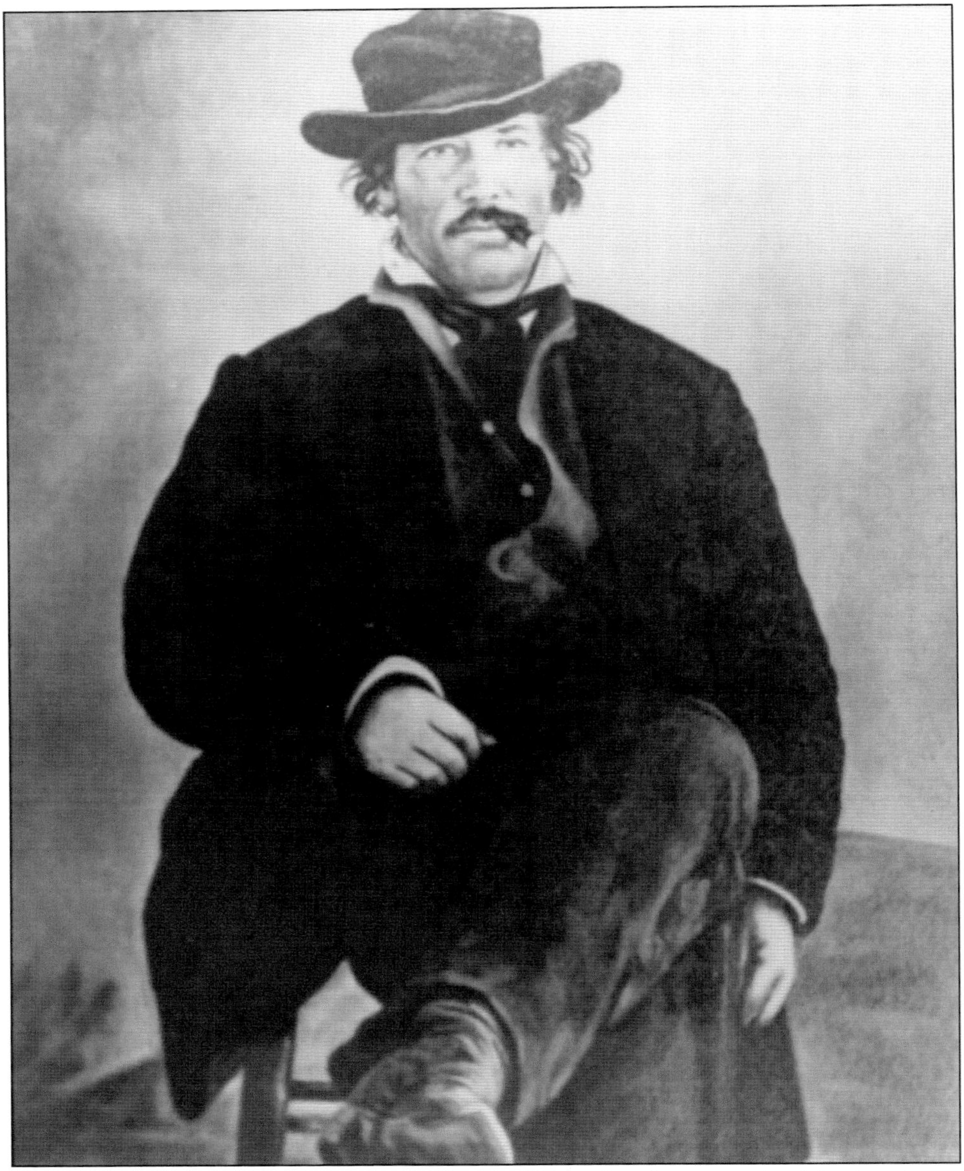

Lucien B. Maxwell was born in 1818 to a well-to-do Illinois family just south of the frontier town of St. Louis. An early youth spent trapping, trading, and scouting through the West with Kit Carson provided him with the tools to handle most situations. But management of his father-in-law's 1,714,465-acre land grant was fraught with problems. During Maxwell's tenure, from 1847 to 1870, Plains Indians raided livestock, prolonged drought dried up water sources, and the discovery of gold led to an influx of undesirables. Yet, through it all, Maxwell's control was as firm as his handshake, and the grant prospered. When Carson died in 1868 and a railroad survey foreshadowed encroachment on his land, Maxwell must have thought it time to cash in. He was no longer young and by then had bought out Beaubien's heirs for the land he had not inherited. After the Civil War, few Americans were wealthy, so the grant was sold to British investors for $1,350,000. Maxwell used the proceeds to buy abandoned Fort Sumner, where, in 1875, after an extraordinary life, he died. (Arthur Johnson Memorial Library.)

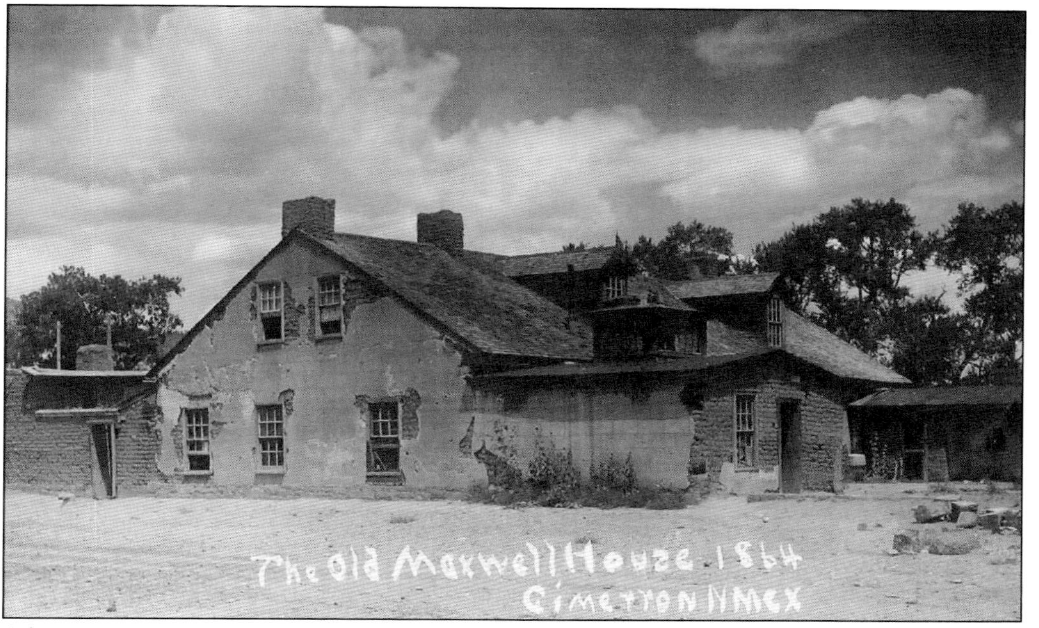

After moving to Cimarron in 1857, Maxwell managed his extensive land holdings from a lavish home at what is now the northeast corner of South Collinson Avenue (after English grant investor John Collinson) and Sixteenth Street, north of the St. James Hotel. This c. 1910 Troutman Studio photograph shows the guest quarters after a 1906 fire destroyed the private family rooms; a second fire in 1924 destroyed the rest. (George Seward Gumaer Collection, Donald Gumaer.)

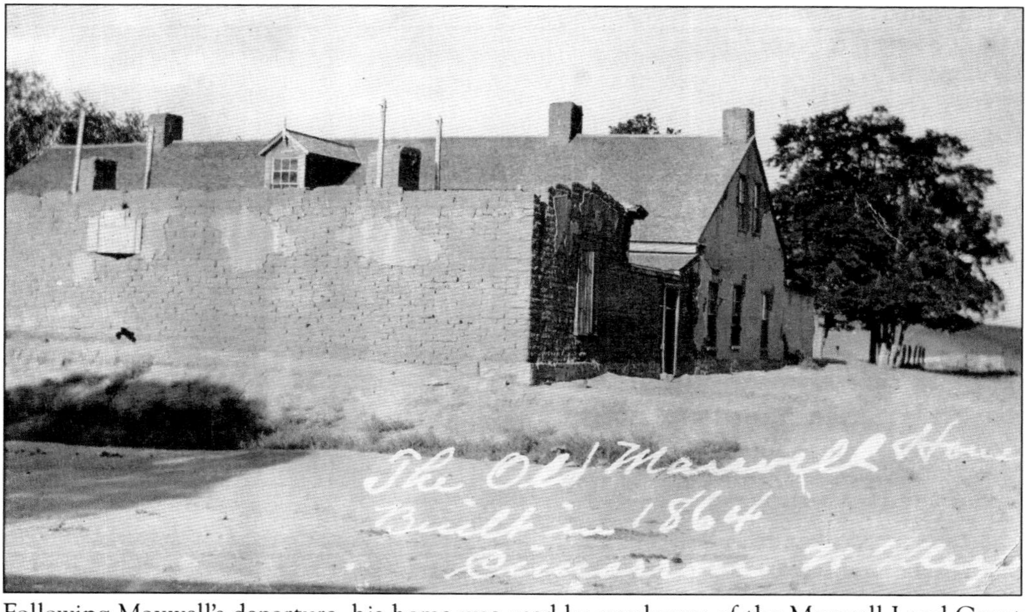

Following Maxwell's departure, his home was used by employees of the Maxwell Land Grant Company. One of the best-remembered is Raymond R. Morley, who in November 1872 accepted the $4,500-a-year post as manager and moved into the "Cimarron House." Morley became editor of the *Cimarron News and Press* and while working as a surveyor for the Santa Fe Railroad in 1878, he secured construction rights over Raton Pass. (Authors' collection.)

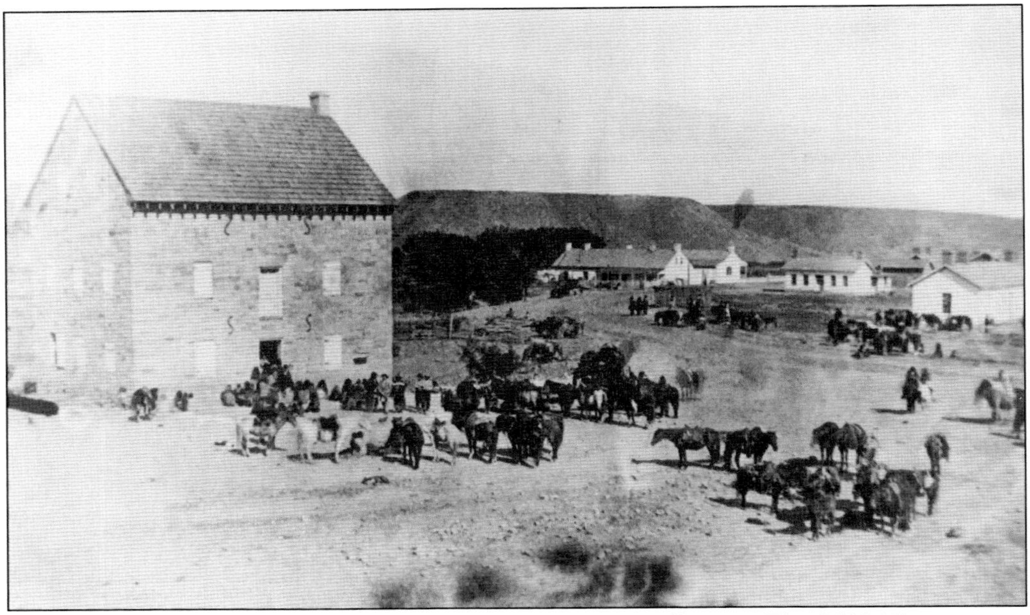

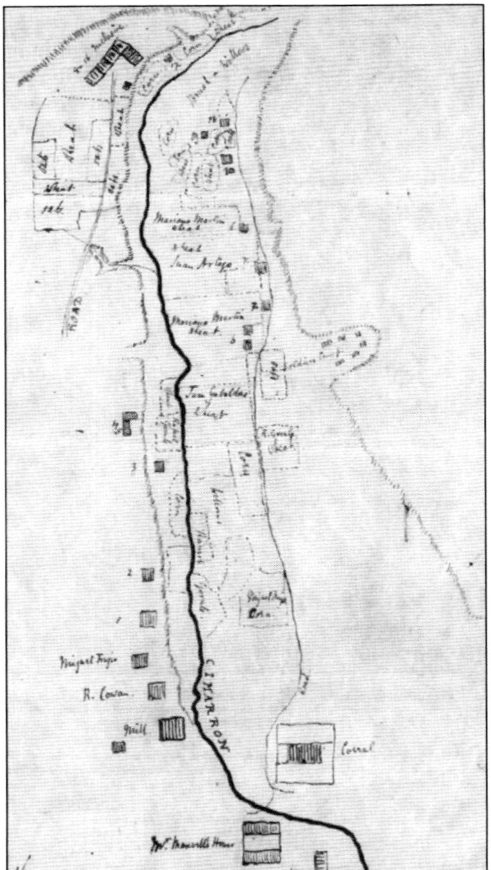

The Aztec Mill—now The Old Mill museum—was an automated gristmill constructed for Lucien B. Maxwell between 1860 and 1864 at a cost of $48,000 by B.M. Blackmore, millwright Emory Williams, and mason James Truax based on inventor Oliver Evans's patented design. The 1868 view above shows a group of Jicarilla Apaches gathered at the mill, along with the Maxwell mansion in the center distance, the predecessor to Henry Lambert's saloon, and the county courthouse at far right. The 1865 hand-drawn map at left shows the acequia, or irrigation ditch, (mislabeled as "Cimarron") that supplied water to the mill. Surveys maps of the 1920s identify it as the "Old Mill Ditch." Maxwell's house, corral and mill, and Dold store are labeled. To the top of the map (west) extend fields designated as corn, oats, or wheat. This map—one of the earliest of Cimarron—was first published in *Translating Property: The Maxwell Land Grant and the Conflict Over Land in the American West, 1840–1900* by María E. Montoya. (Above, The Old Mill; left, University of New Mexico Center for Southwest Research.)

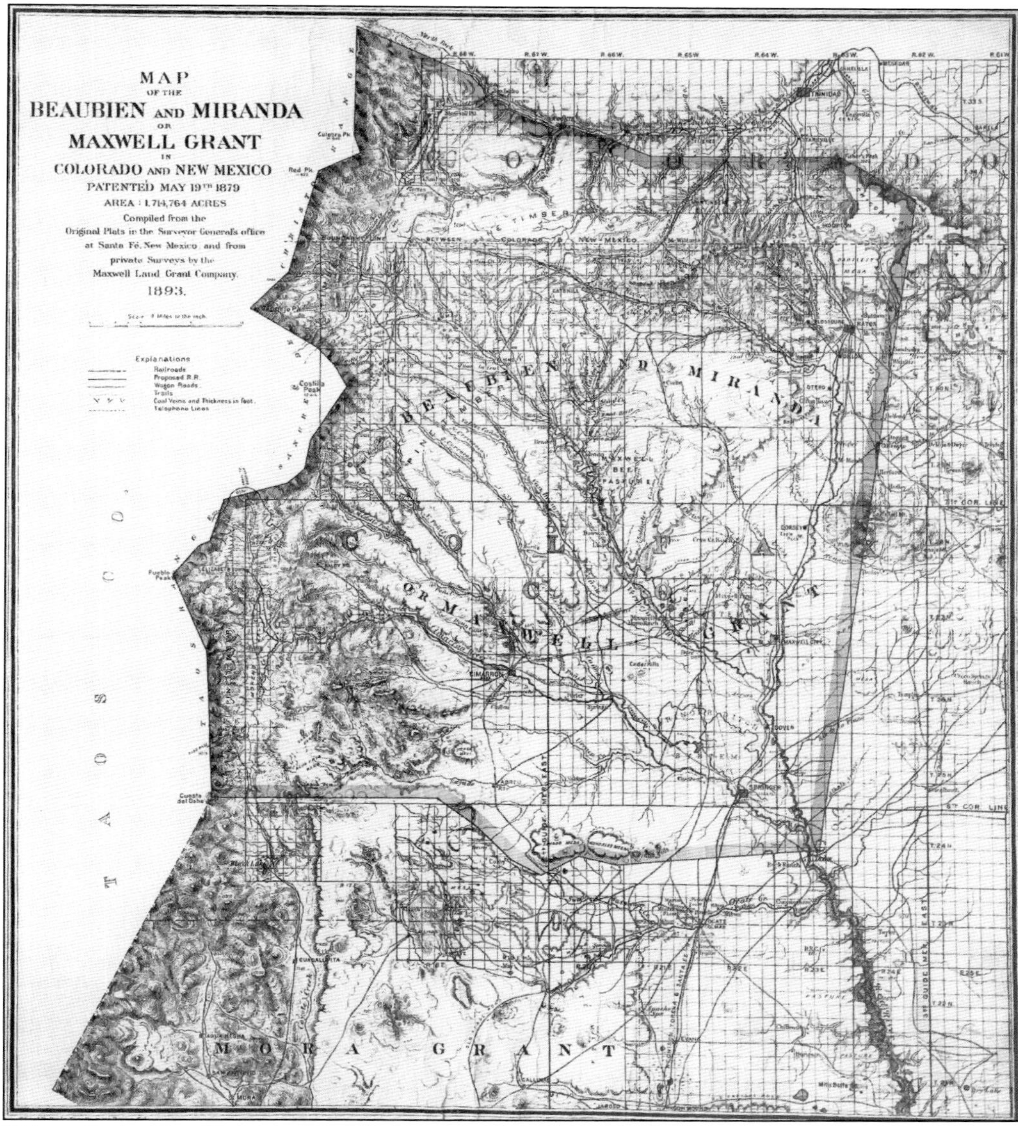

When Carlos Beaubien and Guadalupe Miranda were awarded their land grant in 1841, even though no specific boundaries were laid out, it was believed that the grant was limited under Mexican law to 22 square leagues, or 96,000 acres. When the new land grant owners requested an "official" but friendly survey, they relied upon evidence offered by many of those who rode with Maxwell as he oversaw his ranch, such as RIchens L. "Uncle Dick" Wootton. Phrases such as "from this large boulder here to the peak on that ridge" became an official boundary. When Congress unwittingly approved the boundaries in 1860 and again in 1879, they became legal and were confirmed by the US Supreme Court in 1887. Measuring roughly 50 miles wide by 55 miles long, the Beaubien-Miranda, later known as the Maxwell, Land Grant was the largest in US history (outlined by the shaded border). This 1893 map clearly shows the mountainous terrain along the western and northern borders that funneled water through rivers toward its southeastern corner. After 1858, Maxwell controlled the grant from his headquarters in Cimarron, located roughly in the center of the map. (The Old Mill.)

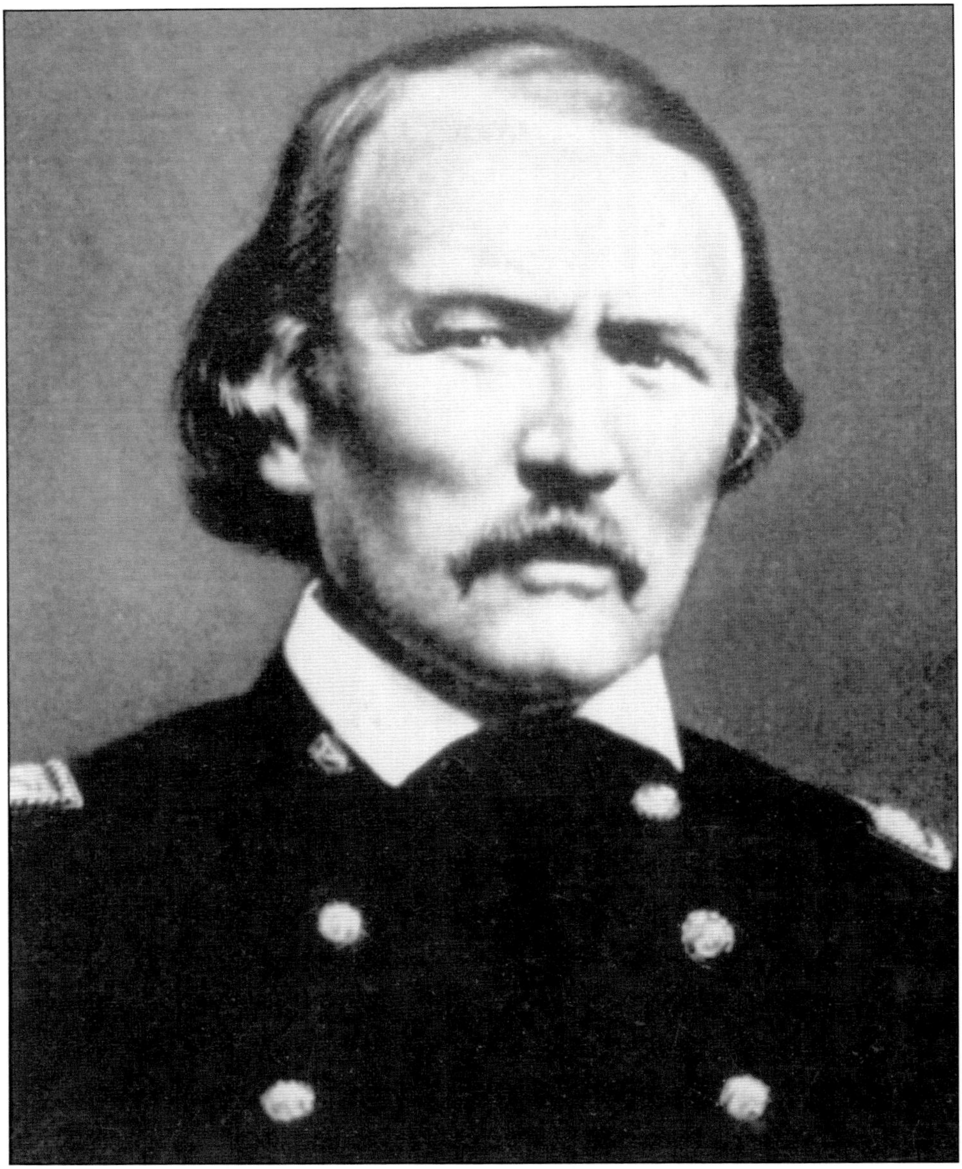

For young Kit Carson (1809–1868), the excitement of growing up on the Missouri frontier was nothing compared to the tales told by men returning from the mountainous wilderness beyond. The death of his father when he was eight caused Kit to forgo schooling, and by age 14, he was learning the saddle-making trade. But the work was boring, so two years later Kit ran away with a caravan to Santa Fe, perhaps with his master's blessing for the reward notice read in part: "One cent reward will be given to any person who will bring back said boy." The next decade was spent trapping from the Rockies to California, learning the ways of the mountain man and the cultures of the Indians. Although remaining illiterate, Carson learned to speak Spanish and seven Native American languages. In the 1840s, he met Lucien B. Maxwell, and the two accompanied Frémont on his expeditions. When Maxwell agreed to start a settlement in Rayado to manage Beaubien's grant, Carson joined him. Much of Carson's later life was involved with Indian affairs, for which he has been praised by some and vilified by others. (Arthur Johnson Memorial Library.)

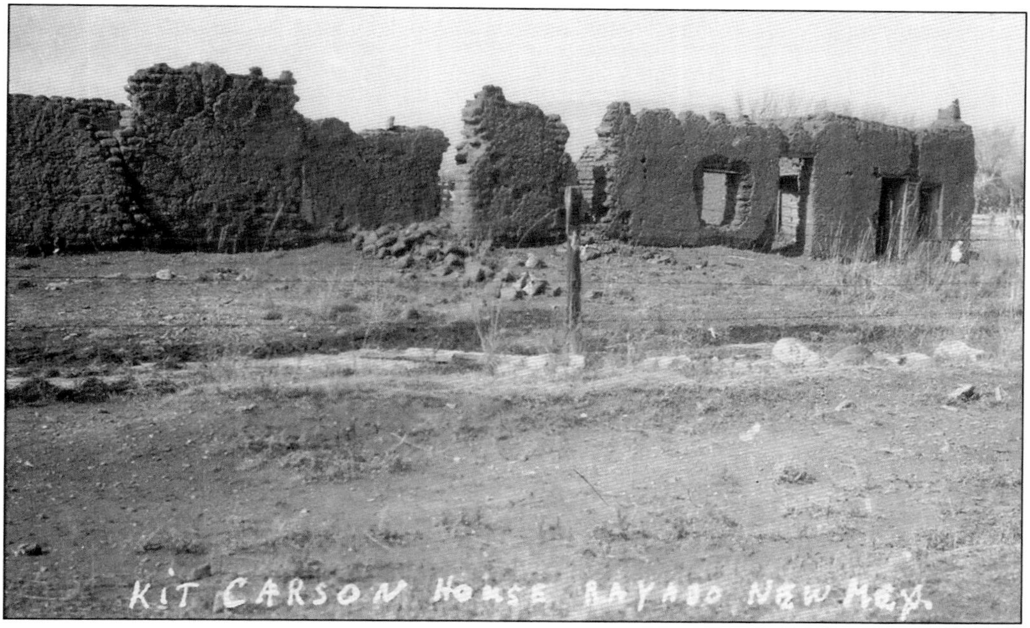

The settlement of Rayado was established 11 miles south of present-day Cimarron by Lucien B. Maxwell and his friend Christopher "Kit" Carson in 1849. Maxwell's sprawling home included some 20 rooms around a commodious courtyard. This photograph shows the ruins of Carson's adobe home, three rooms of which were intact prior to a 1949 reconstruction. The headquarters of the 189,000-acre Express UU Bar Ranch is also at Rayado. (Authors' collection.)

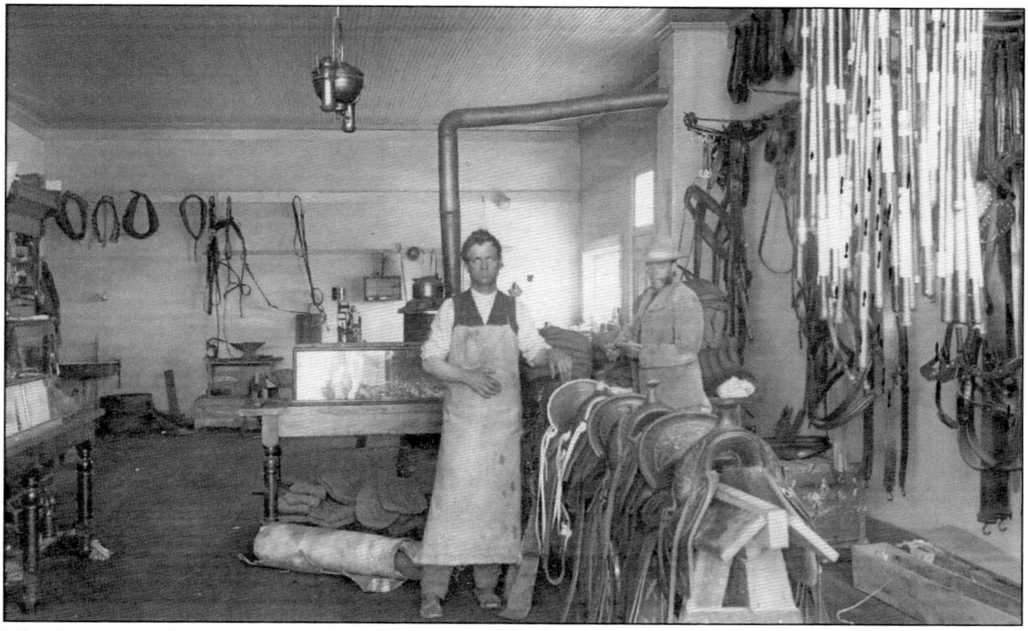

The Carey Hardware and Livery Stable was constructed in 1872 on the west side of South Sherman Avenue across from the National Hotel. The foundation of a house owned by probate judge Robert H. Longwill in 1875 is still visible in the yard. The Carey building later served as the office of the *Cimarron News and Press* and since the 1920s has been a private residence. (The Old Mill.)

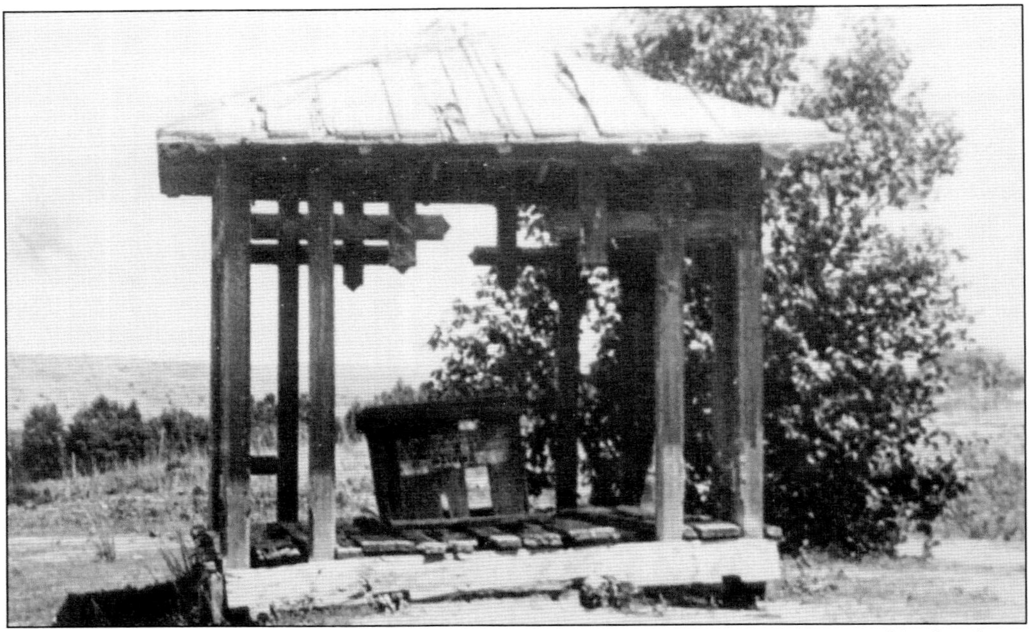

Life in early Cimarron revolved around the plaza. The plaza well dug in 1871 was used by freighters along the Santa Fe Trail until 1880 when railroad service replaced the need for the trail. The gazebo was reconstructed in 1962 from photographs of the original structure. The plaza was a welcome sight for travelers, many of whom would spend the night at the nearby National Hotel (1858) or camp under the stars. (The Old Mill.)

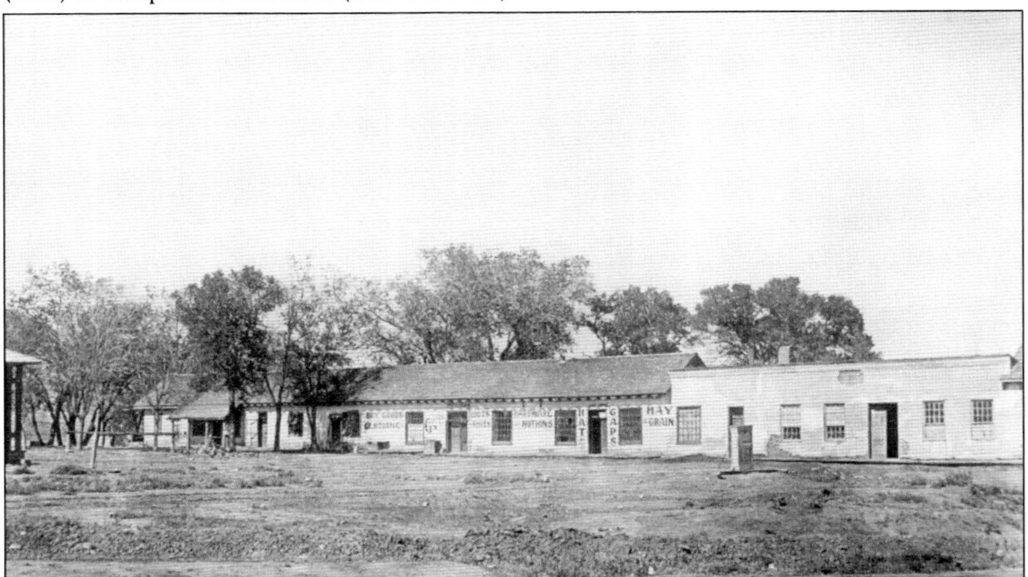

Constructed in 1848, this building was used by brothers Andres and John Dold for their freight line between Missouri and Las Vegas, New Mexico. It later served as a trading post, Indian agency, and commissary for Maxwell. In 1873, it was a general store operated by merchants Porter and Middaugh, and two years later it was the office of the *Cimarron News and Press*. This building is mentioned in Zane Grey's novel *Fighting Caravans*. (The Old Mill.)

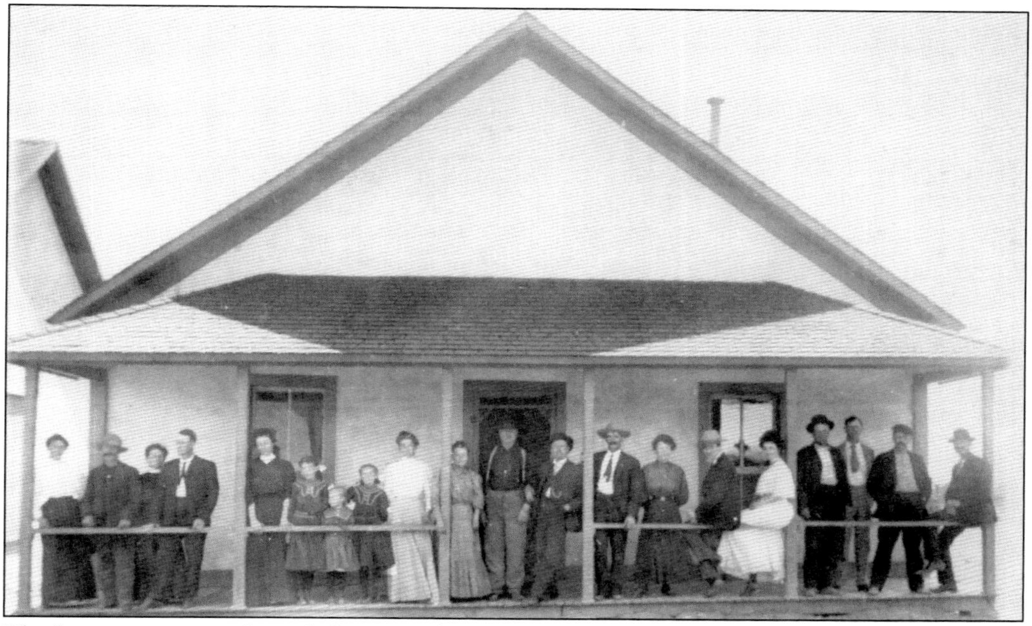

The first stage service through Cimarron began in 1861. Barlow, Sanderson & Company obtained the line in 1866 with a branch route to the gold towns of Elizabethtown and Virginia City starting two years later. This was the company's local office from 1870 until 1880 when the first train arrived in Santa Fe. It was then used by Wells Fargo to connect Cimarron with nearby towns before becoming a mercantile store in the early 1900s. (Audrey Alpers Collection, The Old Mill.)

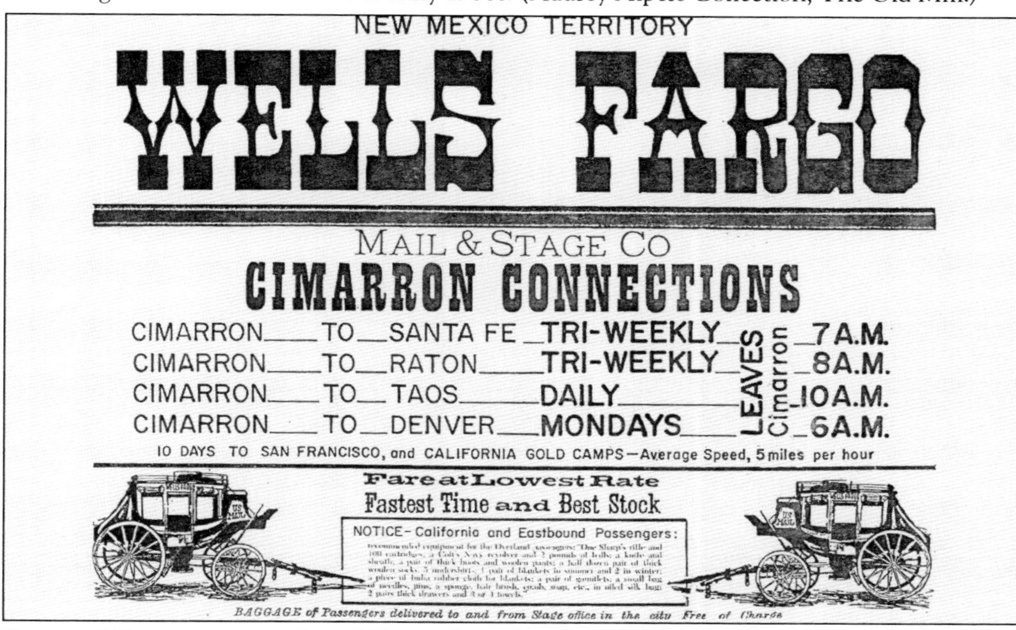

For many Western towns without US postal or railroad service, Wells, Fargo & Company provided passenger and mail service to neighboring communities. The journey by stage to Raton, about 40 miles, would take a day. The journey going to Taos through Cimarron Canyon and over Palo Flechado Pass would require an overnight stop in Elizabethtown. (The Old Mill.)

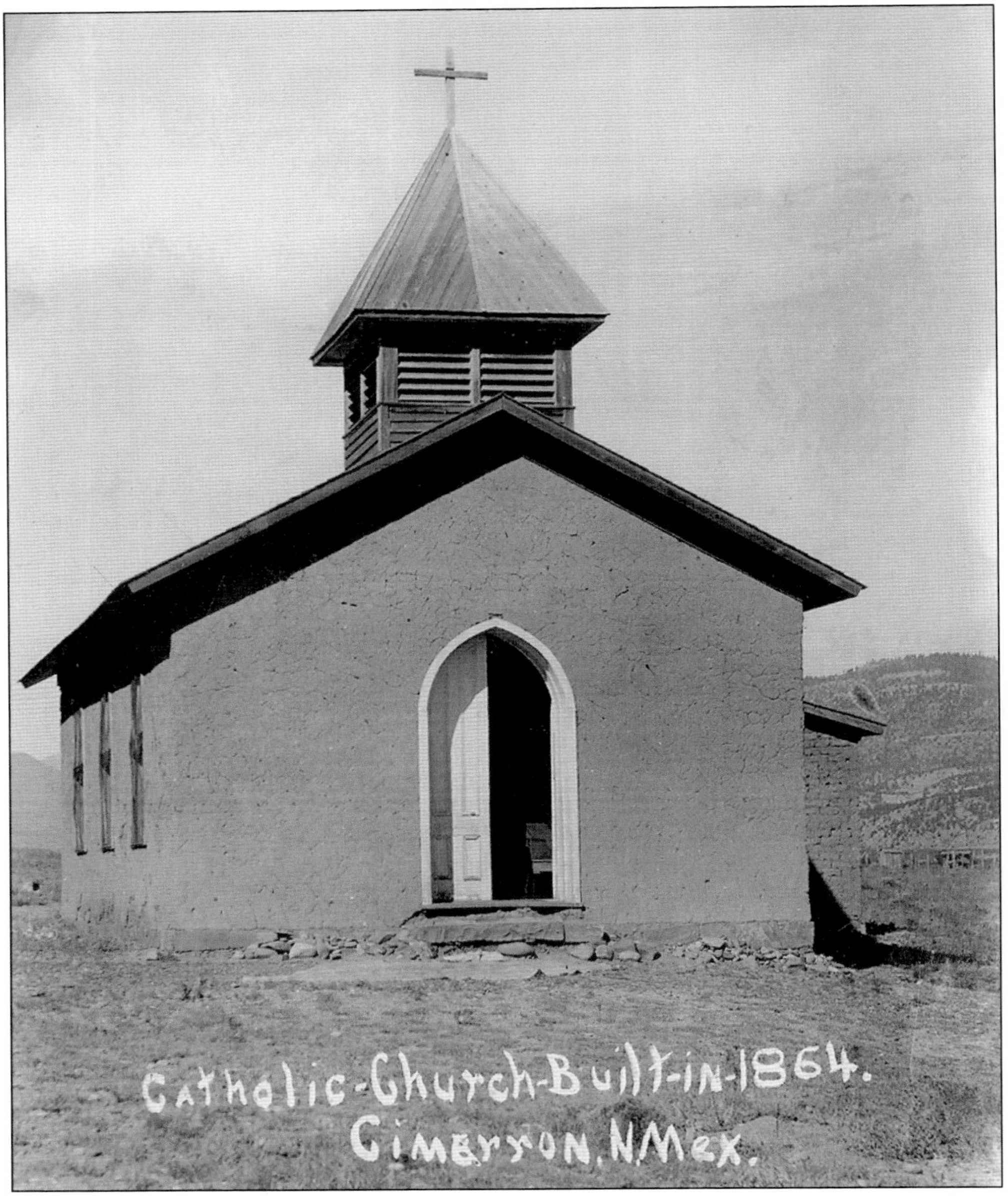

The Immaculate Conception Catholic Church stands a few blocks west of the historic plaza in Old Town Cimarron. The original structure was built in 1864 by Lucien B. and Luz Maxwell in memory of their two deceased children, Verenisa and Julian, and was donated to the Catholic Church in honor of Jean Baptiste Lamy, the first bishop of Santa Fe. It served as a mission of the parish of La Junta in Watrous, Mora County. This c. 1910 Troutman Studio photograph shows a later building constructed in 1879 and deeded to Bishop Lamy for $1. The sanctuary was enlarged in 1909, and a bell tower and entrance now extend from the eastern facade. The church has operated as its own parish since 1954. Eleven miles south at Rayado is the Chapel of the Holy Child in Rayado, constructed by Petra Abreu in 1904 on land now owned by Philmont Scout Ranch. Cimarron is also home to the Cimarron United Methodist Church, First Baptist Church, and Church of Christ. (Authors' collection.)

Three

The Colfax County War

By 1870, Lucien B. Maxwell's land grant was a success, gold had been discovered on Baldy Mountain, the settlements of Elizabethtown and Baldy Town were flourishing, and Cimarron was the site of the local Indian agency. But Kit Carson had died in 1868, and Maxwell, although a wealthy man by having purchased what grant land he had not inherited, was feeling his age. With the railroad to Santa Fe soon to cut across his land, Maxwell decided to sell the grant. The European investors who purchased the property quickly forced settlers and Indians, whom Maxwell had allowed to live freely, to either pay up or move. One of the more vocal defenders of the poor was Methodist minister Rev. Franklin J. Tolby. On September 14, 1875, Tolby's body was discovered next to Clear Creek in Cimarron Canyon, a bullet in the back, although his personal belongings had not been disturbed.

Oscar McMains was appointed minister and, along with local rancher and occasional gunslinger Clay Allison, promptly looked into Tolby's death. A local inquiry indicated that Constable Cruz Vega was involved, and, under threat of hanging, Vega implicated Manuel Cárdenas. The next day, Vega was discovered swinging from a telegraph pole one mile north of town. Then, Cárdenas was routed from jail by a mob and killed. When told of Vega's lynching, Francisco "Pancho" Griego, a relative, confronted Allison in Lambert's saloon and shots were fired. The town lamented the closing of the bar until Griego's body was removed the following morning.

The instigators behind Tolby's killing were determined to be the new grant owners in collusion with Santa Fe politicians known as The Ring. When Washington got wind of the trouble out West and that the governor was involved, Pres. Rutherford Hayes replaced Gov. Samuel Axtell with Civil War general Lew Wallace, who quickly doused the flames. Still, embers smoldered even after the US Supreme Court upheld the legality of the grant in 1886. The last person considered a casualty of the Colfax County War was Richard Russell, who was shot in Stonewall, Colorado, on August 27, 1888. His widow, Marion Sloan Russell, is remembered for her diary *Land of Enchantment*.

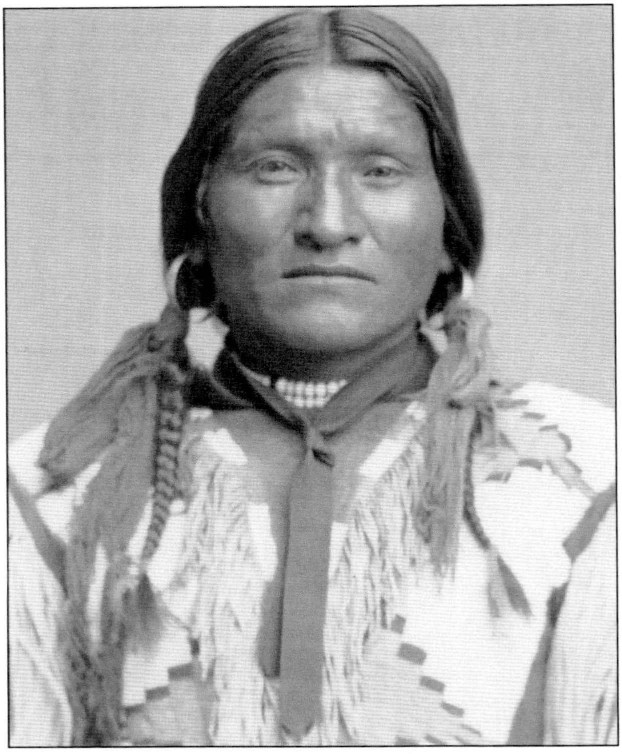

The Cimarron Agency was established in 1860 to serve local Jicarilla Apaches and Utes who lived on long-occupied land now under the control of the Maxwell Land Grant. When the land grant was sold to English investors, the new owners tried forcibly to remove the settlers and Indians, which led to the Colfax County War. With the closing of the agency in 1876, the federal government unsuccessfully attempted to remove the Jicarilla Apaches to the Mescalero Reservation in southern New Mexico. Santiago Largo was one of five Jicarilla Apache leaders who travelled to Washington, DC, in 1880 to seek a permanent reservation for his people, which they finally received in 1887. (Charles Milton Bell, National Anthropological Archives, Smithsonian Institution, BAE GN 2570 A.)

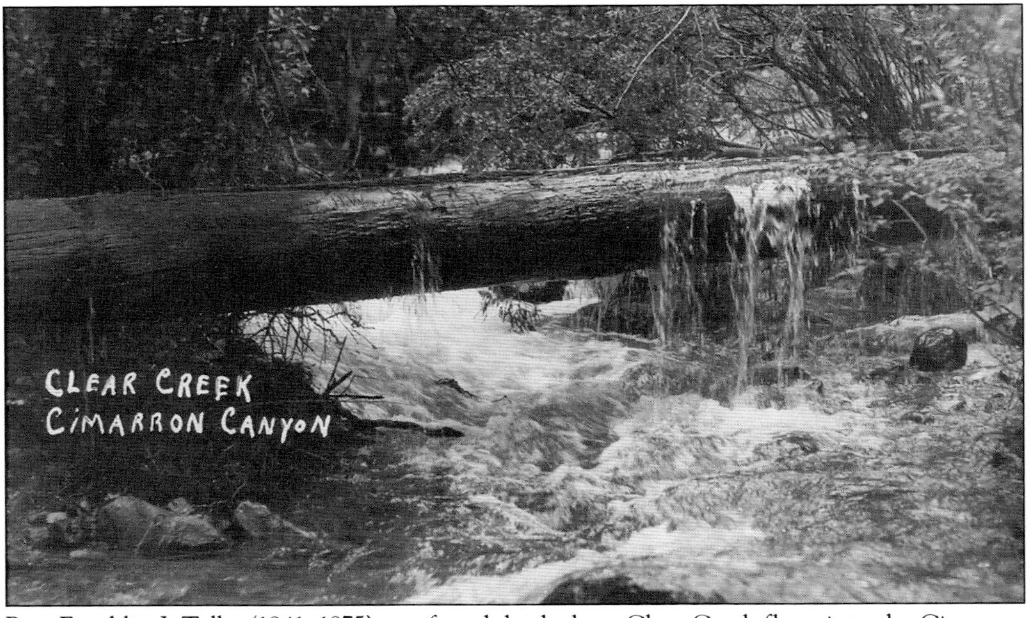

Rev. Franklin J. Tolby (1841–1875) was found dead where Clear Creek flows into the Cimarron River. For decades, this drinking log at mile marker 292 has marked the approximate spot where the assassination occurred. Tolby is memorialized by the Tolby Campground in the Cimarron Canyon State Park, the Tolby Trail in the nearby 33,116-acre Colin Neblett Wildlife Management Area, and 11,539-foot Tolby Peak west of Philmont near Mount Phillips. (Authors' collection.)

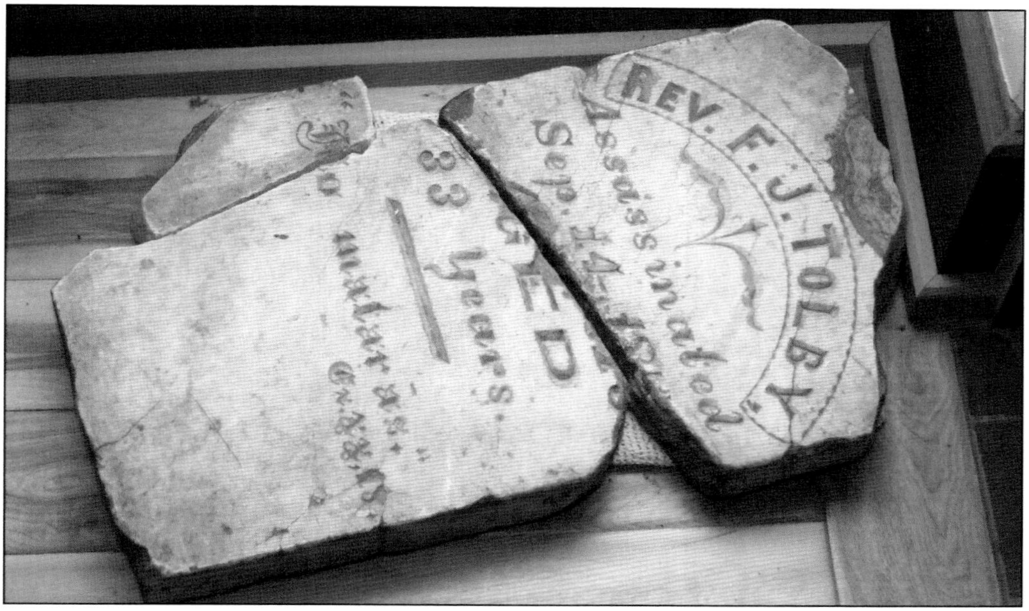

Reverend Tolby was laid to rest in Cimarron's Mountain View Cemetery. His original vandalized headstone is presently on display in the lobby of the St. James Hotel. Lost for some time, it is said to have suffered ignominious service as a doorstep for years before it was rediscovered and preserved. After his death, the Methodist church was renamed the Tolby Memorial Church in his honor. (Authors' collection.)

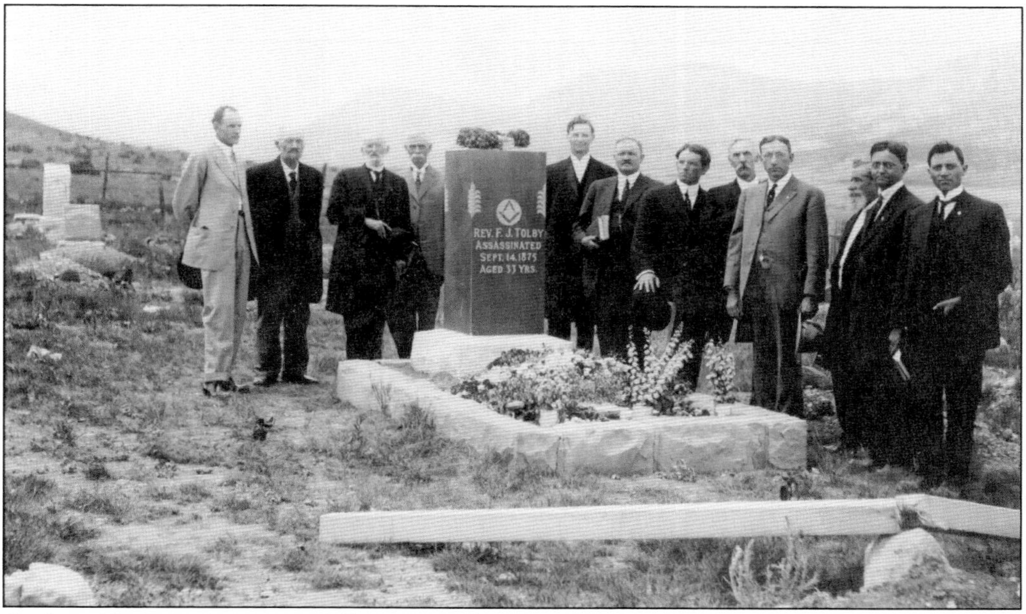

On June 29, 1913—known as Tolby Memorial Day—members of Cimarron Lodge No. 37 Ancient Free and Accepted Masons and Tolby Memorial Church have gathered in the cemetery to unveil the monument that replaced Tolby's original headstone. Officiants included H.G. Frankenburger and Manly M. Chase. The Tolby monument is immediately northwest of the grave of Colfax County pioneer Michael Stubblefield (1842–1878). (The Old Mill.)

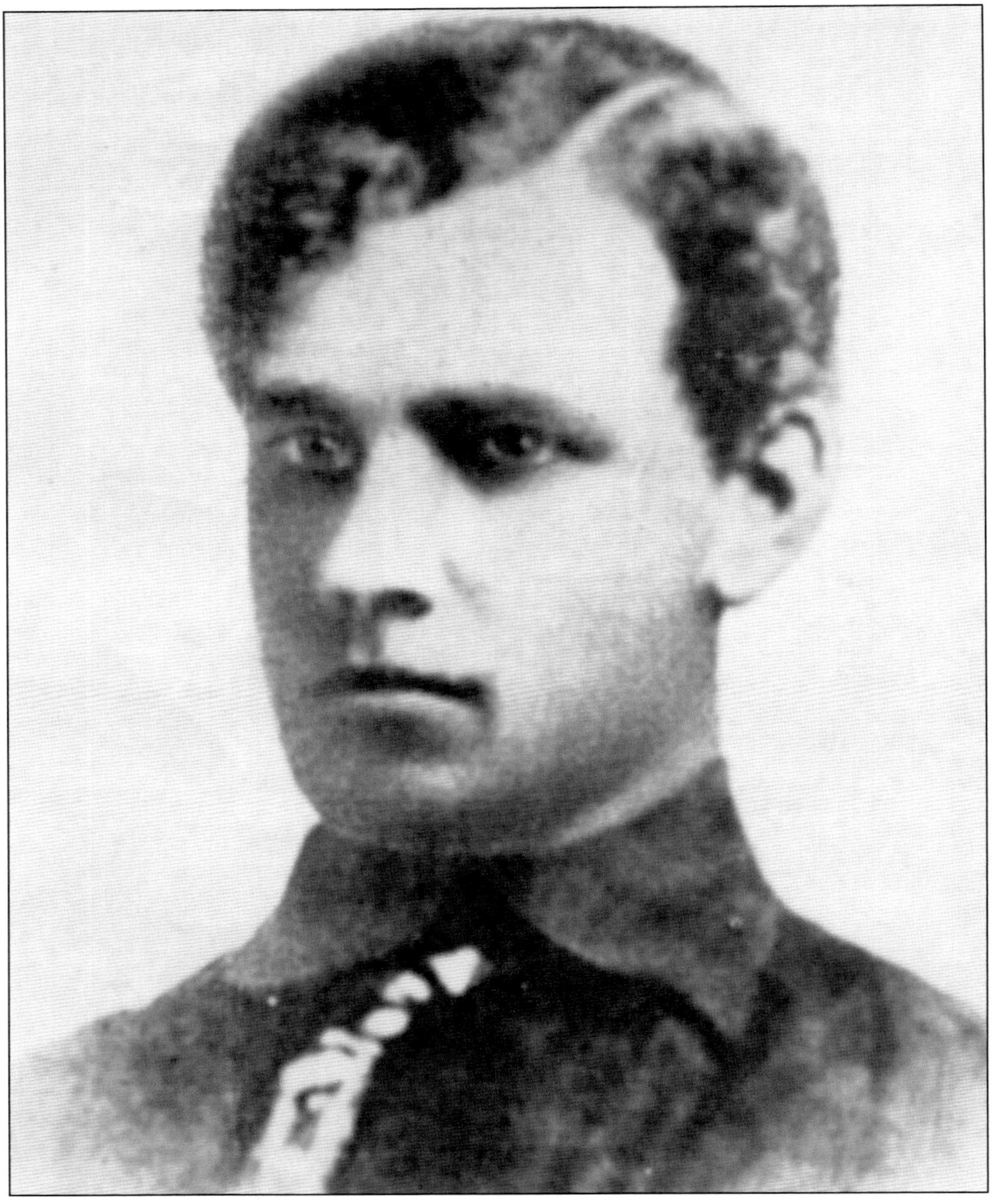

Robert "Clay" Allison (1840–1887) grew up on a cattle and sheep farm in Tennessee. When the Civil War broke out, he joined the Confederate army, mustering out as a prisoner of war in 1865. He soon moved to the Brazos River Valley of West Texas and signed on as a drover for Charles Goodnight and Oliver Loving's famed cattle drive. On the journey, he met Lucien B. Maxwell, and by 1872, he had started ranching 10 miles north of Cimarron. Allison's reputation as a gunslinger began when he killed John "Chunk" Colbert, a wanted man, in a gunfight in 1874. He was not, as often described, an outlaw, but would certainly hold his own in a fight, even those he started while drinking. He is reported to have said, "I never killed a man who didn't need killing." During the Colfax County War, Allison played a major role, first throwing the printing press of the *Cimarron News and Press* into the river, then heading up the search for the killers of Reverend Tolby. (The Old Mill.)

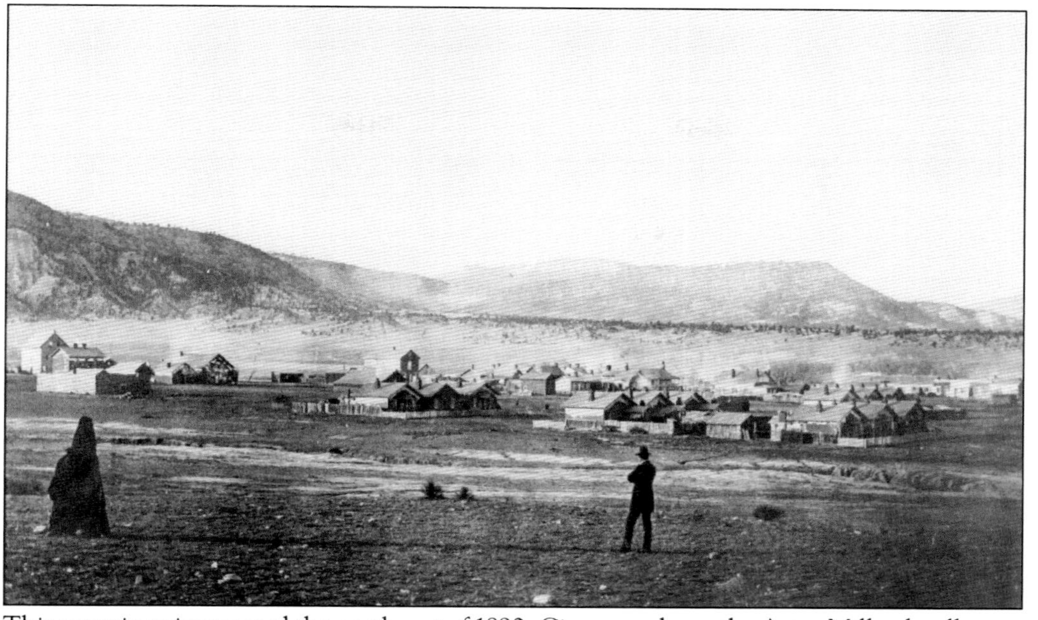

This sweeping view toward the northwest of 1890s Cimarron shows the Aztec Mill, schoolhouse, jail, and Swink's Gambling Hall to the left. Land grant manager's houses, in three clusters of three, appear in the center and right foreground. Long shadows to the northeast with smoking chimneys and a lack of snow suggest the gentleman is enjoying a late fall afternoon. (Audrey Alpers Collection, The Old Mill.)

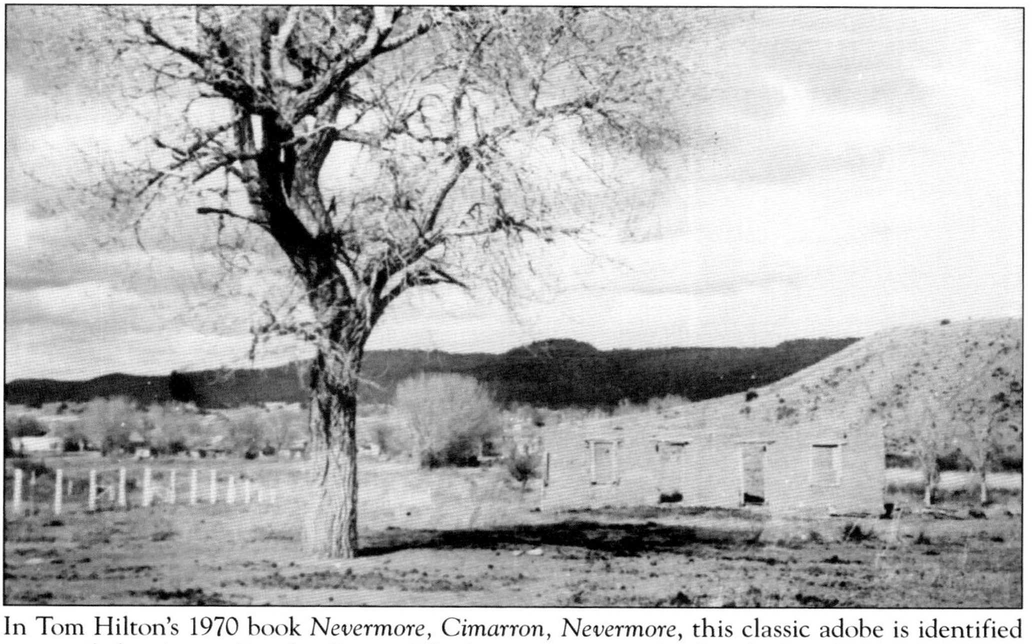

In Tom Hilton's 1970 book *Nevermore, Cimarron, Nevermore*, this classic adobe is identified as once belonging to Pancho Griego. The location is just a few hundred yards from Lambert's Saloon, where Griego was killed in a duel with Clay Allison on November 1, 1875. Though now in ruins (again), the house was later used by other Cimarron citizens. Longtime resident Jane Garcia remembers sweeping out the kitchen's dirt floor as a child. (The Old Mill.)

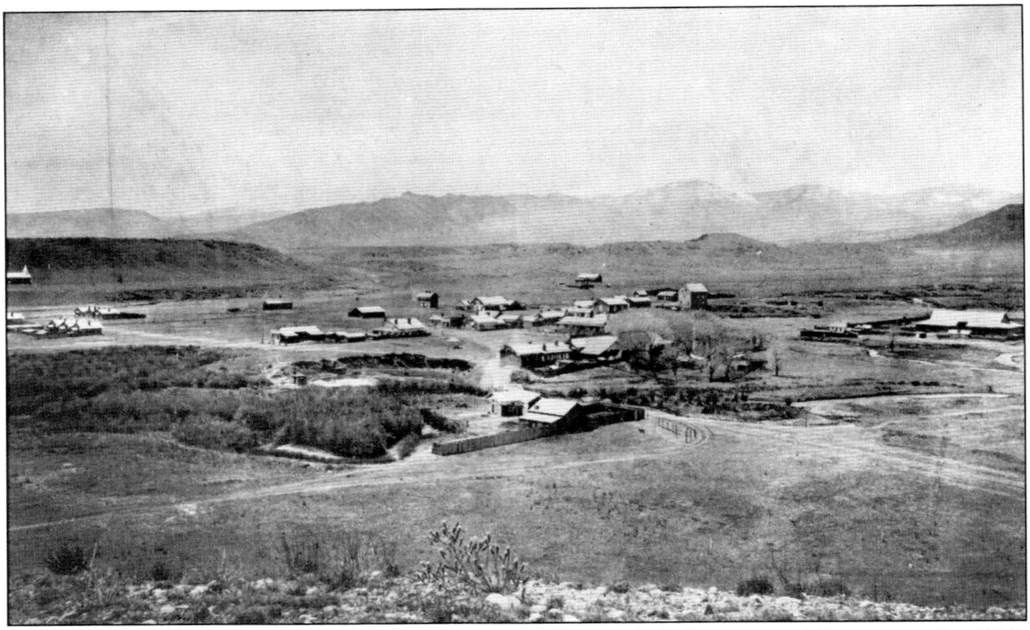

Looking southwest from atop C Hill in about 1877 provided this view of Cimarron. In 1938, Edith Tinson—daughter of Grant Company officer Henry Tinson—provided a key to the image. The church in the far left distance was built in 1872 and was used as a schoolhouse before 1887, when it was destroyed by a windstorm. The Maxwell Land Grant stables are at the far right. (The Old Mill.)

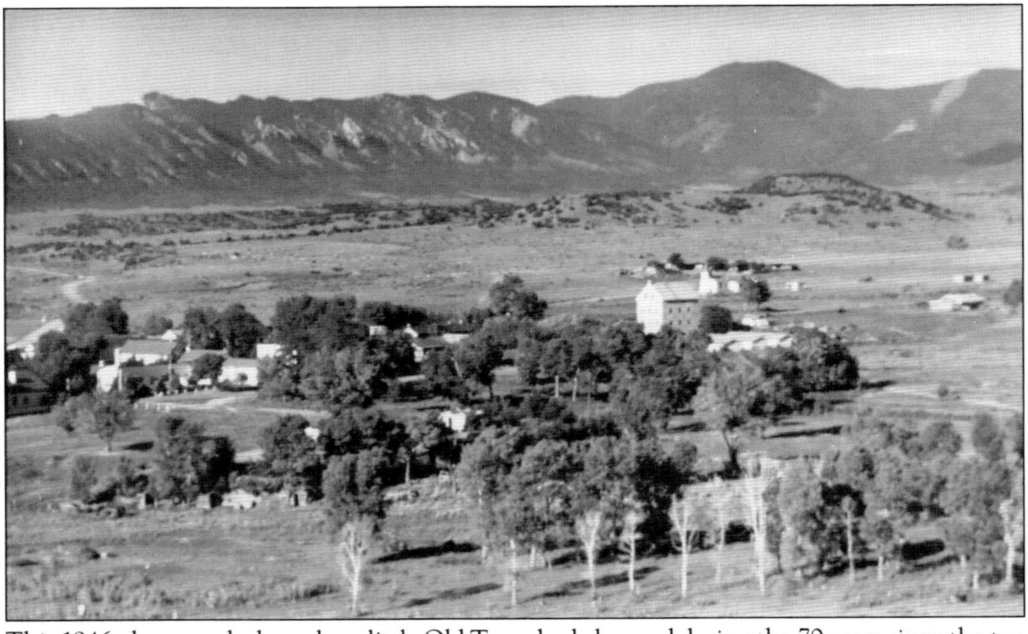

This 1946 photograph shows how little Old Town had changed during the 70 years since the top image was recorded. Aside from a few trees hiding original structures, only the absence of Maxwell's stables and the replacement of the Santa Fe Trail entering the northeast corner of the plaza by a bridge over the Cimarron River farther west show the passage of time. (The Old Mill.)

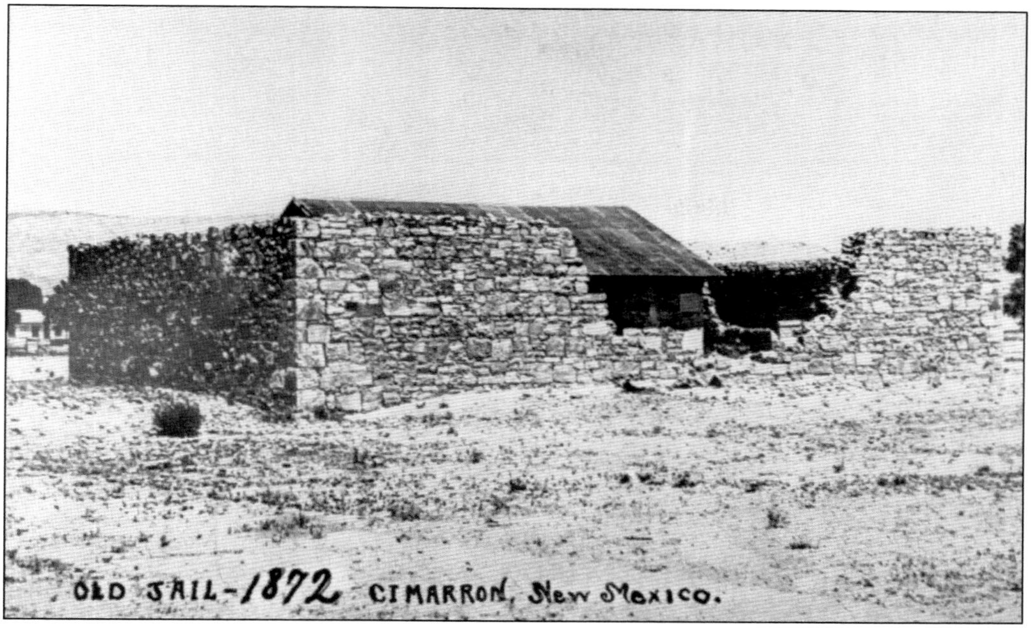

Western jails were not as quaint as portrayed in movies. They were often stone structures, dark and dank, with solid metal doors and small windows that let in little light or air. Cimarron's jail was built in 1872 and had an outer wall four feet thick and ten feet high. Despite this, an attempted jailbreak in the 1900s resulted in the outer wall being dynamited. The jail was used until the 1960s. (Arthur Johnson Memorial Library.)

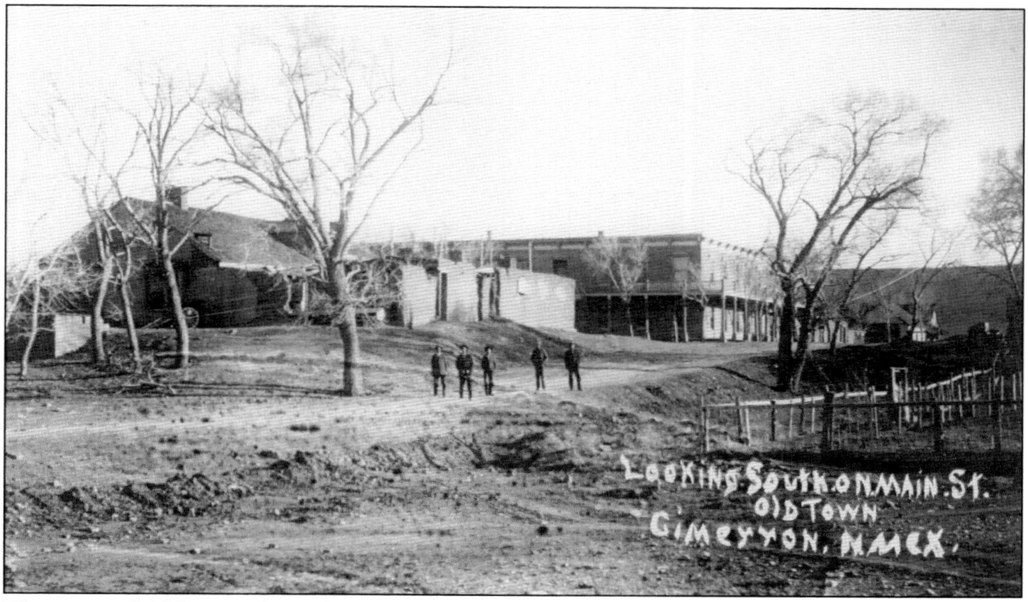

This view of Old Town from the north shows the ruins of Maxwell's house, the St. James Hotel, the former stage office sunlit in the distance, and Mary Lambert's fenced-in garden on the right. The Santa Fe Trail entered from the left between Maxwell's house and the hotel before turning south. Access to Old Town today is along Collinson Avenue, where the men are standing. (The Old Mill.)

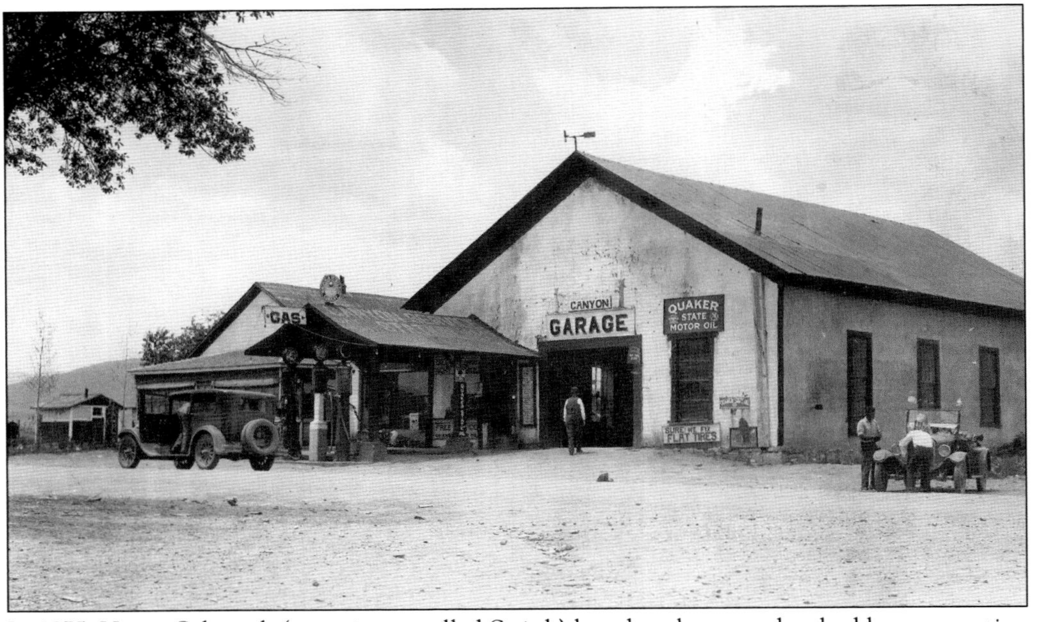

In 1875, Henry Schwenk (sometimes spelled Swink) bought a brewery that had been operating since 1854 and turned it into a gambling hall and bar, in competition with Henry Lambert's saloon on the opposite corner. When Henry's son Fred bought the property, the Canyon Lunch café was added next door. In later years, the buildings also did duty as a service station (seen here), a community meeting place, a mercantile store, and a motel. (Raton Museum.)

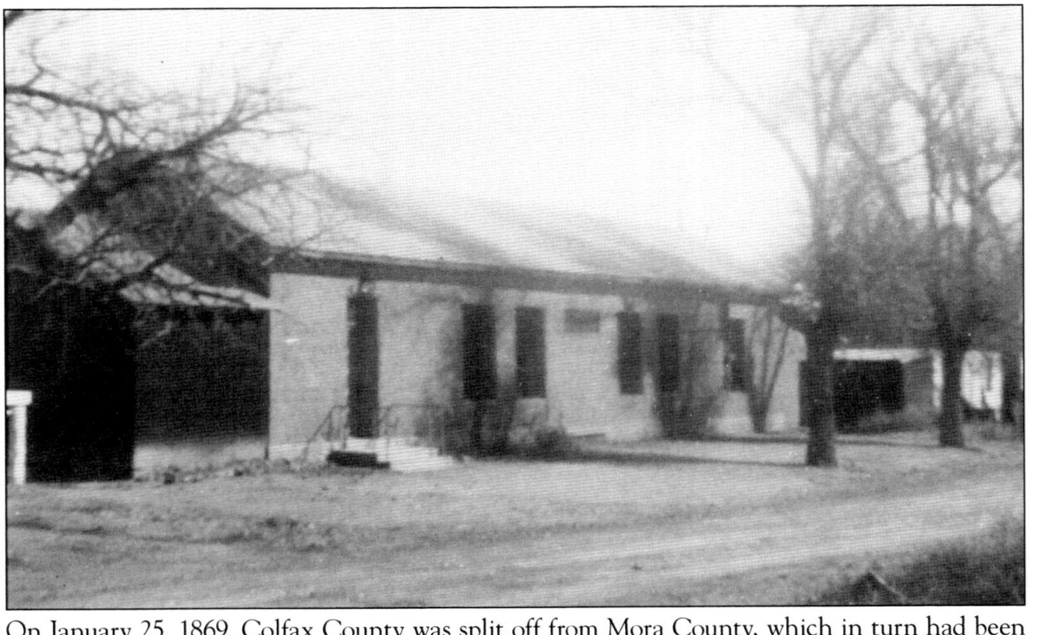

On January 25, 1869, Colfax County was split off from Mora County, which in turn had been created from Taos County 10 years earlier. With the gold rush on Baldy in full flower, the county seat was established at Elizabethtown. In 1872, when most claims had played out, the county seat moved to Cimarron; this building served as the county courthouse. As the railroad moved through New Mexico, Springer and finally Raton became the county seat. (Authors' collection.)

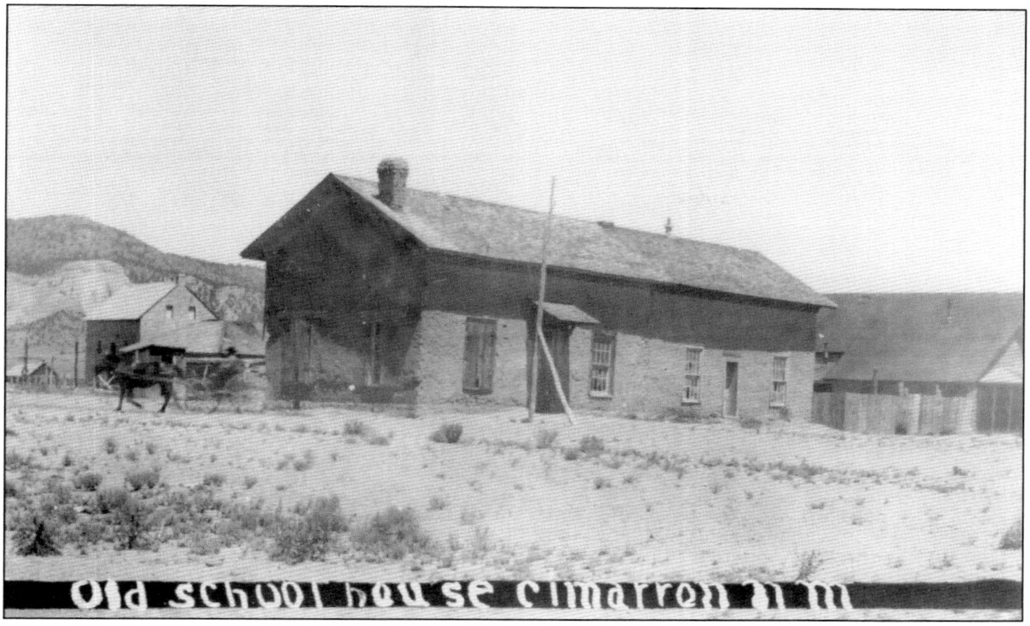

This adobe building was Cimarron's first purpose-built schoolhouse before the New Town school was completed in 1909. Miss Margaret Cavanaugh typified Cimarron's schoolteachers. A graduate of the Territorial Normal School at Las Vegas (now New Mexico Highlands University), she first taught here in 1906 and taught in Baldy Town and attended training institutes during the summer. This building was destroyed by fire in May 1923. (Troutman Studio, The Old Mill.)

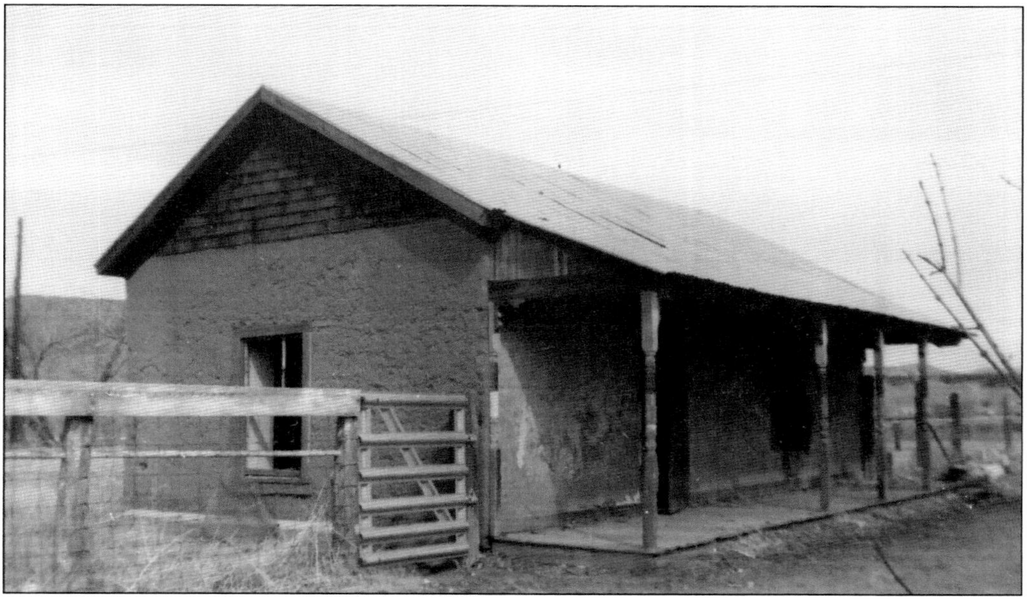

This adobe building once stood in Old Town near the historic county courthouse. Adobe as a construction material has been used for thousands of years. Bricks formed from sandy clay mixed with water and straw or another binding agent are cured in the sun, then used to form walls. The adobe bricks used to build the two-story St. James Hotel on the following pages are 12 by 18 by 4 inches in size. (The Old Mill.)

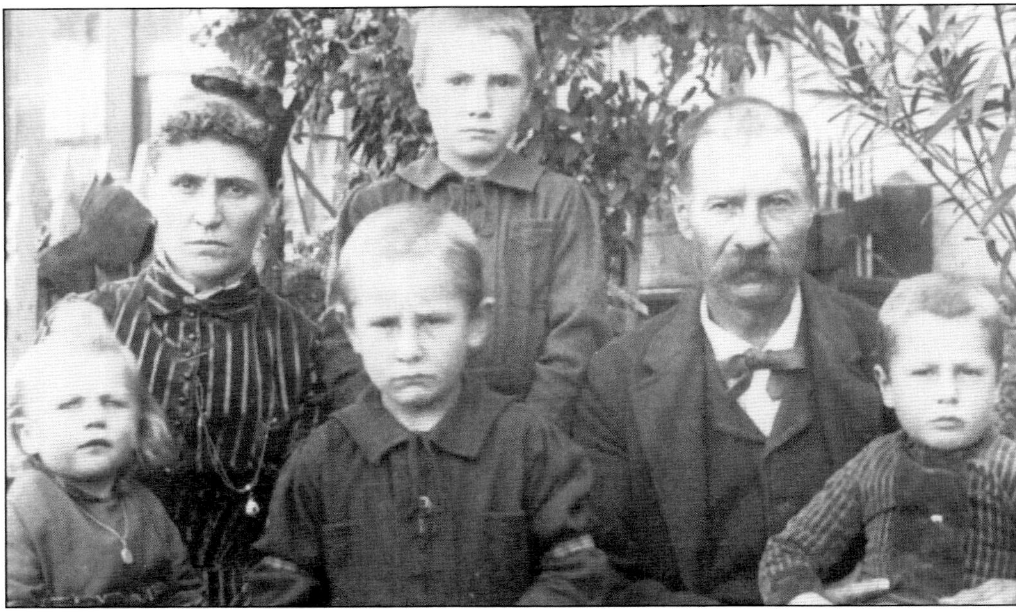

In 1871, Frenchman Henri (later changed to Henry) Lambert sold his small hotel in Elizabethtown and moved to the growing community of Cimarron, where in 1883 he married second wife Mary Elizabeth Davis (1858–1926). In 1891, the Lambert family, from left to right, includes Johnnie (1889–1892) (in his mother's arms), William Henry (1883–1953), Frank Davis (1885–1952), and Henri (1838–1913) holding Charles Fred (1887–1971). Son Eugene Twitty (1893–1975) was born soon thereafter. (Arthur Johnson Memorial Library.)

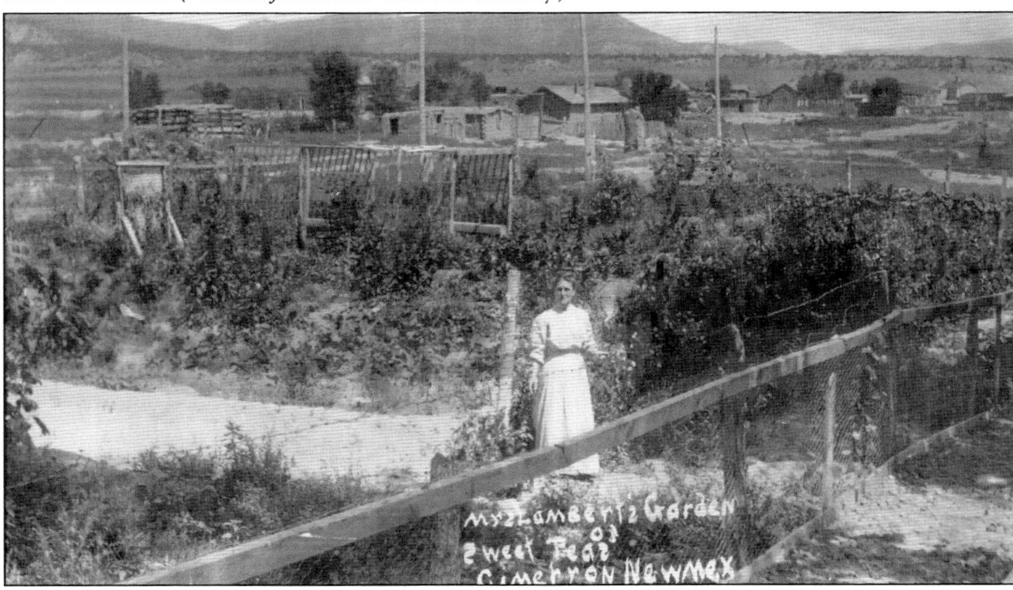

This northwest-facing Troutman Studio photograph shows Mary Lambert and her dog Rags in her garden of sweet peas, with the Gapito Duran and Whiteman homes in the distance. The garden was on the west side of South Collinson Avenue immediately northwest of the St. James Hotel. The ghost of Lambert—distinguishable by her rose perfume—is said to protect Room 17 on the second floor. (Authors' collection.)

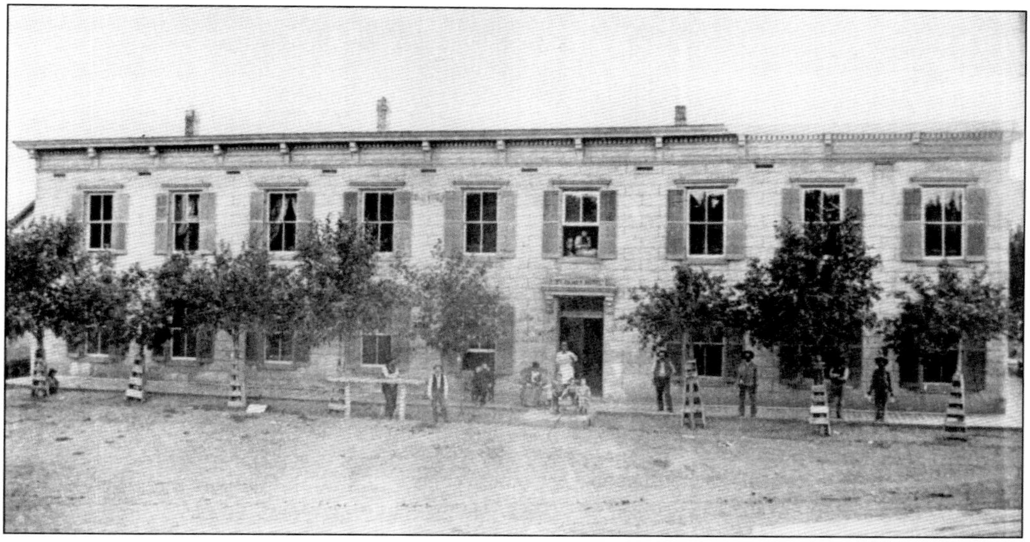

By 1875, Henry Lambert had purchased a popular saloon near the plaza that achieved notoriety during the Colfax County War when Clay Allison gunned down Pancho Griego. In 1880, Lambert began expanding his saloon to the north and east, and it became the St. James Hotel two years later. This photograph shows the hotel shortly after opening, with Henry in his chef's uniform in the doorway and his wife and children beside him. (Arthur Johnson Memorial Library.)

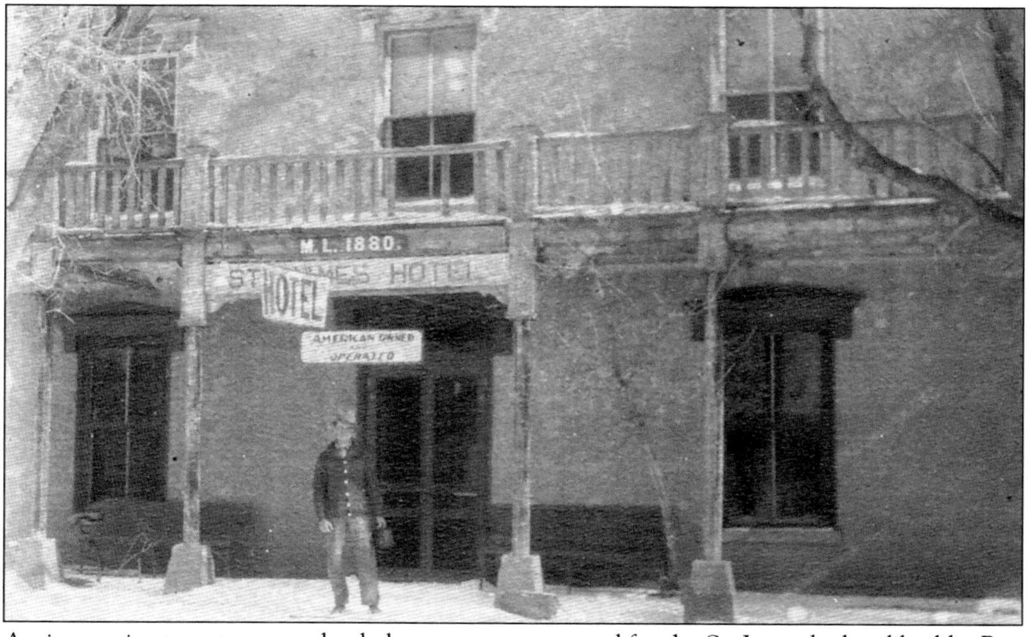

An impressive two-story wooden balcony was constructed for the St. James by local builder Roy Tosier in 1905, as remembered by Fred Lambert. This view of the north facade includes a sign reading "American Owned and Operated." The inscription "M. L. 1880" above the doorway is believed to represent "Monsieur Lambert" and the year Henry initiated his conversion of the old saloon into the legendary hotel. (Lambert family.)

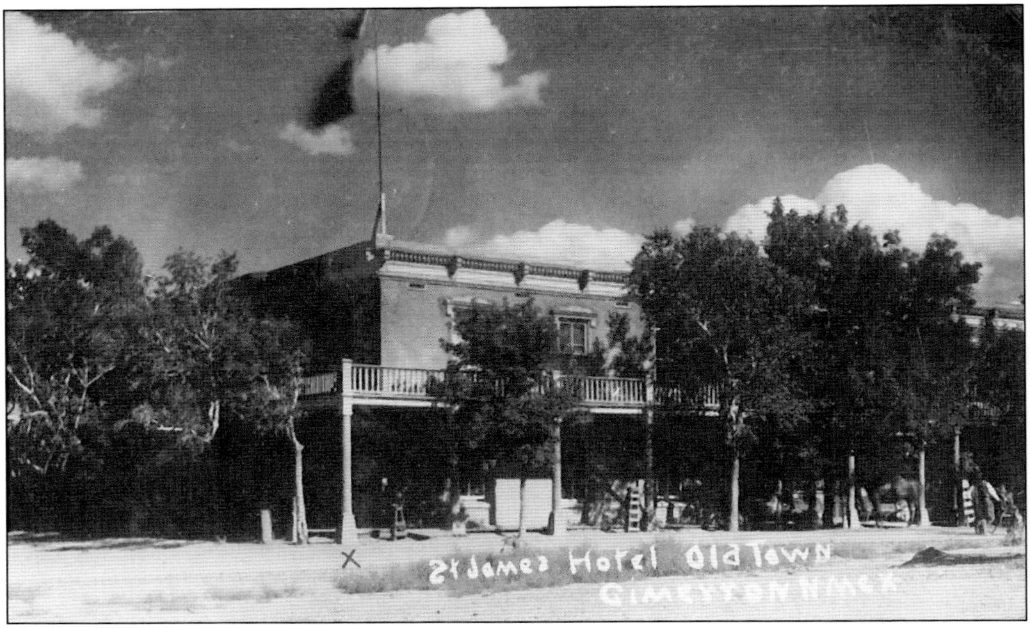

The original saloon comprises the right half of the building hidden behind the trees. The hotel was renamed the Don Diego Hotel in 1932 by new owner F. W. Haegler. A 1960s remodel added new rooms bordering a swimming pool, and for some 20 years afterward the historic section of the hotel was closed, save for the bar. The St. James name was restored in 1985. (George Seward Gumaer Collection, Donald Gumaer.)

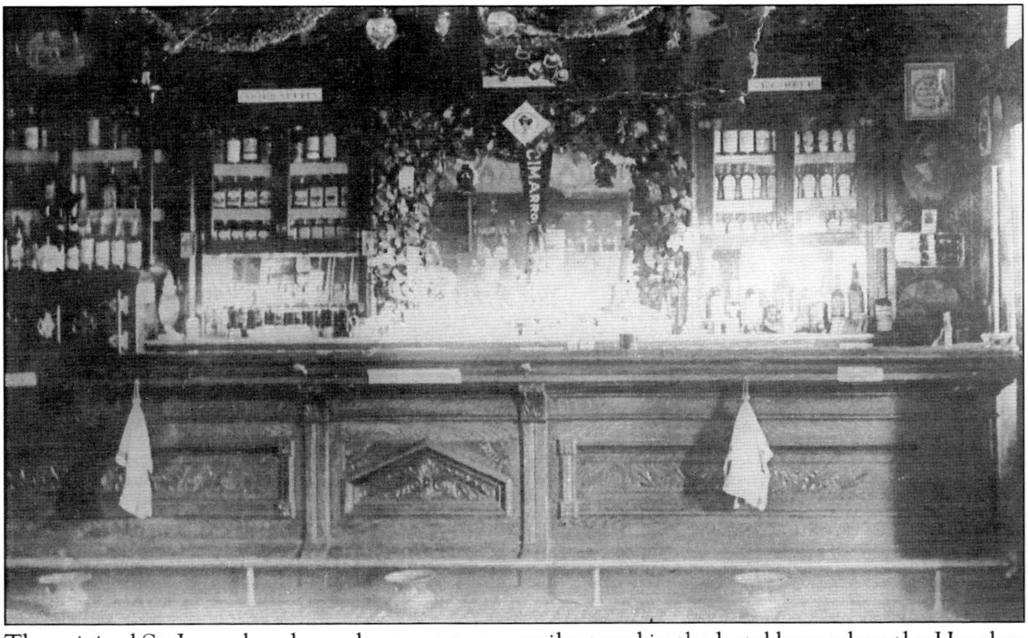

The original St. James bar shown here was temporarily stored in the hotel barn when the Haeglers bought the hostelry and renamed it the Don Diego. The bar was later sold and moved first to the Parks Inn in Taos and then to the Hacienda Motel in Questa. According to Max Evans in *Madame Millie*, the bar is now in the Holiday Inn in Las Cruces. (Lambert family.)

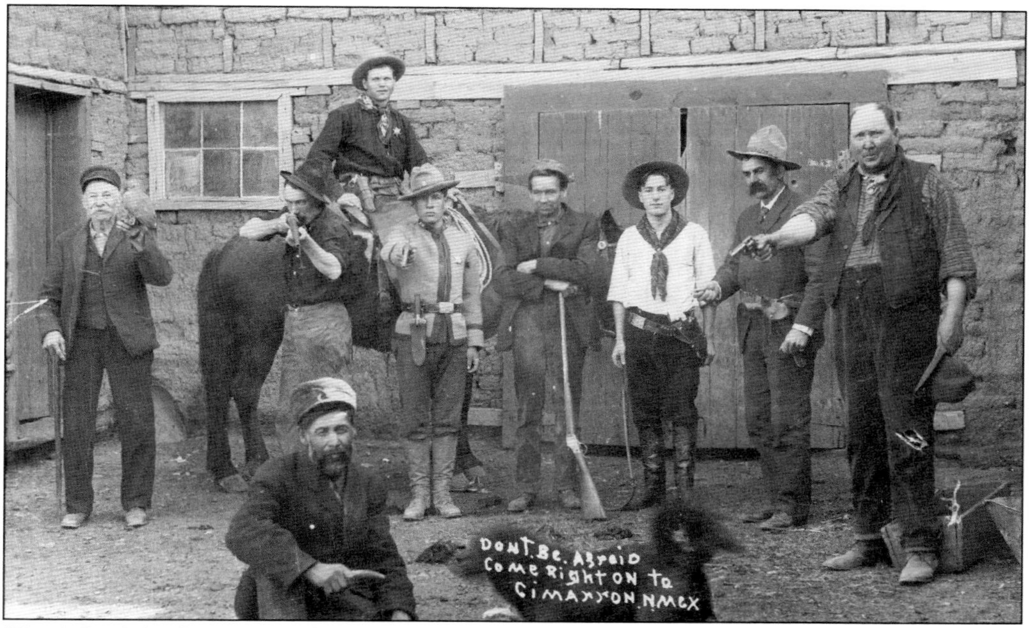

"Don't Be Afraid. Come Right on to Cimarron, N. Mex." is written on this staged photograph showing the southeast corner of the wagon yard on the site of the present hotel annex. Those identified include Henry Lambert (far left), Otaviano Espinoza, William Lambert, Gene Lambert, Fred Lambert, and "Old man Waddle & his boy." It was also published in *The History of the Don Diego Hotel and its Famous Founder, Cimarron, New Mexico.* (Arthur Johnson Memorial Library.)

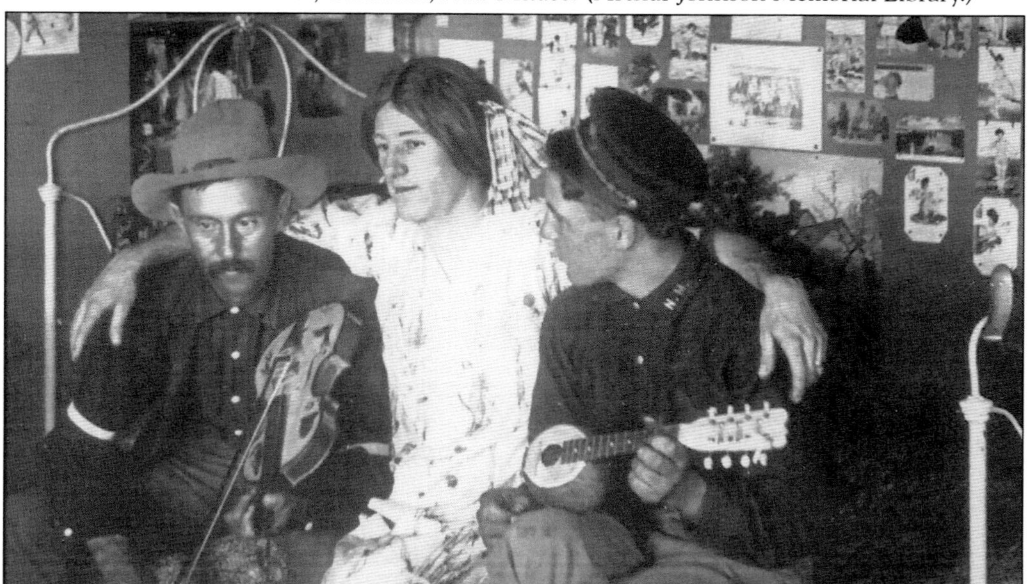

Fred Lambert led a storied and eventful life; from his birth in the St. James to his 50-year law enforcement career, Lambert witnessed the passing of the Wild West firsthand. He and adventuresome Katie Hoover (1886–1964) married in 1913, he became a noted author and Western artist, and he organized The Old Mill museum. This comical 1906 photograph shows John Brackett (left), Fred (center), and brother Gene in Fred's room in the hotel. (Lambert family.)

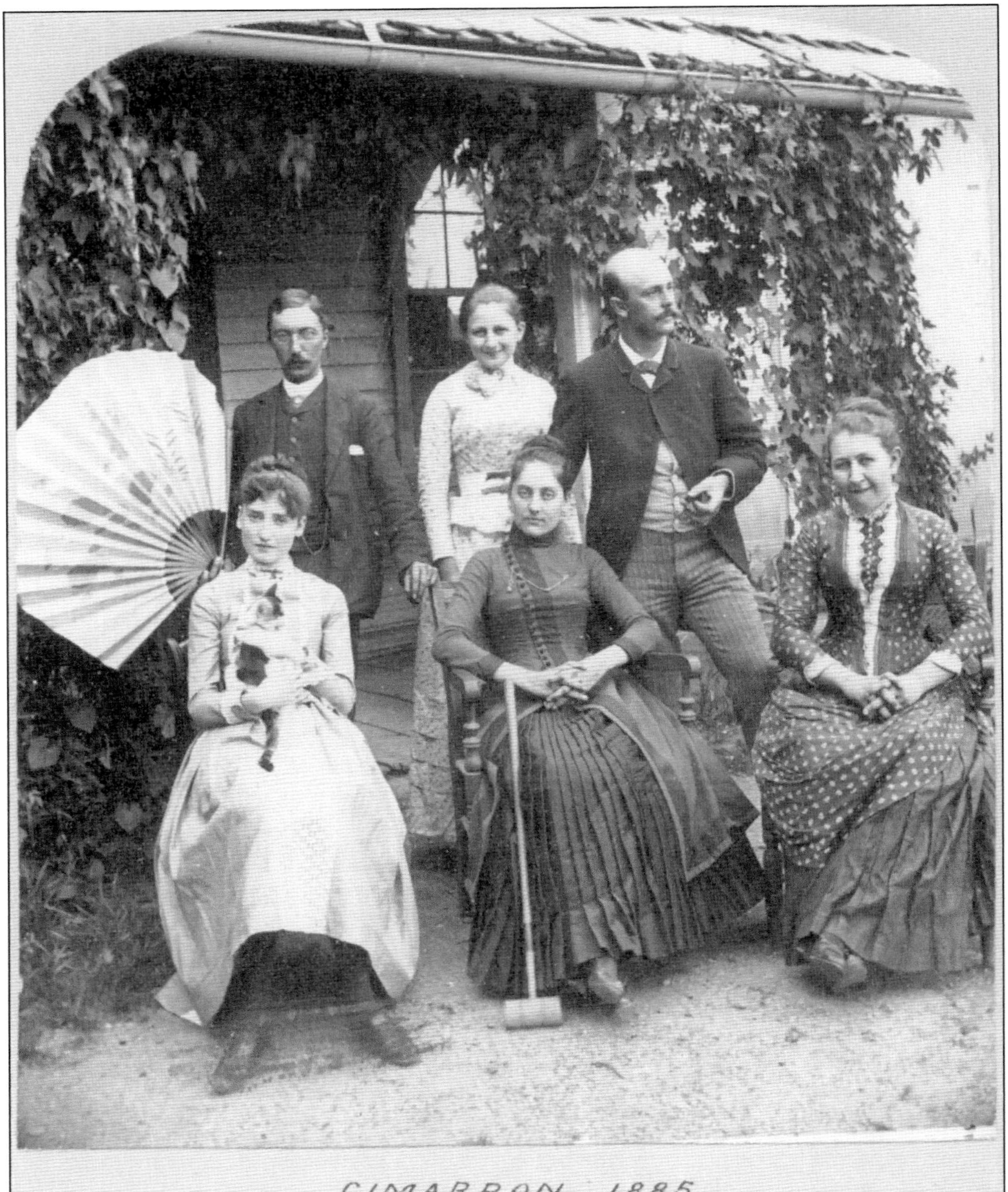

Croquet, once called the "Queen of Games," in which a hard wooden ball is struck by a wooden mallet through a wire hoop, or wicket, on a grass court, originated in France but flourished in England in the mid-19th century. Because the game generally required a close-cut lawn, only those who could afford a gardener played, with those being the upper class. When the game moved to America via the British colonies, it likewise became a symbol of the well-to-do. Whether the ladies and gentlemen in this 1885 photograph actually played croquet is unknown, but the mallet, oriental sunshade, patient cat, and formal poses certainly present the appearance of wealth in an otherwise hardscrabble town. Note the maid in the shadows peeking behind the post. (On page 92, ex-Gov. Lew Wallace plays croquet on the front lawn of the Chase Ranch.) (The Old Mill.)

Four

The Railroad Era

The speculators who purchased Lucien B. Maxwell's Grant promised stockholders that a railroad would come to Cimarron and boasted of the business opportunities soon to be had in the area. There was gold mining on Baldy Mountain, the Cimarron Valley was rich in water for farmers and cattlemen, the hills were a vast source of lumber, and coal had been discovered on John Dawson's ranch just a dozen miles north of town. But the troubles of the Colfax County War lingered in the minds of many, and investors stayed away. Reorganization of the original Maxwell Land Grant and Railway Company of 1872 into the "new" Maxwell Land Grant Company in 1880 did little to help. In that year, the Atchison, Topeka & Santa Fe Railway completed track from Raton to Lamy, just south of Santa Fe, but Cimarron was bypassed, with the route directed through the town of Springer 20 miles to the east.

It was not until 1906 that the St. Louis, Rocky Mountain & Pacific Railway Company built a spur line from Raton to Cimarron, with a later extension through the canyon to Ute Park 15 miles to the west. Stops on the main passenger line included Nash, at the canyon mouth, and Harlan two miles farther west. A plan to extend tracks to Elizabethtown, Taos, and the West Coast was later dropped. The logo chosen for the StLRM&P was a popular Navajo symbol used in healing, the swastika, hence the moniker "the Swastika Line." Ironically, the tracks of the railroad were taken up during World War II and were reused in the war effort.

Only one year after the StLRM&P inaugurated its line, the Cimarron and Northwestern Railway Company began laying track up the north fork of Ponil River. In 1908, the rich timberland from Cimarron 22 miles along the Ponil was opened for logging. Towns such as Ponil Park, Ring, and Bonito housed track workers and lumbermen who were paid in scrip, redeemable only at company stores. Today, these once thriving communities have vanished beneath the lush grasses of the Valle Vidal Unit of the Carson National Forest.

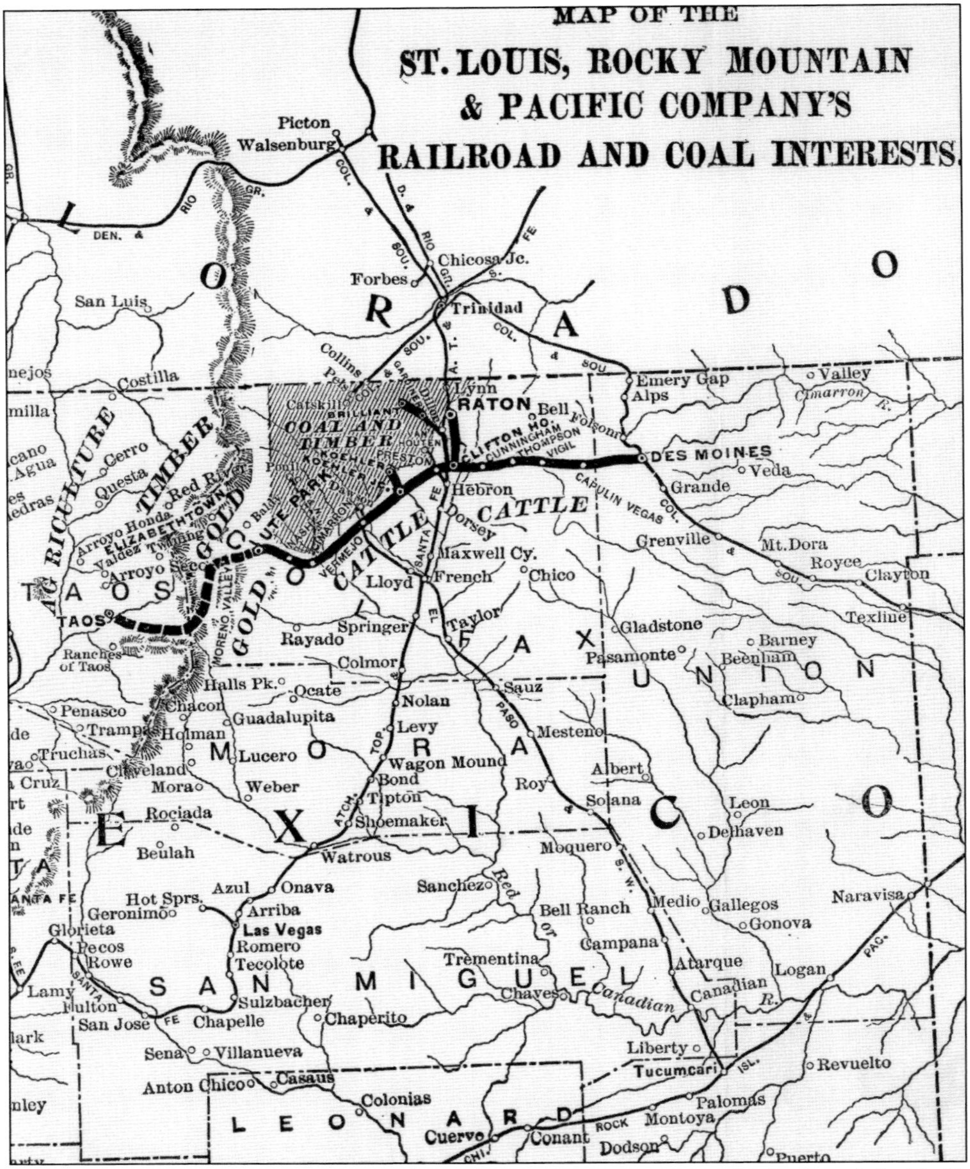

The St. Louis Rocky Mountain & Pacific Railway Company was established on July 11, 1905. This map excerpt from the 1908 *Manual of Statistics: Stock Exchange Hand-Book* illustrates the coal lands then owned (191,895 acres) or served (328,430 acres), the rail lines owned between Des Moines, New Mexico, through Raton and Cimarron to Ute Park, and the proposed service route extending west from Ute Park to Taos. Other railroads crisscrossed Colorado and New Mexico: the Denver and Rio Grande; Colorado and Southern; Atchison, Topeka, & Santa Fe; El Paso and Southwestern; Chicago, Rock Island, and Pacific; and the Southern Pacific. Timber and coal railroads such as the Cimarron & Northwestern and the New Mexico Midland were formed as affiliates of these railroads or by lumber and mining companies. Not surprisingly, this map bears a strong resemblance to modern highway maps of the area. A glimpse into early-20th-century rail travel is still available to Amtrak riders, including the thousands of Scouts who arrive at and depart from the former Atchison, Topeka, & Santa Fe depot (1903) in Raton. (Authors' collection.)

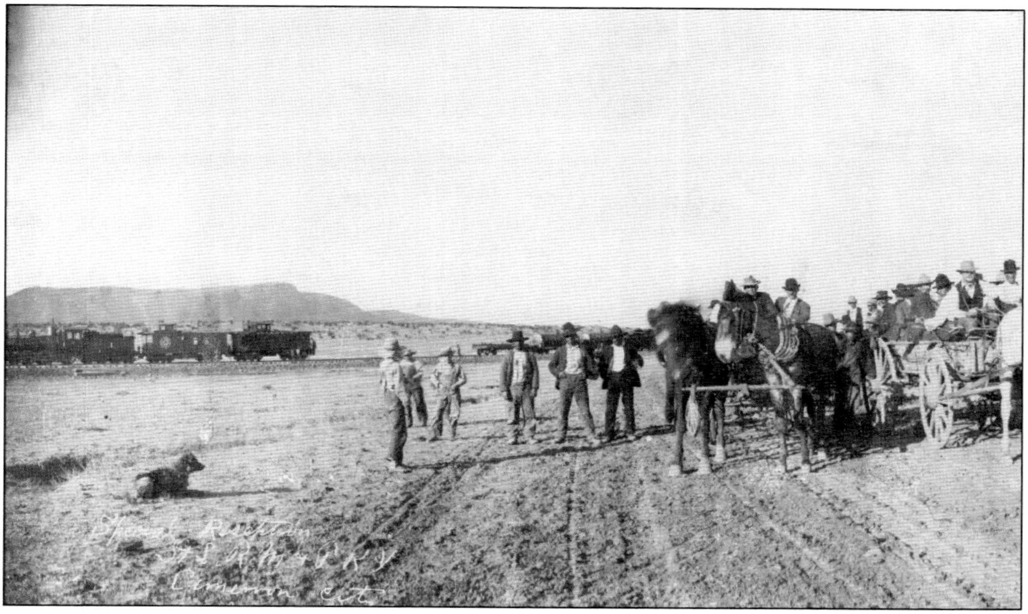

An enthusiastic crowd was on hand to meet the first train into Cimarron: "Special Reseption [*sic*] / St L. R. M. + P Ry / Cimerron [*sic*] City / June 26th 1906." Regular passenger and freight traffic was established later that year between all points on the line, which eventually encompassed 105 miles. The company was sold to the Santa Fe Railroad in 1913 and in 1915 was renamed the Rocky Mountain and Santa Fe Railway Company. (The Old Mill.)

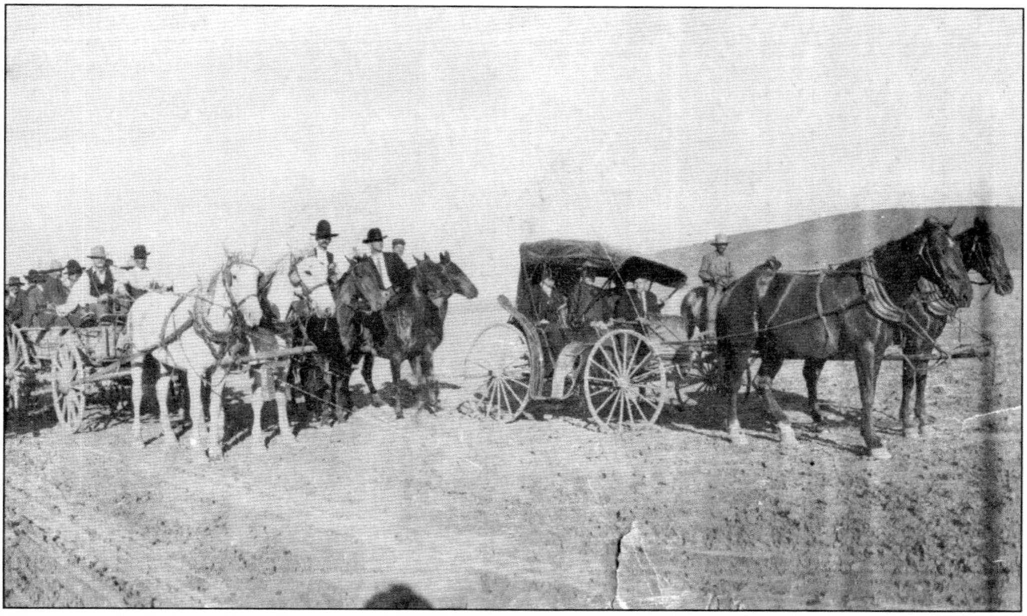

The arrival of the railroad promised a renewal in Cimarron's fortunes. A glowing tribute to her prospects appeared in the March 4, 1908, *Cimarron Citizen*: "We have business houses that any city in the Territory might be proud of . . . Being just a half mile from Heaven, we have some of its climate. [E]verything but exorbitant tax assessments and the small pox is to be found at Cimarron." (The Old Mill.)

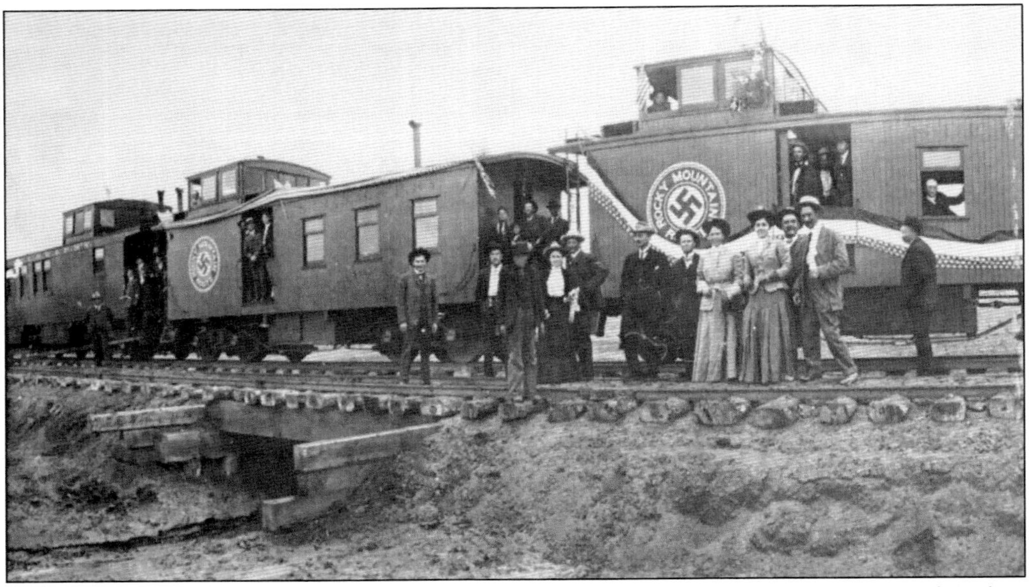

After 14 months of grading and construction by the Utah Construction Company of Ogden, the railroad was completed in January 1907. Although construction from Raton to Cimarron was over relatively flat terrain, passage through the rocky Cimarron Canyon to Ute Park was as challenging as any project in the Southwest. This inaugural train—extending to the opposite page—included three cabooses, a tank car, and passenger train engine No. 1. (Audrey Alpers Collection, The Old Mill.)

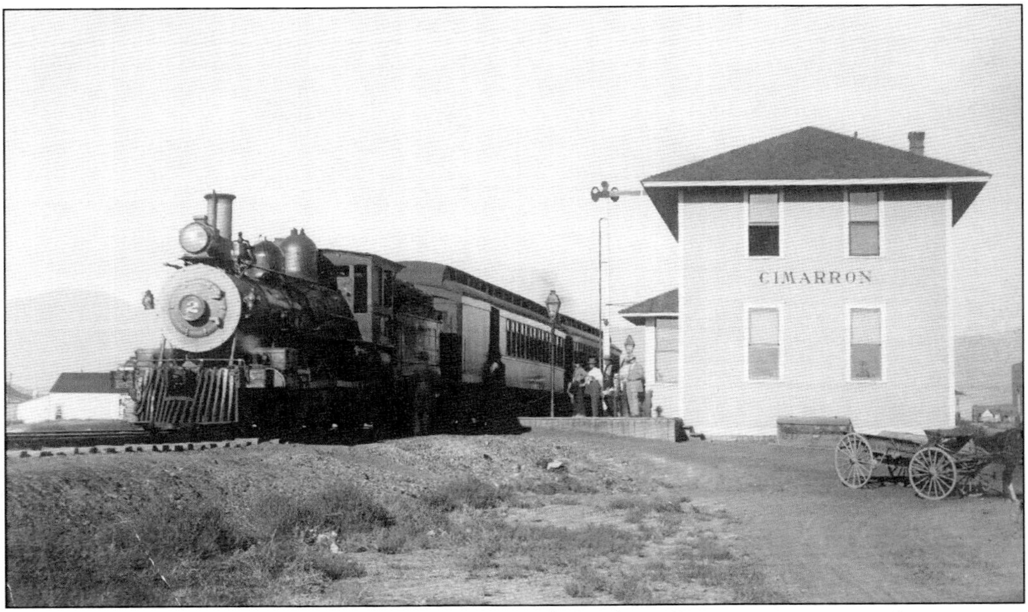

In mid-1907, the St. Louis, Rocky Mountain & Pacific Railway Company constructed a two-story station on the north side of the track at the foot of Washington Avenue. Above a stone basement, the steam-heated, 24-by-55-foot frame structure adjoined a 16-by-75-foot platform. The ticket office and waiting room are on the ground floor, with railroad offices and a bedroom upstairs. Passengers are here seen preparing to board the Raton-bound train. (The Old Mill.)

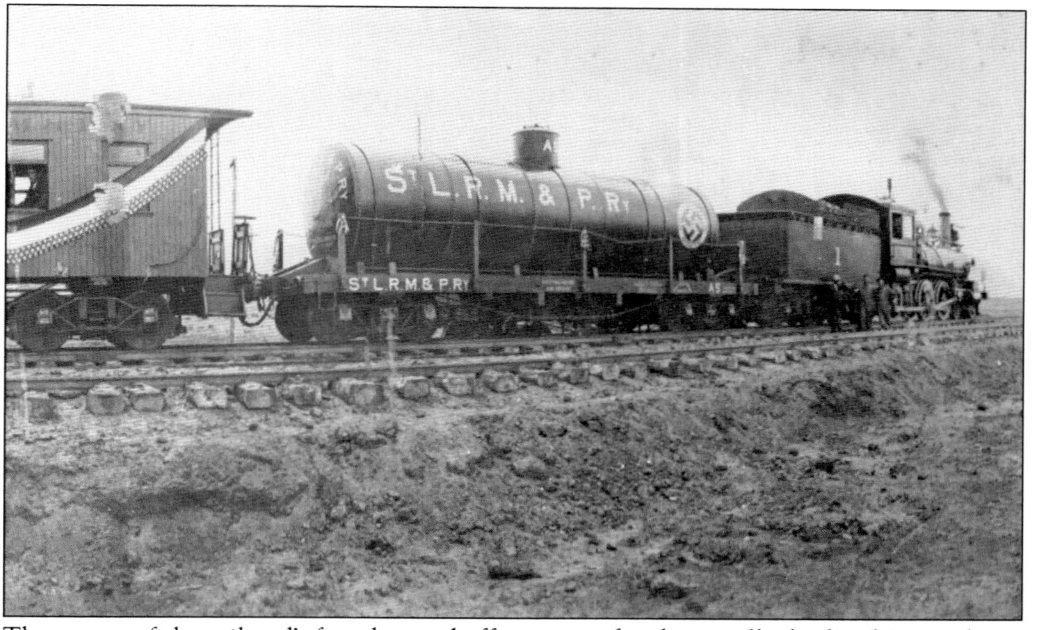

The names of the railroad's founders and officers were familiar to all who lived in northeast New Mexico: Henry Koehler, Jan Van Houten, Charles Springer, Hugo A. Koehler, and Arthur H. Officer. Springer and Officer also helped establish the Cimarron Valley Land Company, which secured rights in 1907 to construct the Eagle Nest Dam, the most transformative project undertaken. (Audrey Alpers Collection, The Old Mill.)

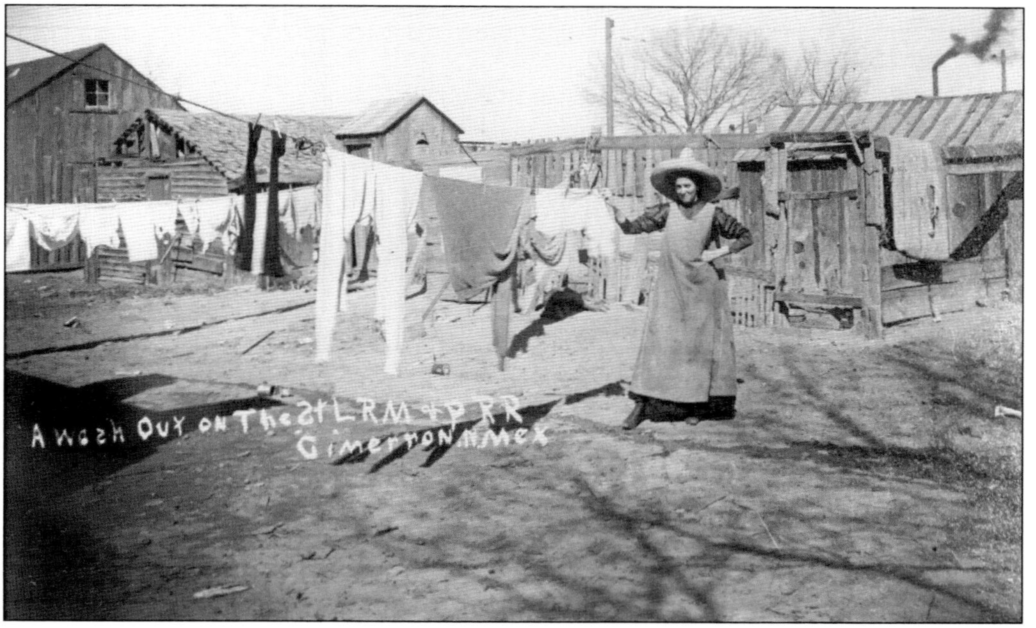

Titled "A Wash Out on the St L R M & P RR," this Troutman Studio photograph symbolizes the contented life led by then modern pioneers in turn-of-the-century Cimarron. One wonders how long the undergarments would stay white under the billowing smokestack of the sawmill in the distance. (The Old Mill.)

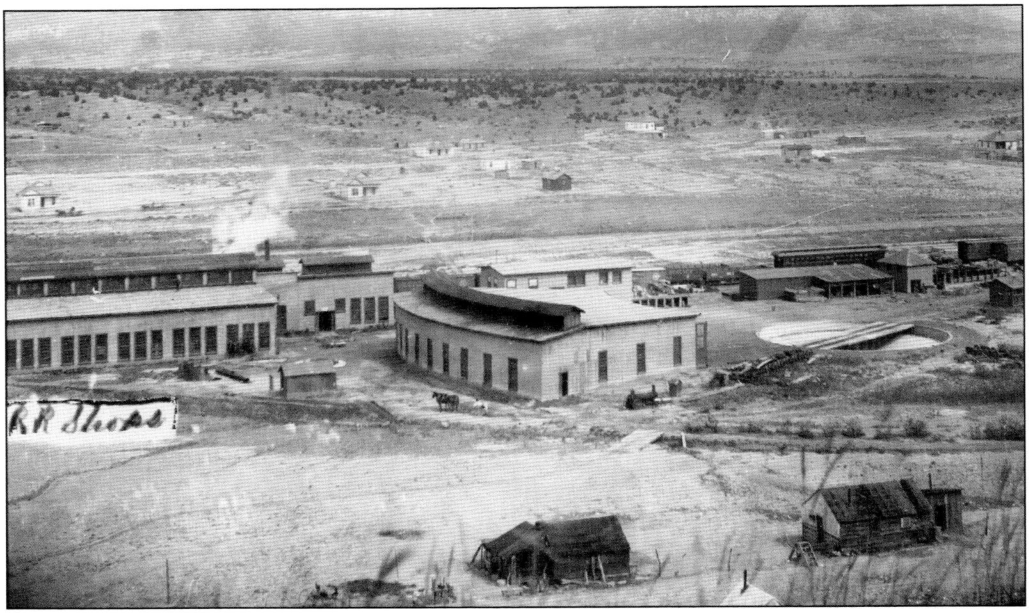

The St. Louis, Rocky Mountain & Pacific Railway roundhouse (1907) used for servicing its engines sat at the east end of town where a wye split off from the main line west to Ute Park. Nearby were stockyards for loading cattle. The shops were dismantled in 1914; all that remains today is the turntable pit that facilitated the storage of engines in different bays of the roundhouse. (Hickman family.)

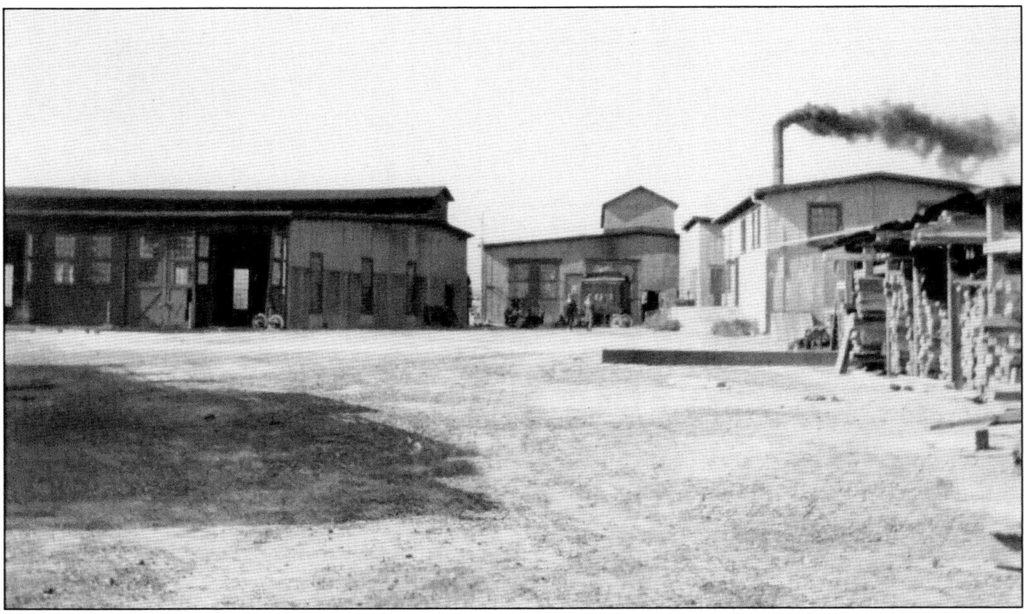

After the St. Louis, Rocky Mountain & Pacific Railway arrived, the Continental Tie & Lumber Company added a spur line from Cimarron up Ponil Creek to harvest the abundant lumber resources along its route. Cut and trimmed logs were sent by rail back to Cimarron where they were processed into finished boards at the company's sawmill. The CT&L office was east of town where the StLRM&P tracks turned west. (Raton Museum.)

General passenger agent W.A. Gorman distributed this long-anticipated passenger train schedule announcing passenger service between Raton, Cimarron, and Dawson effective December 10, 1906. The train's average speed between Cimarron and Raton was 15 miles per hour. If the schedule was in effect in 1911, then the photograph below was taken about 9:30 in the morning. The northbound time for Koehler may seem in error, but Koehler Junction sat on the main line whereas Koehler was at the end of a spur west of the junction. The train always stopped at the junction first before picking up passengers at Koehler. As shown on the letterhead, the railroad also was known as the "Rocky Mountain Route." (Hickman family.)

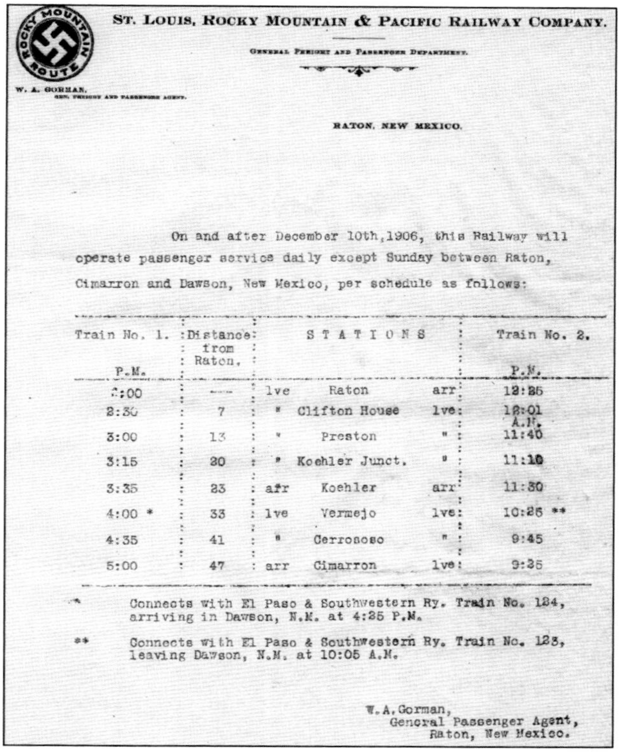

ST. LOUIS, ROCKY MOUNTAIN & PACIFIC RAILWAY COMPANY.

GENERAL FREIGHT AND PASSENGER DEPARTMENT.

W. A. GORMAN,
GEN. FREIGHT AND PASSENGER AGENT.

RATON, NEW MEXICO.

On and after December 10th,1906, this Railway will operate passenger service daily except Sunday between Raton, Cimarron and Dawson, New Mexico, per schedule as follows:

Train No. 1. P.M.	Distance from Raton.		STATIONS		Train No. 2. P.M.
2:00	---	lve	Raton	arr	12:35
2:30	7	"	Clifton House	lve	12:01 A.M.
3:00	13	"	Preston	"	11:40
3:15	20	"	Koehler Junct.	"	11:10
3:35	23	arr	Koehler	arr	11:30
4:00 *	33	lve	Vermejo	lve	10:25 **
4:35	41	"	Cerrososo	"	9:45
5:00	47	arr	Cimarron	lve	9:35

* Connects with El Paso & Southwestern Ry. Train No. 124, arriving in Dawson, N.M. at 4:25 P.M.

** Connects with El Paso & Southwestern Ry. Train No. 123, leaving Dawson, N.M. at 10:05 A.M.

W.A.Gorman,
General Passenger Agent,
Raton, New Mexico.

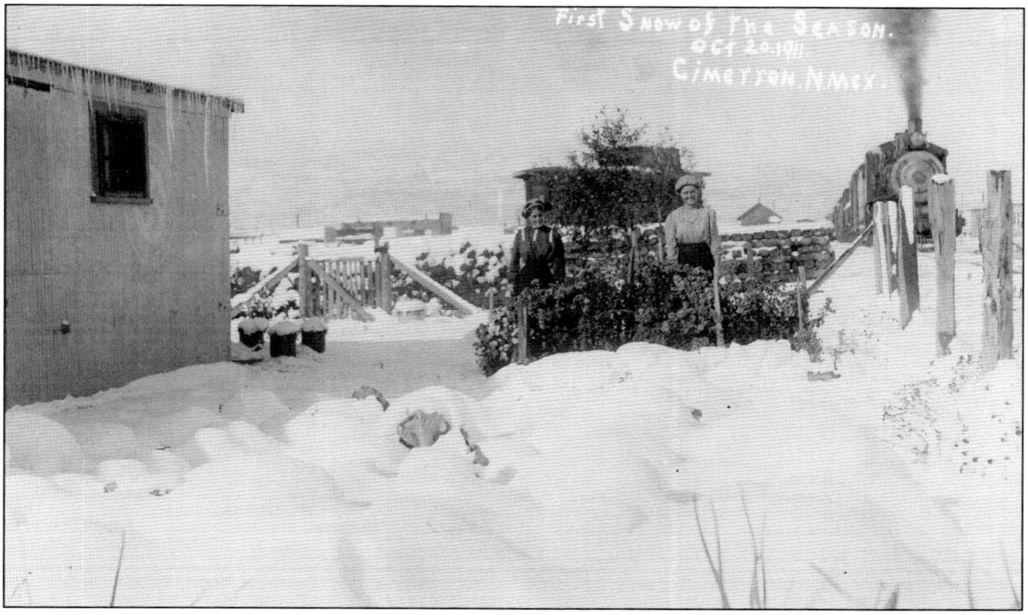

Celebrating the "First Snow of the Season" on October 20, 1911, these two ladies standing next to their garden pleasantly ignore the belching steam engine passing nearby. The boxcar on the left served as their home. These women may have been close friends or relatives of the Troutmans, because the house appears in numerous photographs. The view is due west with the Sangre de Cristo Mountains in the distance blanketed in early-autumn snow. (Raton Museum.)

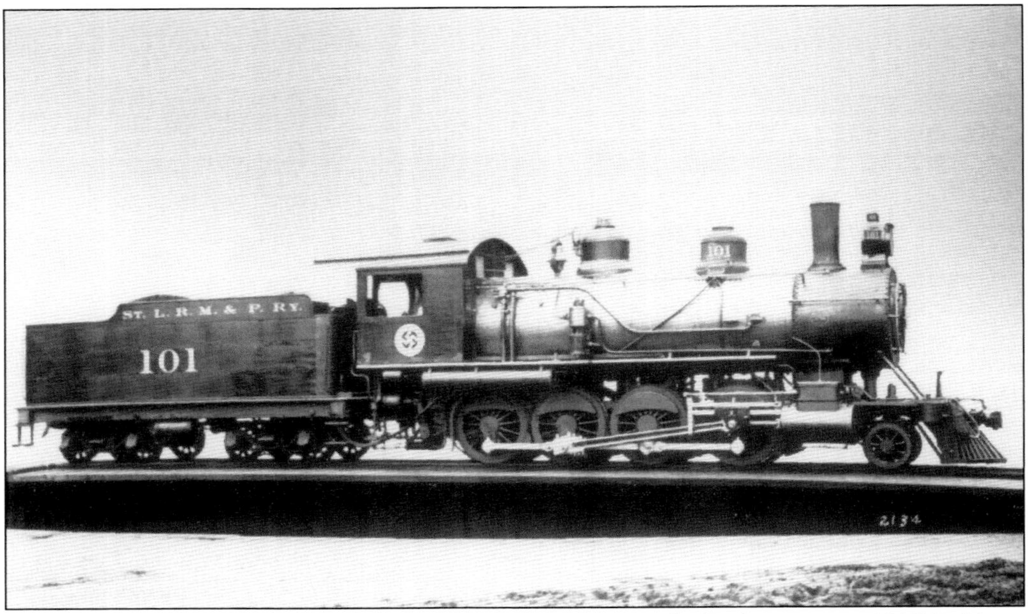

Locomotive 101 of the St. Louis, Rocky Mountain & Pacific Railway was a 1905 Baldwin Consolidation 2-8-0 locomotive, as shown in this Baldwin builder's photograph. It was renumbered 870 in 1924, while under Rocky Mountain & Santa Fe ownership, and was sold in 1940 to the Albuquerque & Los Cerrillos Coal Company. In the 1970s, it was sold to the City of Santa Fe Springs, California, restored, and is on display at Heritage Park. (Philmont Scout Ranch.)

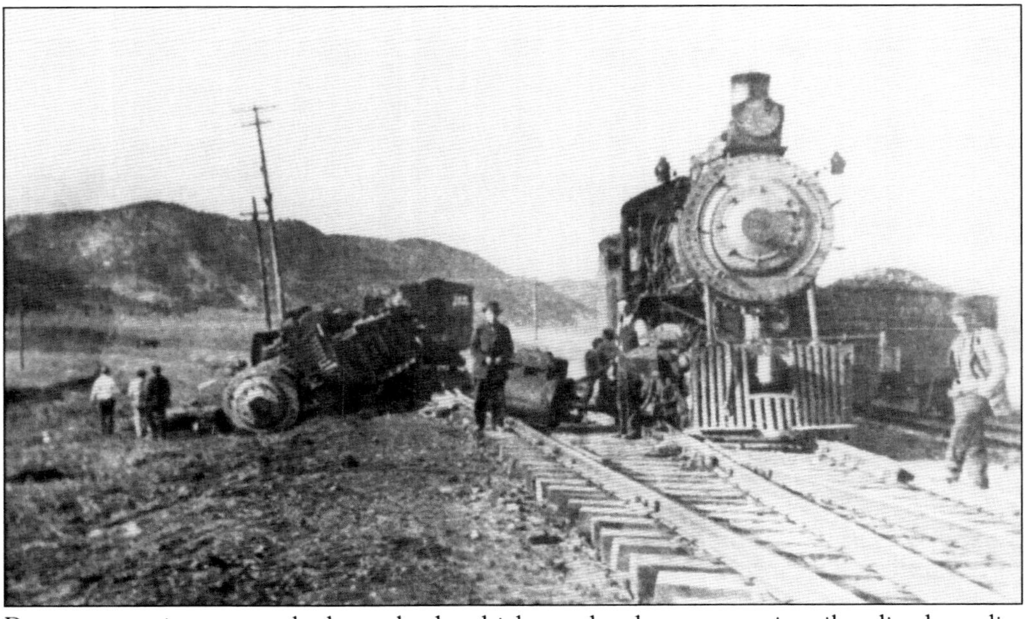

Damage to equipment, tracks, heavy loads at high speed, or human error in railroading have dire consequences, as witnessed in this c. 1911 derailment photograph. According to the inscription, this was a Cimarron & Northwestern Railway locomotive and Santa Fe wreck near Springer. A crane from shops in Raton or Santa Fe would have been dispatched to right the locomotive and restore service. (Philmont Scout Ranch.)

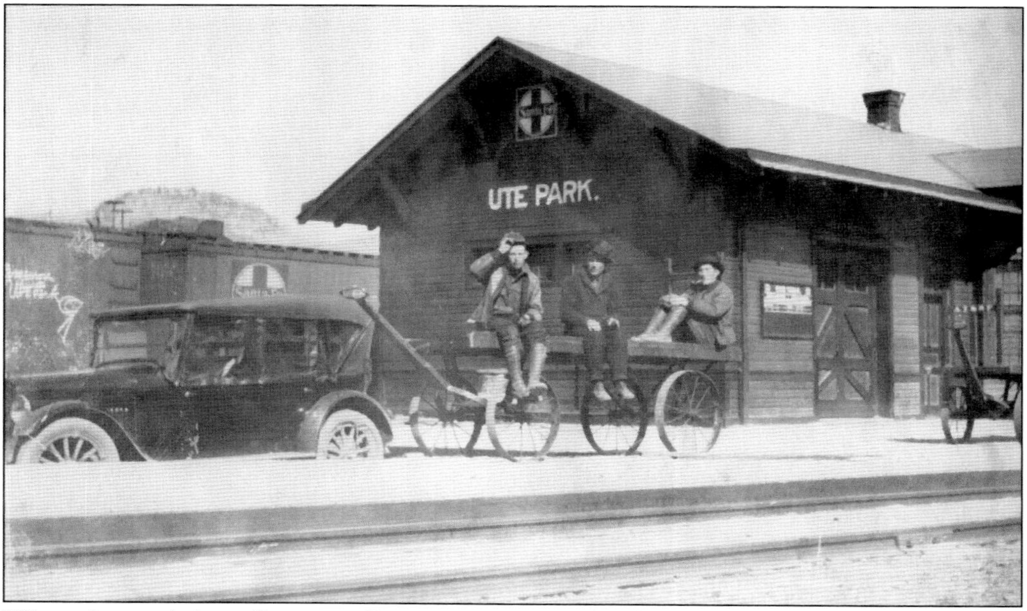

When the track from Raton to Cimarron was completed in the summer of 1906, a line for passengers was immediately extended to Ute Park. By January, the stations, freight house, and icehouses were ready for use, with H.H. Hankins as the local agent. Hankins also operated the Hankins Stage Line between Springer and Taos. By the time of this photograph, the station was under the ownership of the Santa Fe Railway. (Hickman family.)

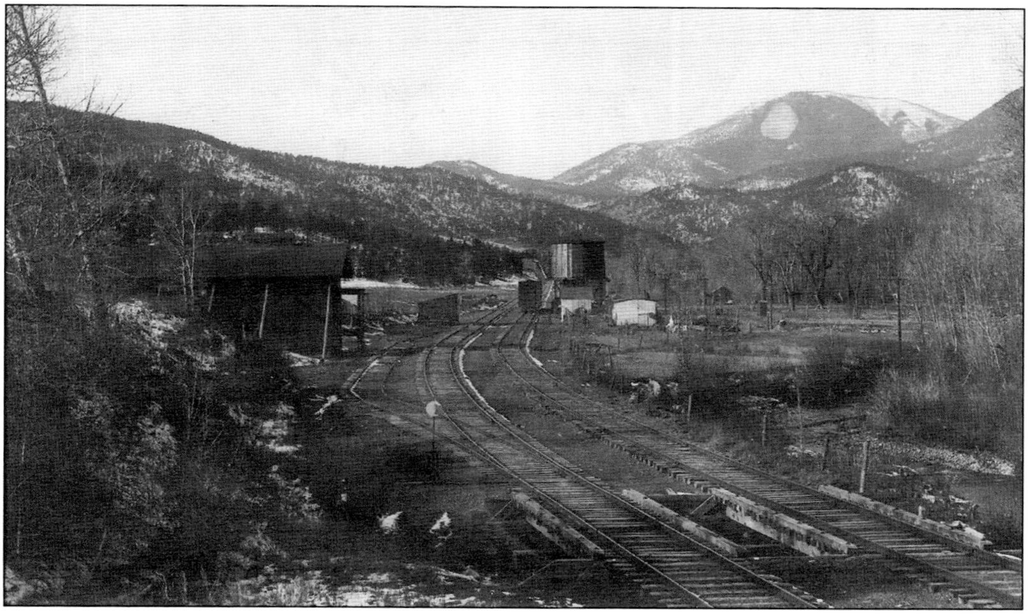

This Troutman Studio photograph of the Ute Park service yard one mile east of the station is one of eight reprinted by the Cimarron Publishing Company as color postcards in 1916. The set was advertised in the *Cimarron News-Citizen*: "Remember your friends and send them post card views of the Cimarron Canon. Sold at leading stores at 2 for 5 cents." The postcard corresponding to this image is "105. Scenic Beauties Near Ute Park, Colfax County, N. M." (Authors' collection.)

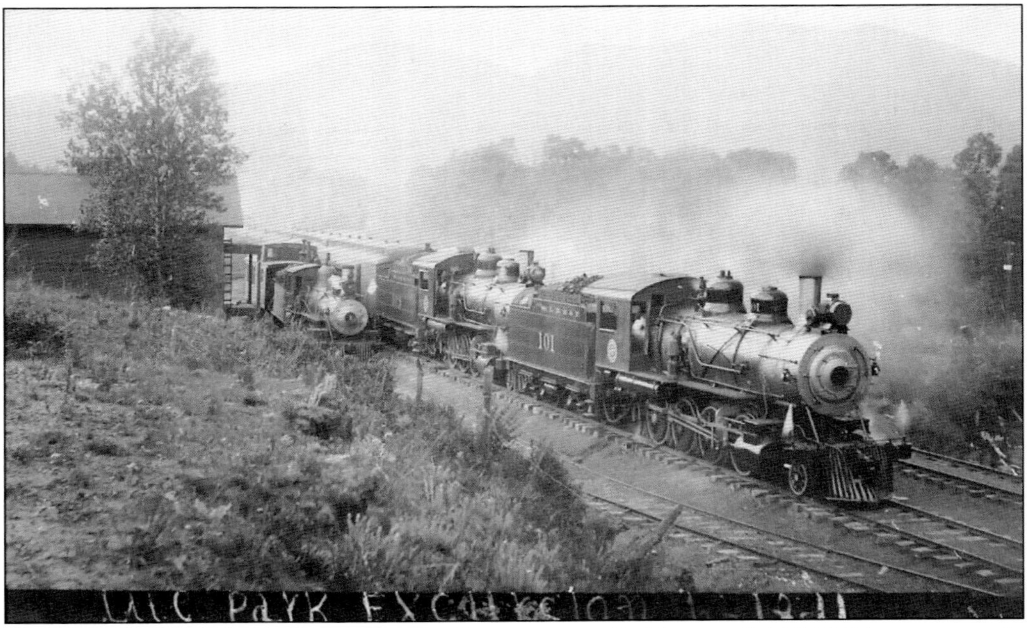

An eastbound passenger train at the Ute Park wye is pulled by two StLRM&P locomotives in mid-June 1911. A smaller local consist is on the adjacent sidetrack. In June 1907, a 12-person railway automobile purchased from the Fairbanks Morse and Company of Chicago was added to the Swastika Route for travel between Cimarron and Ute Park. (George Seward Gumaer Collection, Donald Gumaer.)

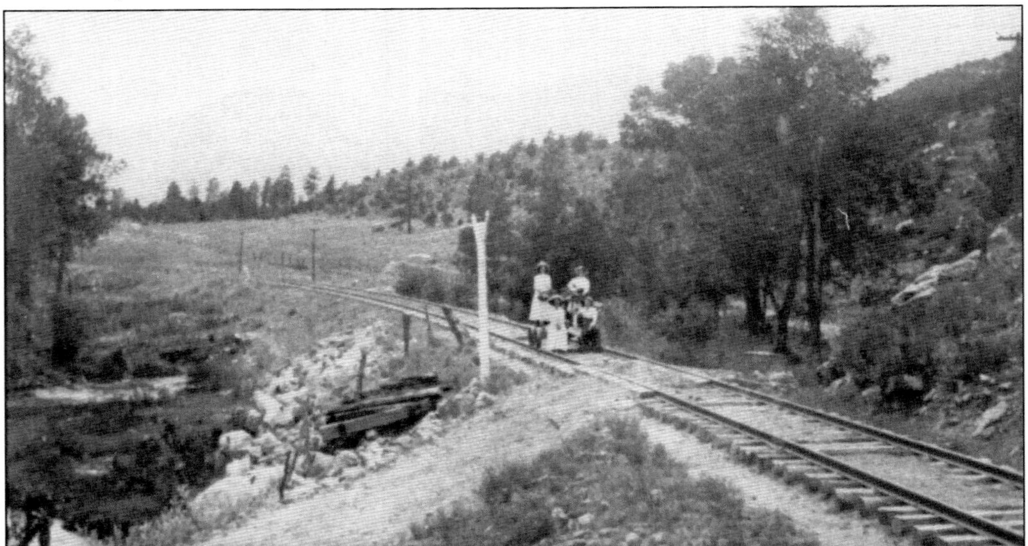

The railroad line from "Ute Park, Gateway to the Golden West" to Cimarron is shown crossing the road from Taos in this delightful photograph. One assumes no train is forthcoming! Touch-Me-Not Mountain appears faintly visible in the distance. Minnette Thompson established the Cimarroncita Ranch Camp for Girls at the former Ute Park railroad resort in 1931, and the Cimarroncita Historic Ranch Retreat remains in operation. (Arthur Johnson Memorial Library.)

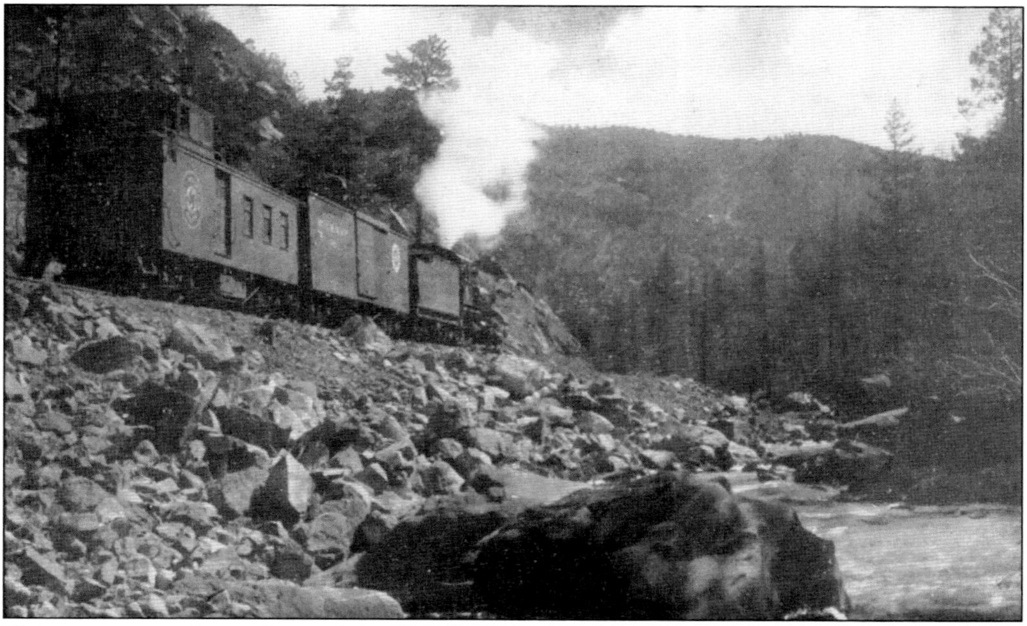

This scenic view shows the eastbound StLRM&P train entering Cimarron Canyon after leaving Ute Park—proceeding toward Cimarron from the previous photographs' views. The location is near Highway 64 mile marker 300 where Scouts cross the river on a footbridge connecting Bear Canyon and the north country (left) to Cimarron River Camp in the south. (Authors' collection.)

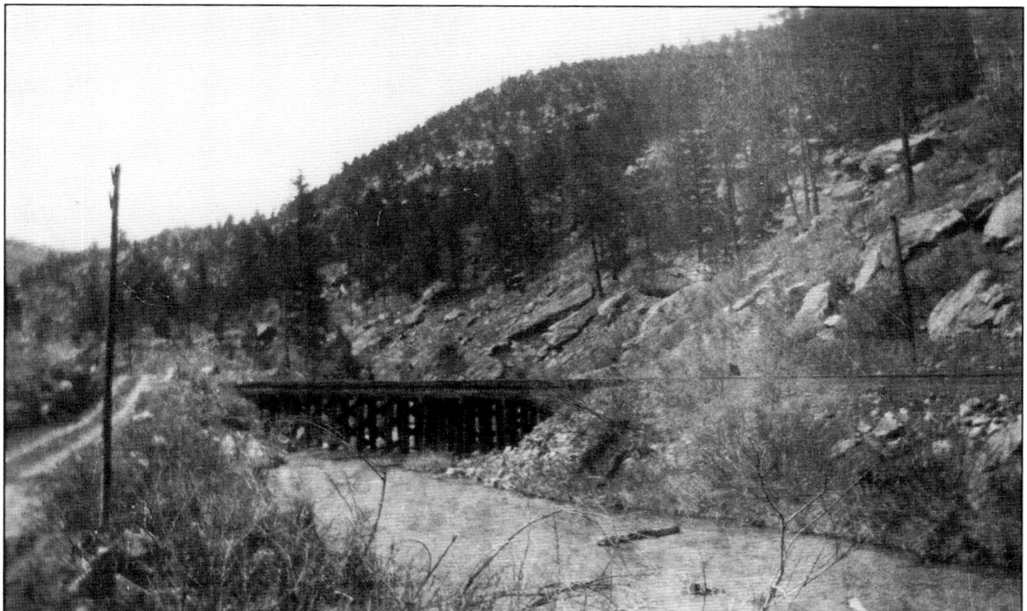

This final view shows the Ute Park-Cimarron line about one mile farther east. The rugged terrain that constantly clashed river, road, and track is clearly evident. Nevertheless, the grade was less than two percent, with few river crossings for either road or rail. The June 15, 1908, schedule lists the Cimarron departure as 7:00 p.m., with a Ute Park arrival at 7:45. After an overnight stay, the 15-mile return trip departed Ute Park at 7:00 the following morning. (Authors' collection.)

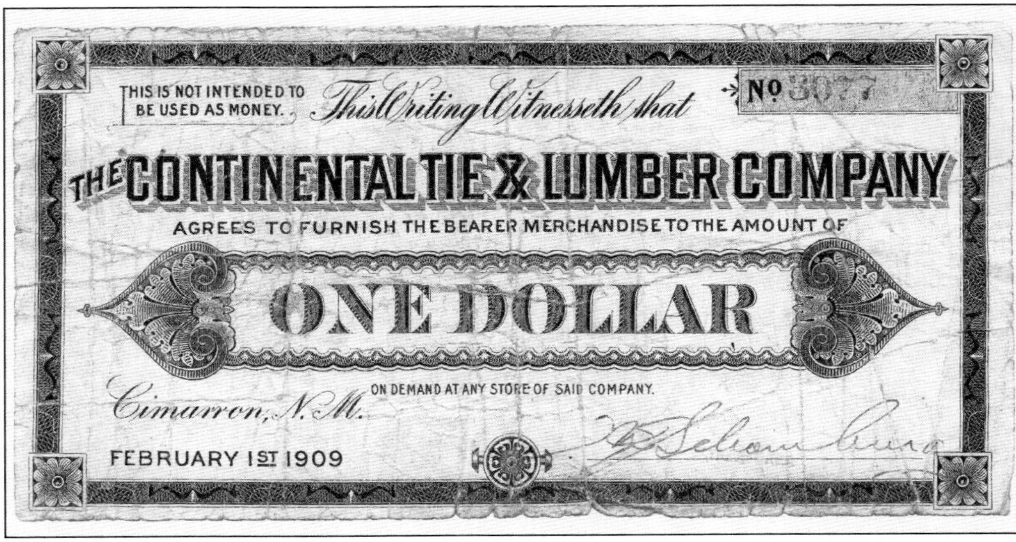

Scrip was currency given by a company as wages to a worker that was usually redeemable only in a company-run store. It was often issued by mining and lumber companies located in isolated places where US coin and currency were in short supply. This $1 scrip from 1909 was issued by the Continental Tie & Lumber Company, which ran rail lines from Cimarron up Ponil Creek. (Philmont Scout Ranch.)

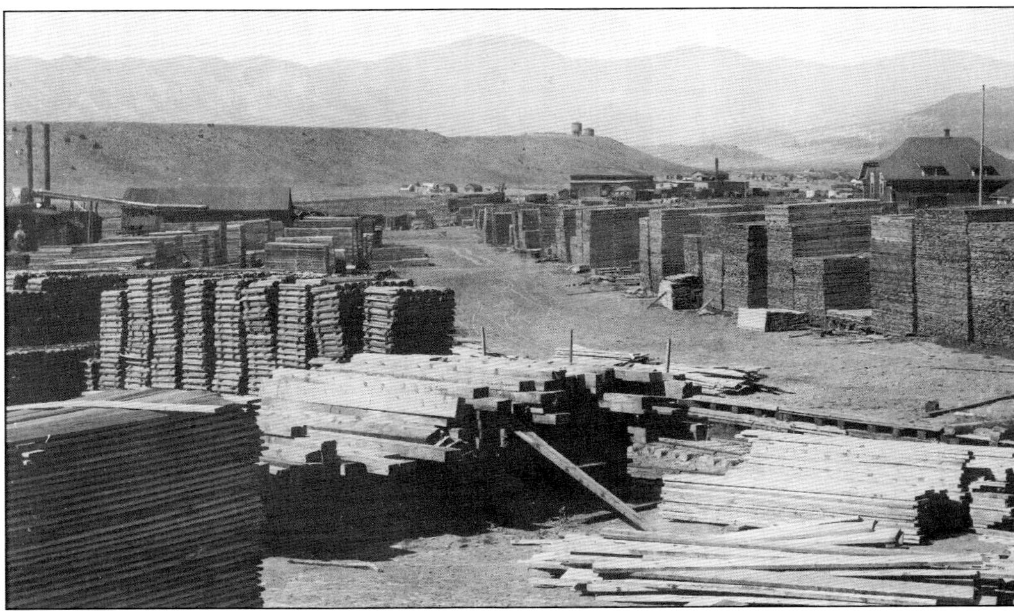

The Continental Tie & Lumber Company lumberyard was east of the present-day intersection of Highways 58 and 64. The Cimarron & Northwestern Railway shop is at far left, and the two-story building at right served as offices for both. The St. Louis & Pacific Railway Company roundhouse and shops are in the center distance. This view dates from 1919; it is a postcard mailed by Alma Troutman. (Authors' collection.)

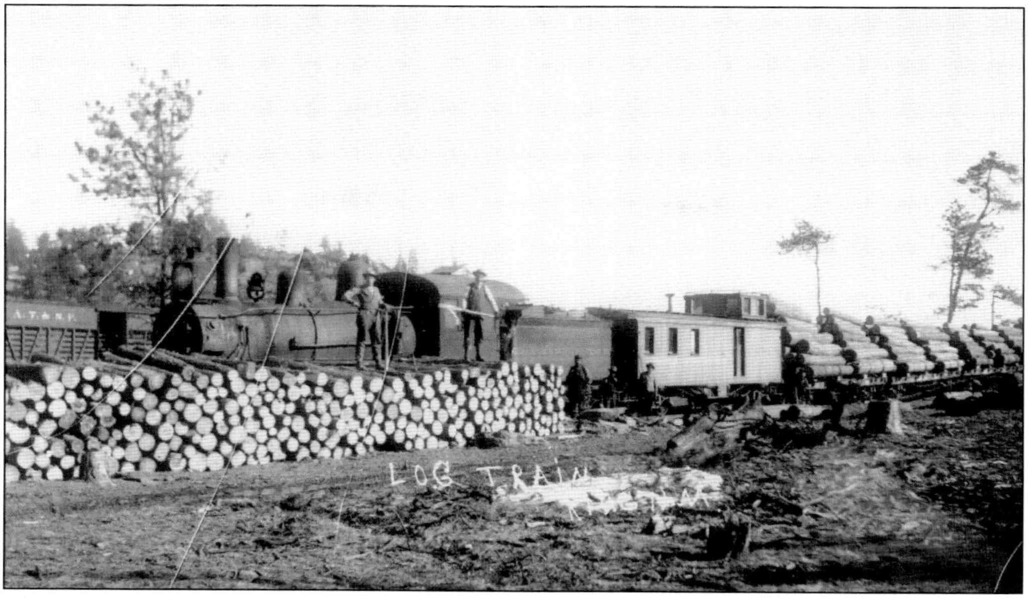

This C&N train is shipping bucked (cut-to-length) logs back to Cimarron to be made into boards. This required debarking, edging, trimming the ends, drying, and finally planing the boards smooth. Before being shipped east, each piece of lumber was then graded depending on the number and size of knots, the presence of bark on edges, splits and other defects, warping or bowing, and the type of wood. (Audrey Alpers Collection, The Old Mill.)

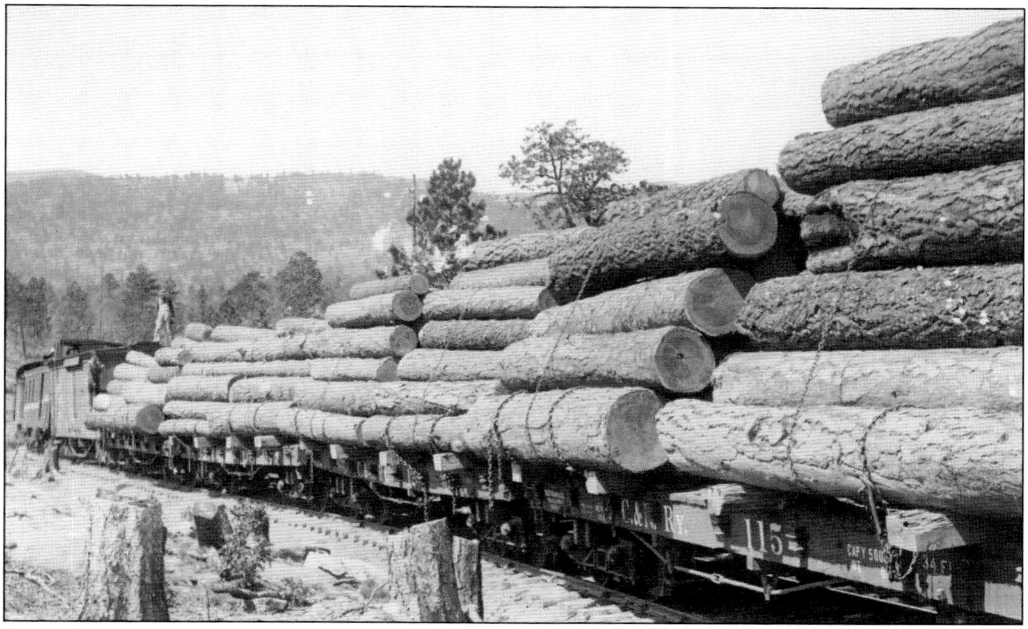

After StLRM&P interest in the Cimarron-Ute Park line declined in the mid-1920s, the CT&L set up a prop yard in Ute Park to supply the renewed mining on Baldy. However, by 1930, the lack of easily accessible timber essentially signaled an end to logging operations in the Cimarron area. Philmont celebrates this brief but important period in Cimarron's history through its backcountry camps at Pueblano and Crater Lake. (The Old Mill.)

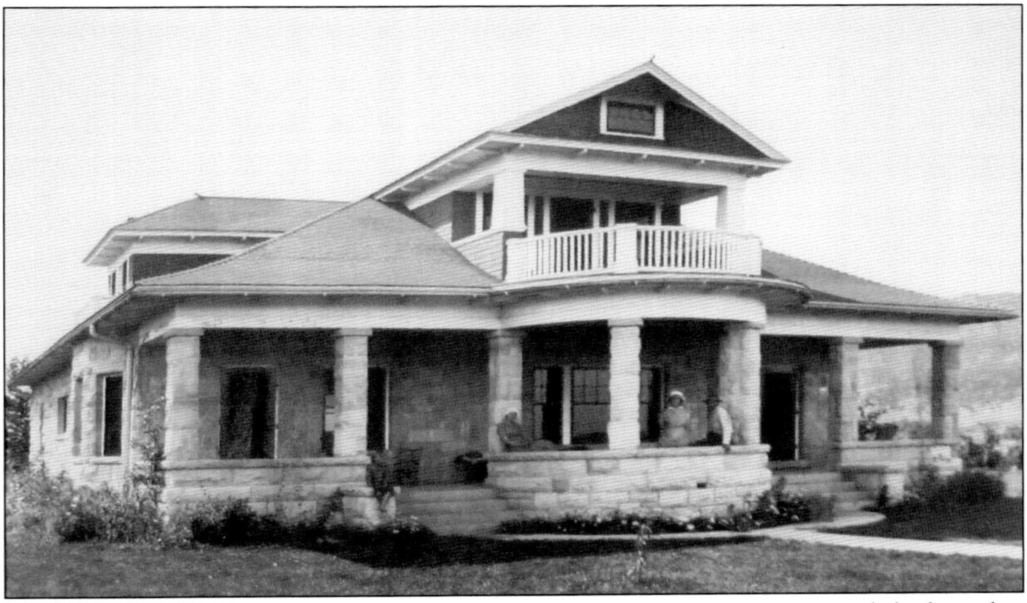

Harvey H. Chandler, manager of the Henry M. Porter ranches, was an accomplished rancher in his own right with land north of the Cimarron River at Turkey Creek Canyon. He and wife Katherine lived in this stone ranch house west of the Catholic church on the old road to Taos. Chandler Canyon, to the south of State Road 204 west of the Six Mile Gate, was named for the Chandler family. (The Old Mill.)

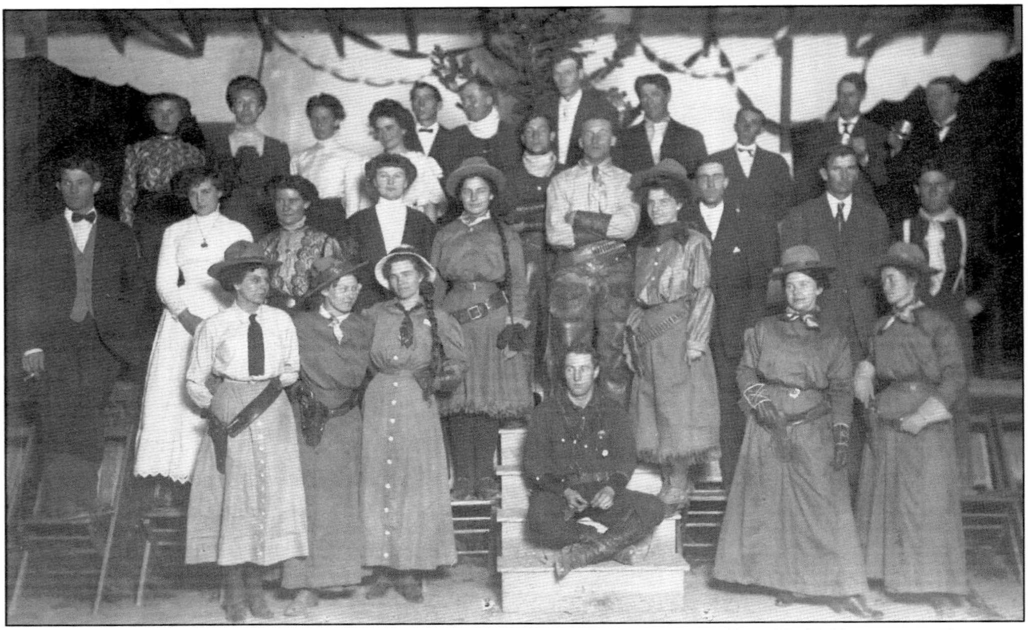

Fred Lambert (seated) is surrounded by his friends at the 1910 Cowboy Ball. Festive gatherings were commonplace in both Old Town and New Town. Cimarron's Star Lodge of the Coming Men of America held all-night dances and feasts in the Aztec Mill and was considered "the most royal entertainers in the southwest." A large CMA logo still graces the north second-story wall in The Old Mill. (The Old Mill.)

Five

New Town

In 1906, with the arrival of the railroad and easy transport of goods from the East, construction of a "New Town" began. Soon, water lines, paved roads, stockyards, a lumber mill, a modern school, a hospital, and numerous businesses appeared. Because the tracks ran north of the river and with people naturally choosing newer amenities over old, Old Town on the south side remained relatively undisturbed. The only major construction projects in Old Town were a cluster of managers' houses and a new bridge to reach them. Compared with other western towns, the landscape of Old Town Cimarron, with its plaza and well, hotels, jail, mill, and other buildings, is uniquely authentic. Today, the Walking Tour of Old Town is a major draw for tourists who wish to step back and experience the past.

Yet, much of New Town also speaks of history. Twelfth Street, known locally as Coco Street (*coco* is colloquial Spanish for "scary" or "monster"), retains its curious assortment of century-old adobes that once served as bars and businesses where the road west to Taos intersected the road east to Springer. After the railroad tracks were removed in 1942, the two roads were rerouted. The road to Taos, which once ran past the hotel in Old Town before veering west past the church, became Highway 64 and now follows the old rail bed into the canyon. The road to Springer, which once ran next to the river, was renamed Highway 58 and now joins Highway 64 at the east end of town.

Many of the buildings north of the highway also date from the time of the railroad. Stores along Ninth Street (Main Street) greeted visitors as they stepped off the train, and prominent business owners built modern houses just a short walk up the hill. The Village Park, which once surrounded the village offices, was also a playground for children, as it is now. Unfortunately, many of the oldest structures, including the nearly dozen hotels and rooming houses that served railroad workers, lumber and cattlemen, and their families, have succumbed to the ravages of time and fire.

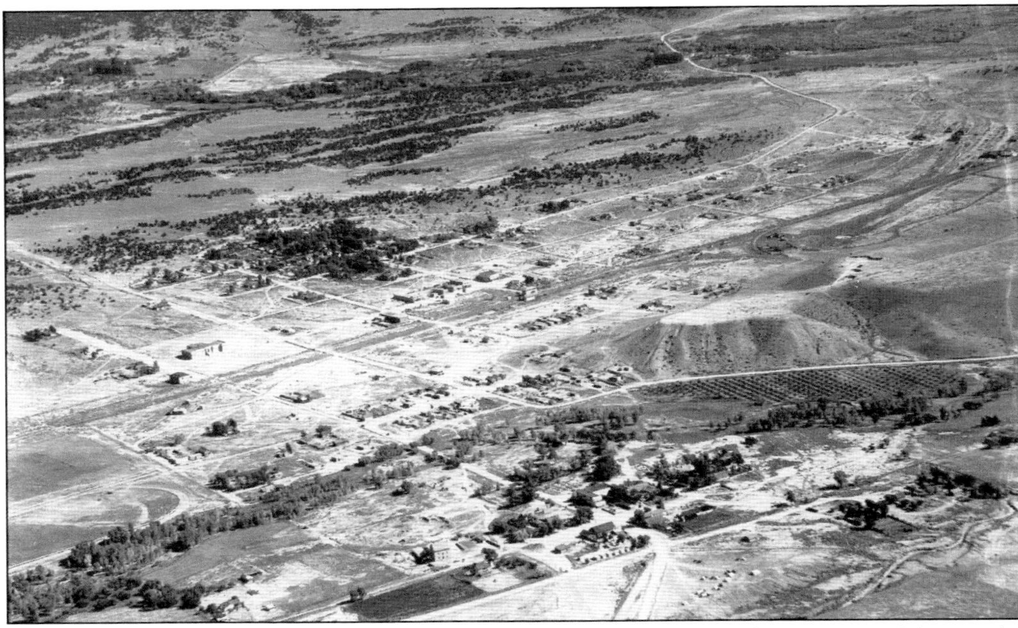

This c. 1944 northeastern-facing aerial view surveys both Old Town and New Town. Of particular note, the railroad tracks and railroad water tower are gone, the roundhouse and adjacent buildings have been dismantled, the Raton road has not yet been rerouted to its present location, the Taos road still winds past the Aztec Mill, and the Springer road skirts the south side of C Hill. (Philmont Scout Ranch.)

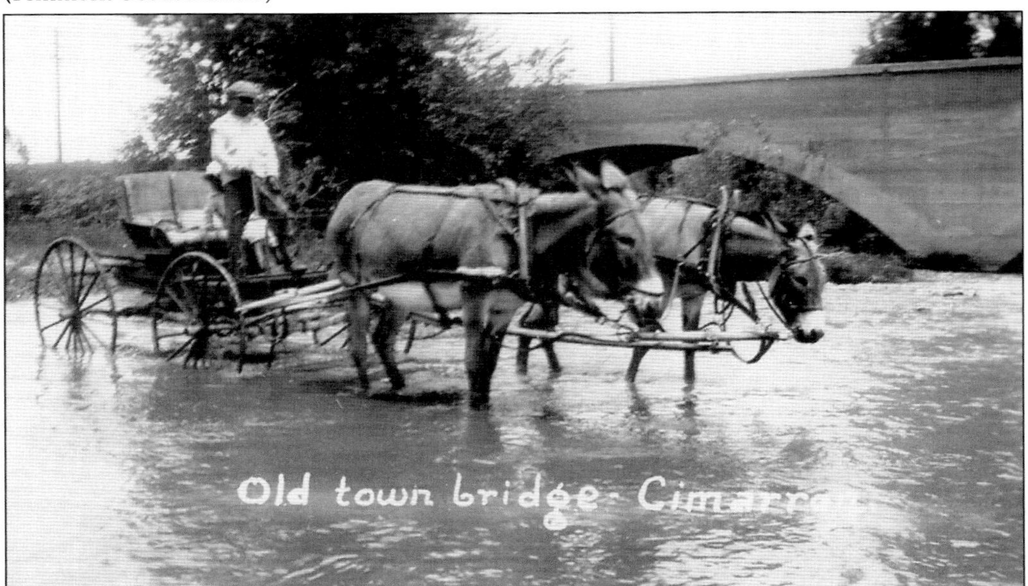

This $5,176, reinforced-concrete bridge was built in 1907 by the Cimarron Construction Company under the direction of Samuel E. Pelphrey and features three 43-foot spans with a 16-foot roadway. The bridge was constructed several hundred feet south of the existing Cimarron River channel, which was then rerouted to parallel new streets. This photograph may have been taken during the record flood on May 2, 1914. (Authors' collection.)

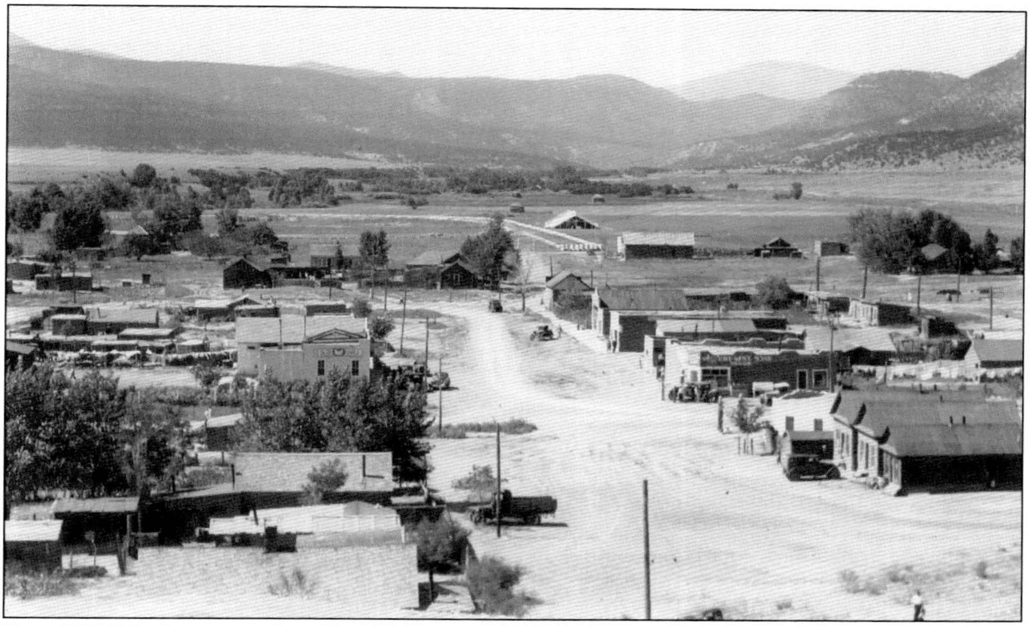

From C Hill looking west along Twelfth Street (Coco Street), one could, by 1934, see Joe Campanella's Blue Eagle bar and Faustin Samora's Cimarron Cash Store on the southwest and northwest corners at South Euclid Avenue. Before the railroad tracks were removed in 1942 and roads later realigned, this was the intersection of the roads to Taos and Springer. (Philmont Scout Ranch.)

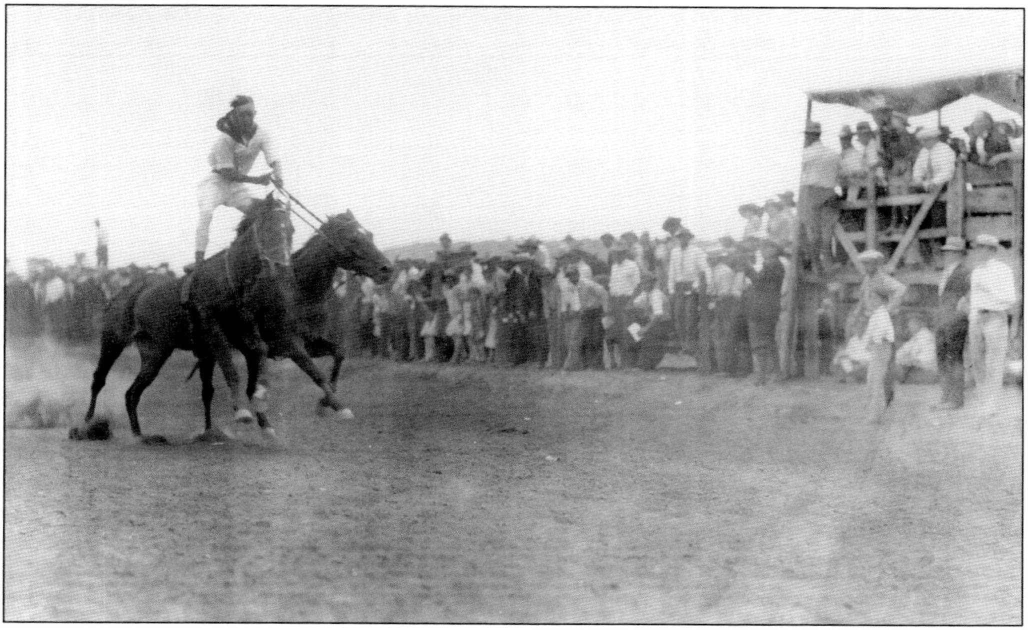

In 1922, the Maverick Club was organized, and in 1935, grounds were secured in the southwest section of New Town. The first annual rodeo was in 1923, four years before this daring rider was photographed. Jack Nairn served as president from 1924 to 1937, before a lifetime appointment to the post. Local ranch hands still participate in the Fourth of July rodeo, with funds generated being awarded as scholarships to the children of Cimarron. (The Old Mill.)

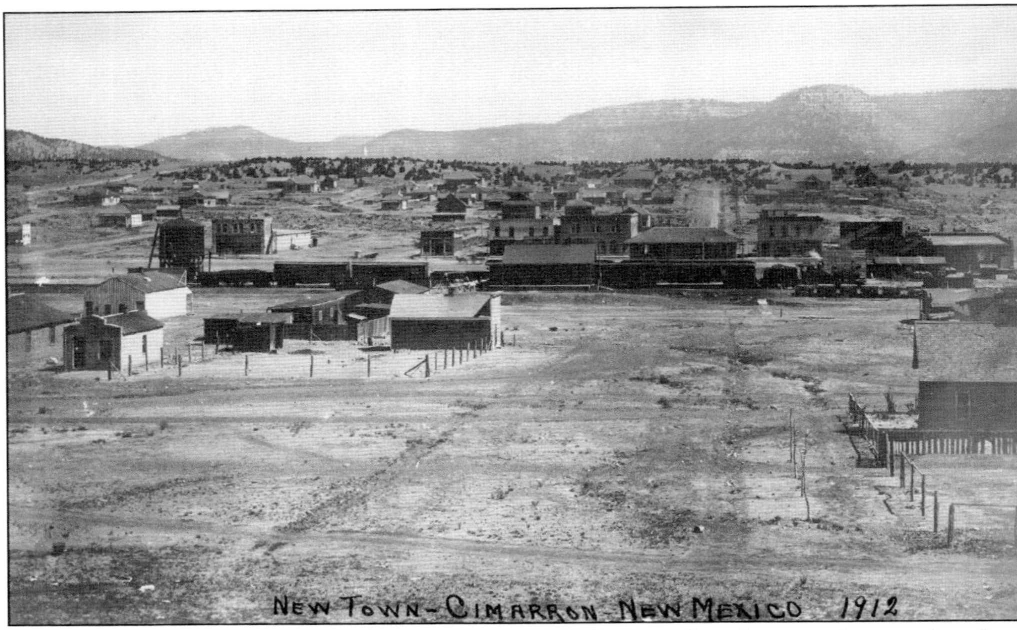

New Town was firmly established and growing in 1912 when this photograph was taken from the base of C Hill looking north along Washington Avenue. Most prominent are the St. Louis, Rocky Mountain & Pacific Railway station and train. C Hill acquired that sobriquet when a giant rock letter C for Cimarron was formed on the north side. The name *Cimarron* has also adorned the hill. (The Old Mill.)

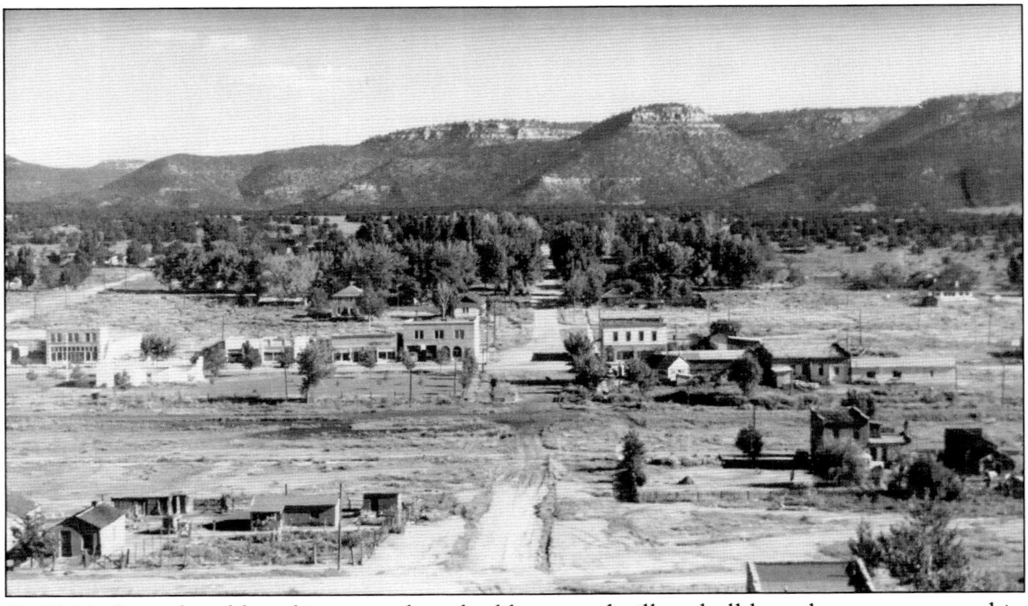

By 1946, the railroad has disappeared, and a library and village hall have been constructed in the park. The most notable difference since 1912 is the lush tree cover in the residential section. The Cimarron Townsite Company in 1907 provided catalpa, locust, hackberry, maple, and poplar trees to anyone who would plant and care for them, and George Webster had likewise offered young cottonwoods in 1908. (The Old Mill.)

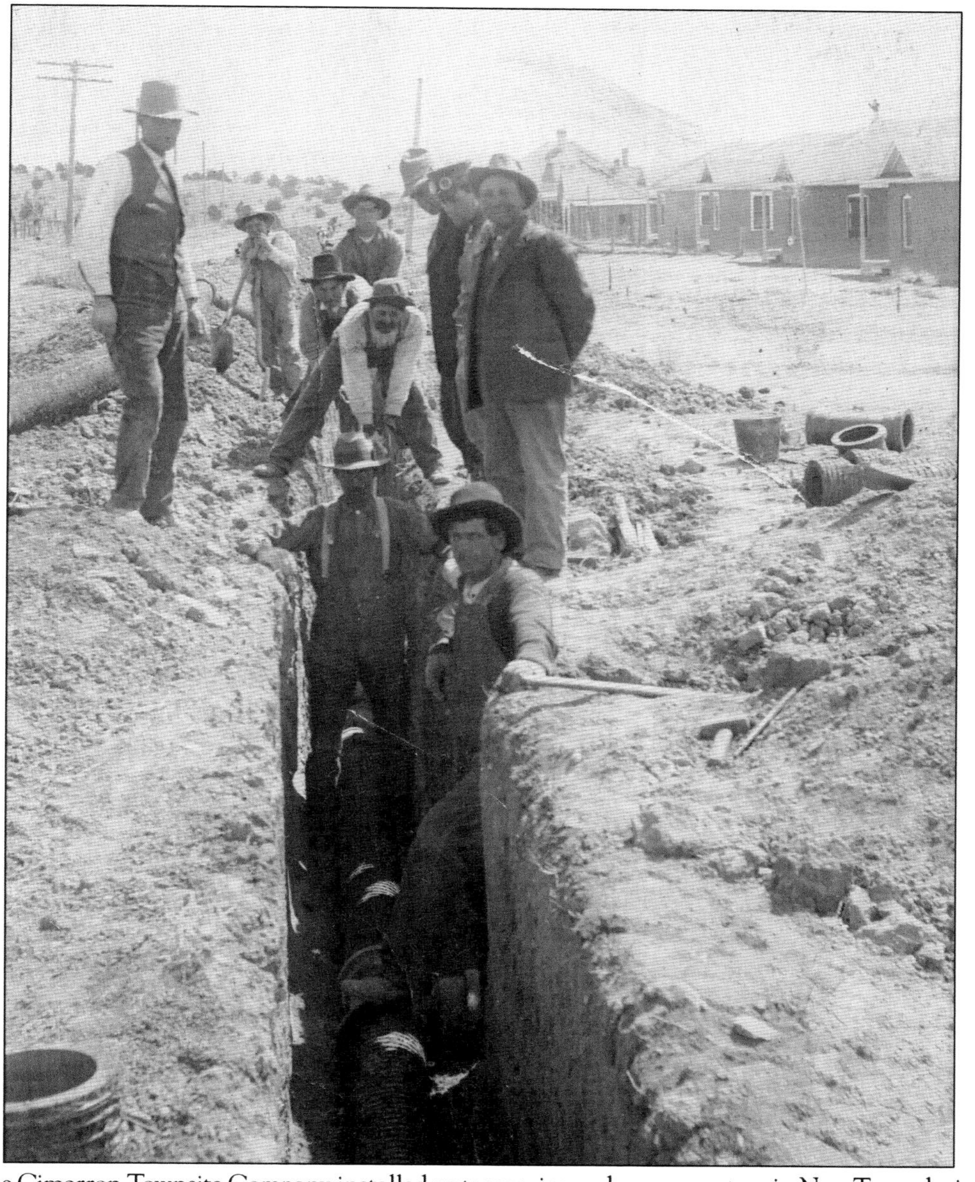

The Cimarron Townsite Company installed water service and a sewer system in New Town during 1907. Plans called for more than 7,000 feet of water line to be installed, with connections for every new residence, with water furnished by the St. Louis, Rocky Mountain & Pacific Railway Company. The 1.5-mile sewer service was forecast to "add much to the cleanliness of our city." By September, four- and six-inch earthen sewer pipe was being placed under Tenth Street and Washington Avenue, and the Oxford Hotel was already connected. The hotel's water connection served another valuable purpose; in March 1908, the proprietors installed a fire protection system consisting of a hydrant and 300 feet of hose. The *Cimarron Citizen* applauded their initiative: "So great is the water pressure that a heavy stream can be thrown many feet in the air above the top of the hotel, and no window in the building will withstand the force of the stream directed against it. This example of enterprise is one that many more of the business men of the city might do well to emulate." (Raton Museum.)

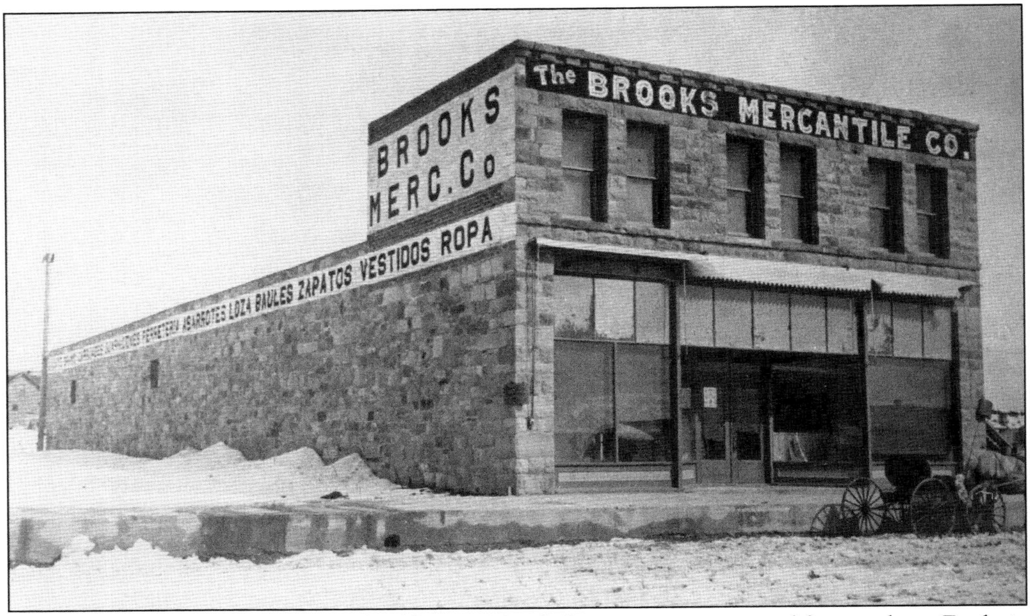

The Brooks Mercantile Company building on Ninth Street was constructed for merchant Frederic Wilder Brooks by Italian immigrant Narciso Federici. Brooks had moved his family to Cimarron from Wagon Mound in the years prior to the coming of the railroad and had operated a store in Old Town west of the St. James. A fire and the relocation of businesses to New Town influenced his move. (Rosso family.)

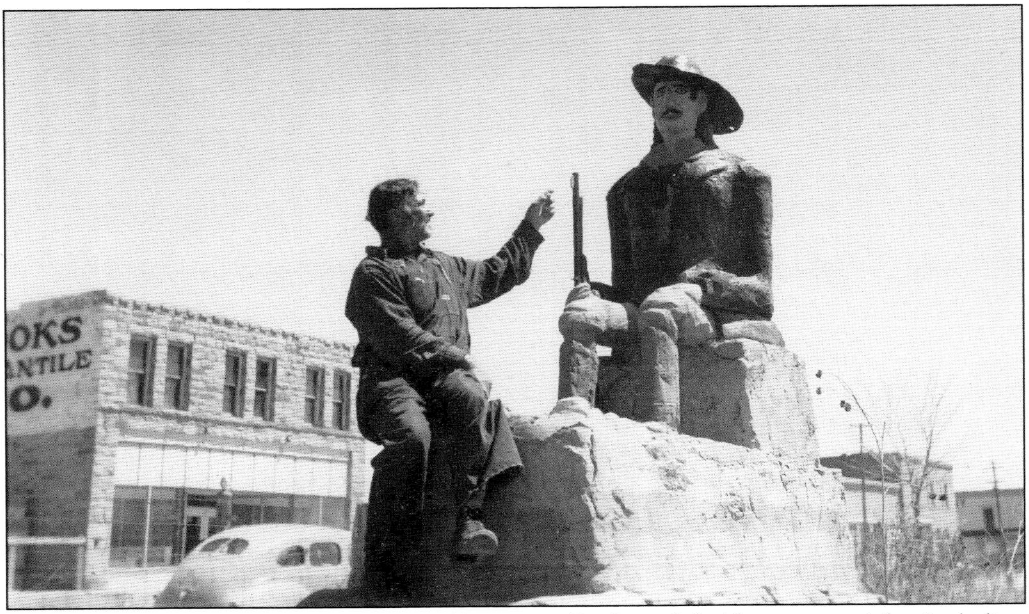

Born in Socorra, New Mexico, in 1872, Domenico Poglianich held numerous jobs, including miner, stagecoach driver, cook, railroad worker, jackhammer operator on the Brooklyn Bridge, gold prospector, logger, cotton picker, and night watchman. He joined the Army in 1902 and served in the Philippines. By 1927, "Professor Dom" was living in Cimarron on veterans pay and built this folk art statue honoring Lucien B. Maxwell in the Village Park in 1935. (The Old Mill.)

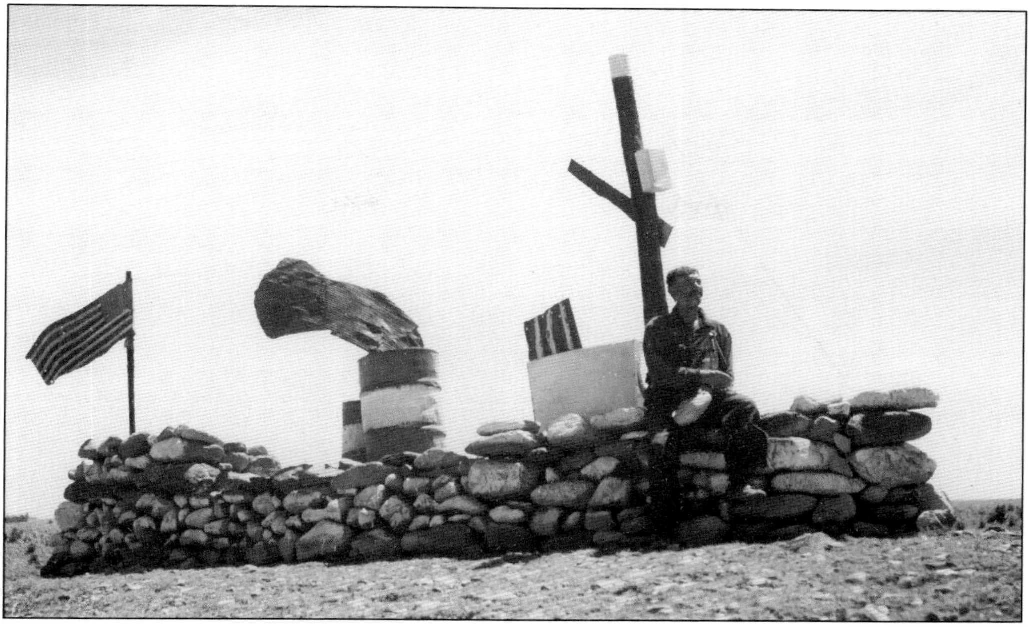

To justify to himself his receiving Army service pay, Professor Dom would walk around town picking up trash. Atop Aztec Ridge south of Old Town, he constructed this stone battleship. On the ground beside it "flies" a large American flag of red, white, and blue glass shards. When asked why the flag was backwards, Dom's reply was, "That's the way the wind was blowin' at the time"—from west to east! (The Old Mill.)

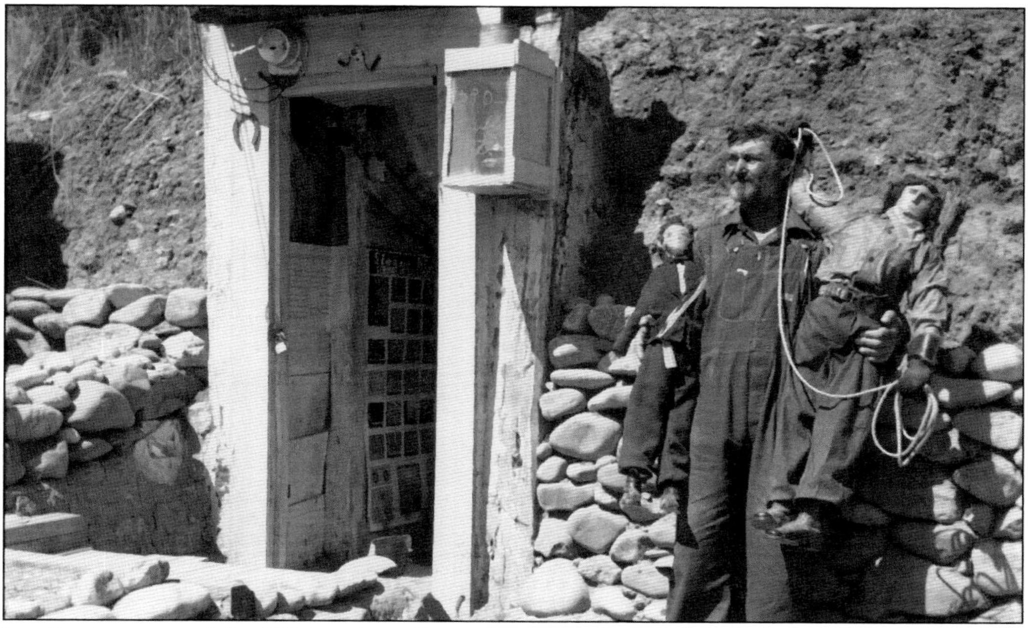

Les Davis, owner of the CS Ranch and himself a war veteran, allowed Dom to live in a cave the "professor" had dug west of The Old Mill. The cave was an elaborate two-story affair with stairs that led to his aboveground "summer shack." Dom also made dolls, two of which are seen here, which would be tied to the front of his Model T during Fourth of July parades. (The Old Mill.)

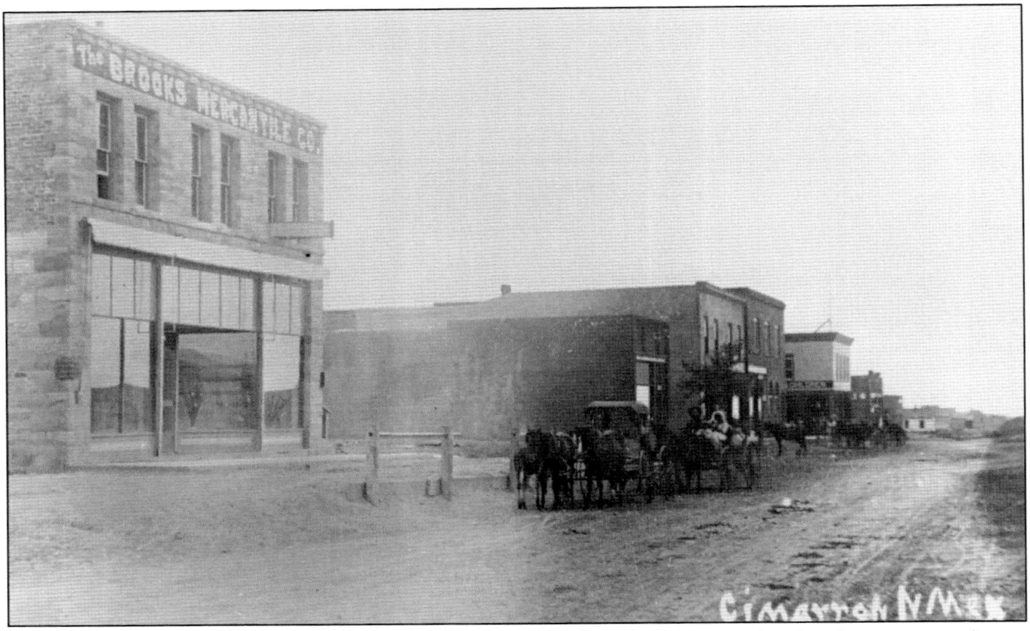

Looking east along Ninth Street around 1910 are the Brooks Mercantile, the drugstore and post office building, the confectionery and hardware building, the bank, Matkin Supply, the furniture store that sold carpets and rugs, and the Antlers Hotel. The photographer was standing close to the intersection of Lincoln Avenue, with the Village Park immediately to the right. (Philmont Scout Ranch.)

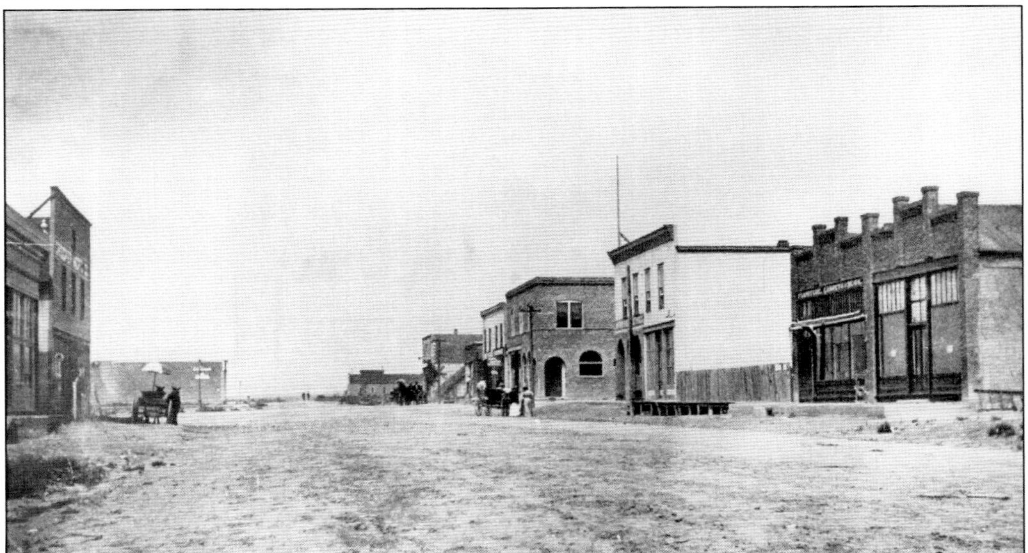

Facing west along Ninth Street, and from left to right, are the Crocker Mercantile, Lail Supply, the Lail and Wilkins Blacksmith shop, Brooks Mercantile, the drugstore and post office, the confectionery and hardware, the bank, Matkin Supply, and the furniture store. The unidentified building at far left was once owned by the Troutman family and is presently the L. Martin Pavletich Studio, then and now featuring one of the most elegant facades in Cimarron. (Rosso family.)

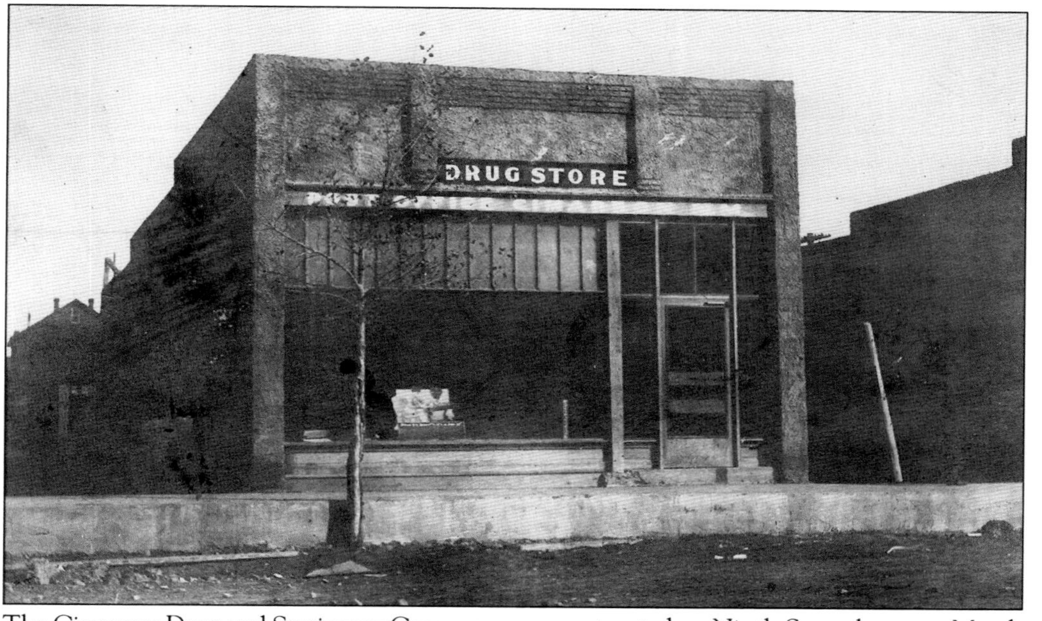

The Cimarron Drug and Stationery Company was constructed on Ninth Street between March and May 1907 for Dr. Horatio Walker and manager Sam P. Officer. Because alcohol was needed for "medicinal purposes," it was the only building on the north side of the railroad permitted to serve liquor. The building later served as a grocery warehouse, pool hall, restaurant, and dry goods store, among others, and is presently an art gallery. (Authors' collection.)

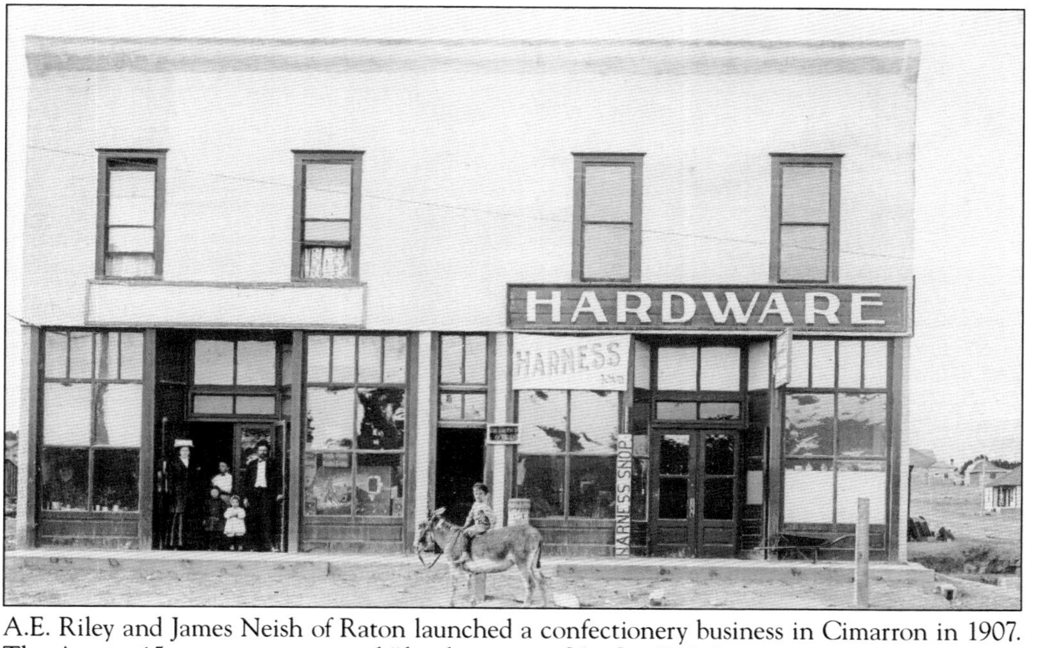

A.E. Riley and James Neish of Raton launched a confectionery business in Cimarron in 1907. The August 15 newspaper reported "for the present [they] will do business in a tent until their building can be erected." Riley purchased a lot east of the drugstore, and the confectionery shared this building with Henry Livran's Hardware Company. Still there, it was shortened in the 1920s following a fire. (The Old Mill.)

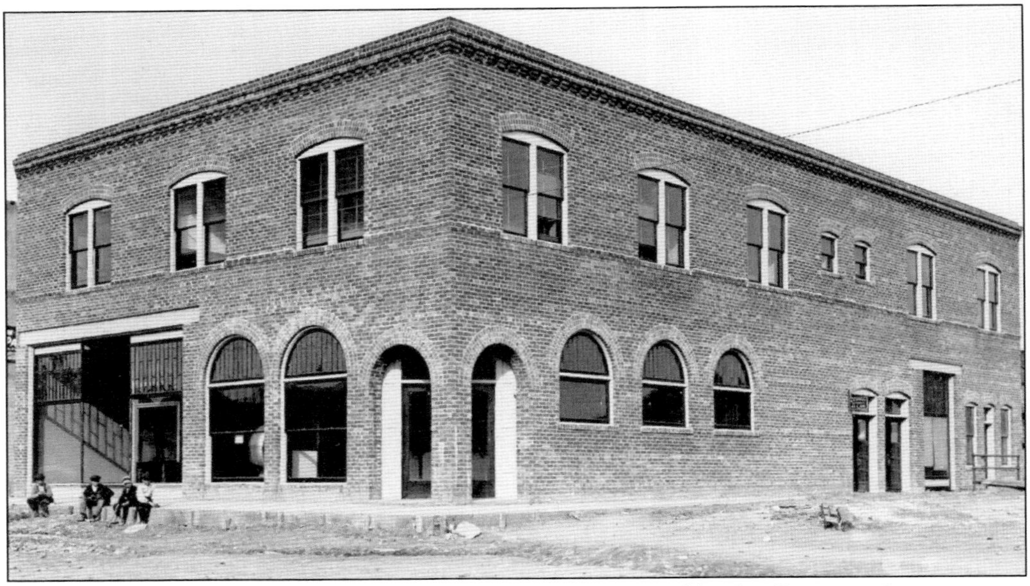

The First National Bank of Cimarron building was constructed by the Cimarron Improvement Company in 1907 at the northwest corner of Washington Avenue and Ninth Street. The two-story brick building was 50 feet by 90 feet, with a nine-foot basement. The ground floor comprised two storefronts; the bank was closest to the street corner and the second used as general office space. The building—which eventually served many purposes—was destroyed by fire in 1977. (The Old Mill.)

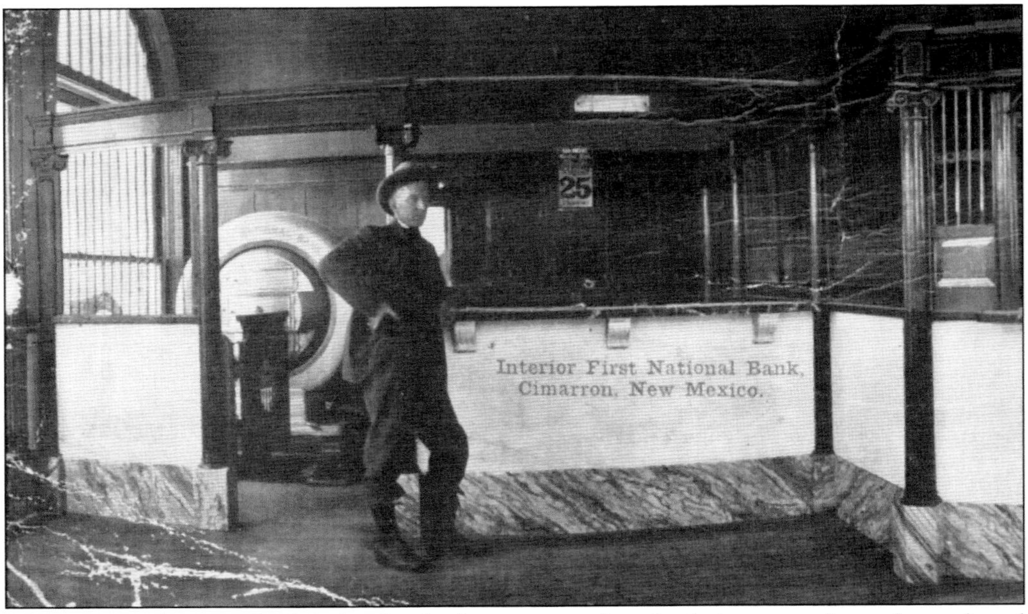

This interior photograph of the bank, which is continued on the facing page, shows the vault and cashier and teller windows. The millwork was entirely of hardwood, the floors were high-quality white pine, and steam heat and city water were available throughout. The town council met regularly in chambers on the second floor. This image was taken on August 25, 1910, a Thursday. (Authors' collection.)

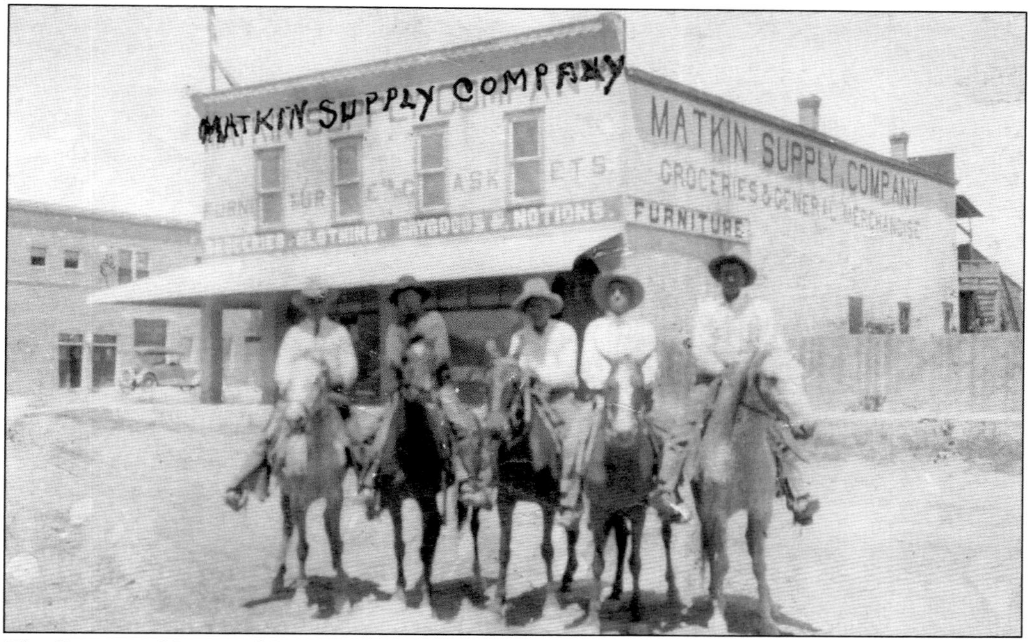

The Cimarron News and Press reported in July 1907 that Otho F. and Stata Sammis Matkin of Goldfield, Nevada, purchased Lots 1 and 2 in Block 25 for $50 from the Cimarron Townsite Company to construct a $6,000, 45-by-75-foot, two-story general merchandise store at the northeast corner of Washington Avenue and Ninth Street. Edgar J. Webb managed Sam Brewer's billiard hall in the Matkin Building when it opened that September. (The Old Mill.)

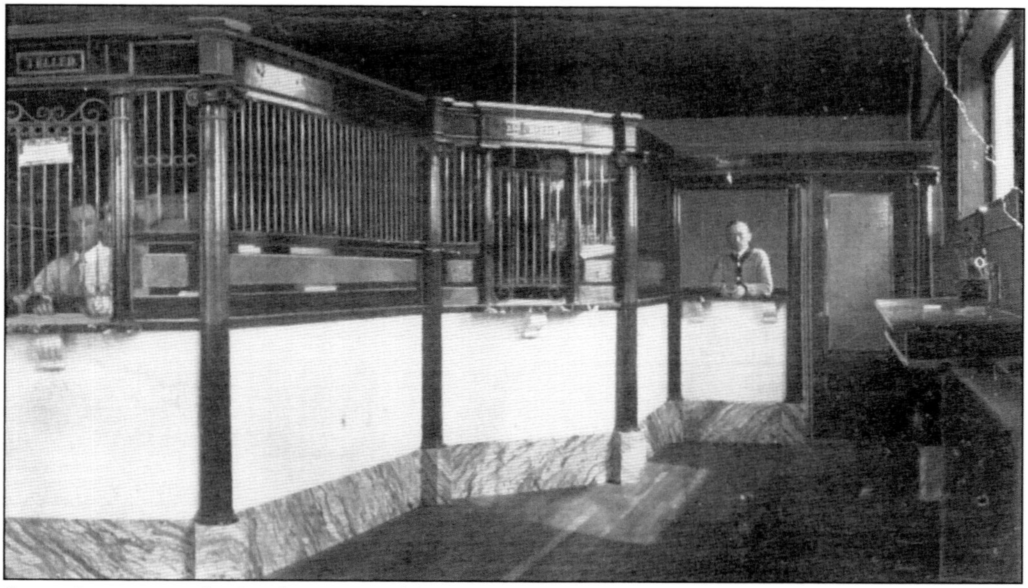

Several rooms in the bank were used by the school board as temporary instructional quarters following the 1916 tornado that destroyed the schoolhouse. Also in 1916 dentist Dr. C.F. Helmig of Raton took appointments in an upstairs office on Fridays and Saturdays. Helmig served as president of the New Mexico State Dental Society in 1920. The far left window served as the post office after it moved from the drug store. (Authors' collection.)

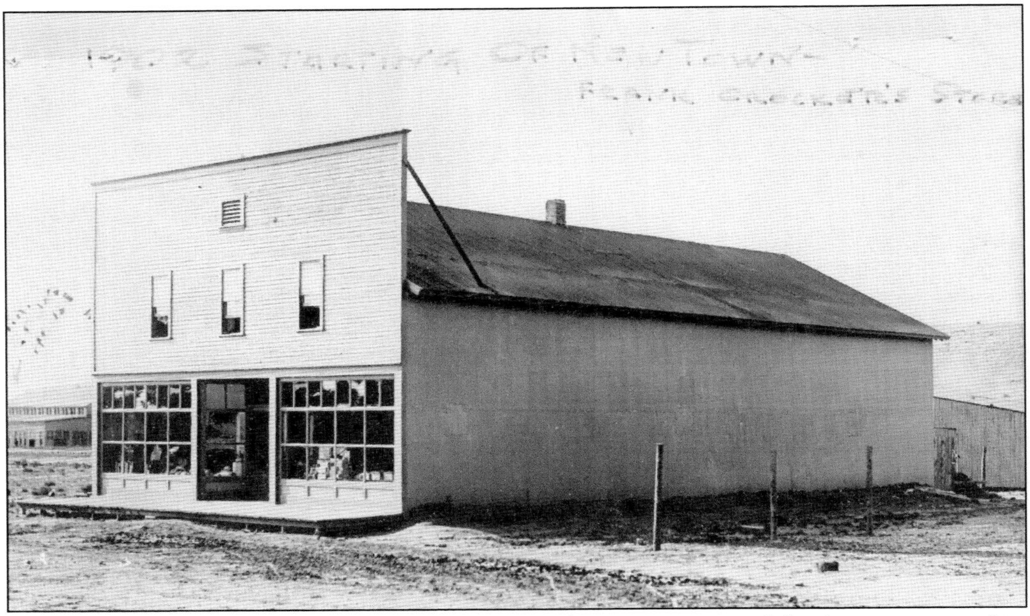

Twins Frank O. and George Ely Crocker's mercantile store was one of the first constructed in New Town near the southeast corner of Washington Avenue and Ninth Street. The roundhouse of the St. Louis, Rocky Mountain & Pacific is visible in the distance past the railroad track. Establishments in New Town were required to be two stories tall; many had false fronts to give that appearance. (The Old Mill.)

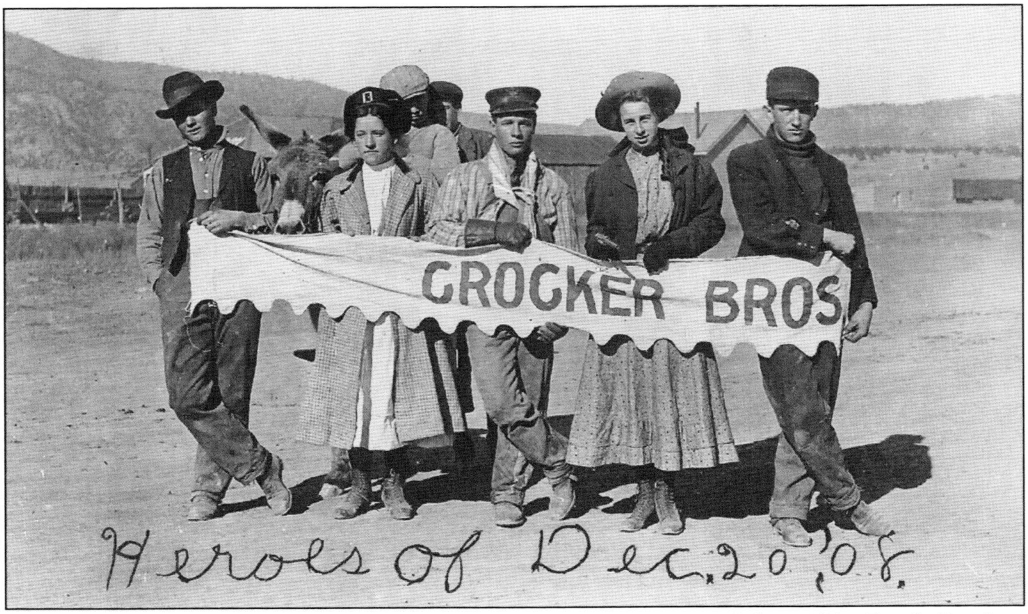

The Crocker Mercantile Company was incorporated in Cimarron in July 1907 by Frank Crocker, George Crocker, and Charles E. Remsberg as a successor to Crocker Brothers. Remsberg, owner of Remsberg Mercantile Company of Raton, became principal owner of the new firm. It is not known what made these seven young people heroes or why one young woman is holding a revolver; Eugene Lambert (center, front) is the only one identified. (Lambert family.)

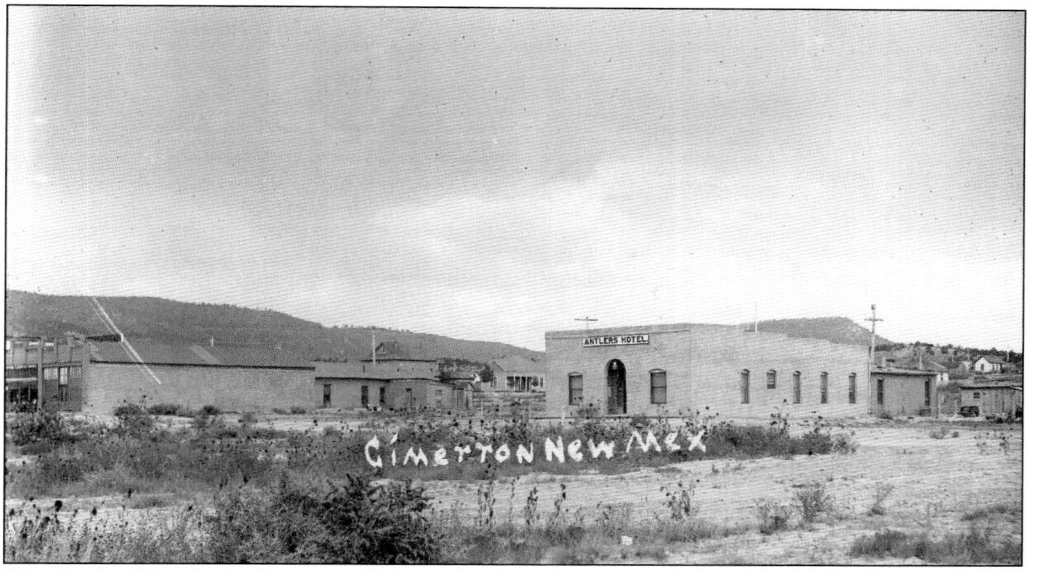

The Antlers Hotel, which eventually became the Cimarron Hospital, was constructed by Narciso Federici after 1906 and was managed during 1915 by S.W. and Ellen Vesey Riggan, parents of schoolteacher Pearl Riggan Sherfick. Mary Todhunter Curtis (1860–1950) succeeded the Riggans in March 1916. Her husband, Zenas A. Curtis (1857–1957), established the Curtis Tool Company to manufacture automobile starters and tools. This c. 1911 Troutman Studio image was scanned from a glass-plate negative. (Authors' collection.)

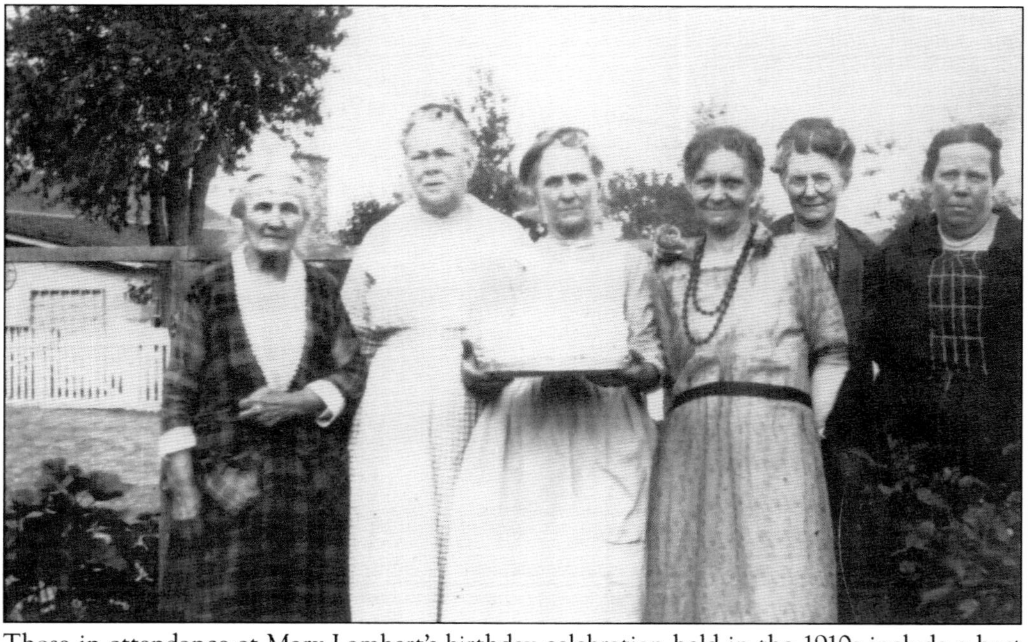

Those in attendance at Mary Lambert's birthday celebration held in the 1910s include a host of well-known and well-regarded citizens. From left to right are Margaret A. Hart Whiteman, Christina Edwards, Mary Elizabeth Lambert, Alice Clara Ritz Heck, photographer Mary Troutman, and Mrs. Lou Chandler. This photograph is from the Victor Grant Collection, which includes a wealth of material on 20th-century Cimarron. (Arthur Johnson Memorial Library.)

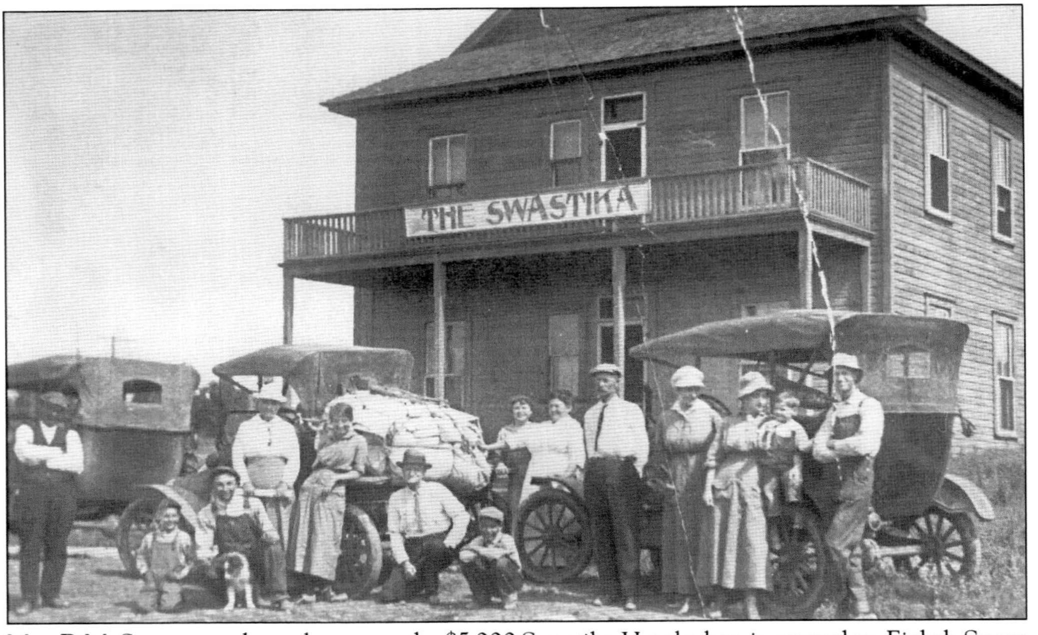

Mrs. D.M. Savage was housekeeper at the $5,000 Swastika Hotel when it opened on Eighth Street in August 1907 as "a club house for the young men of the city, providing bachelor's quarters and a place of amusement and recreation." It was later managed by Howard McDaniel and then by Rudolph and Bea Schwartz. The second story burned in the late 1930s; it is presently a private residence. (Rosso family.)

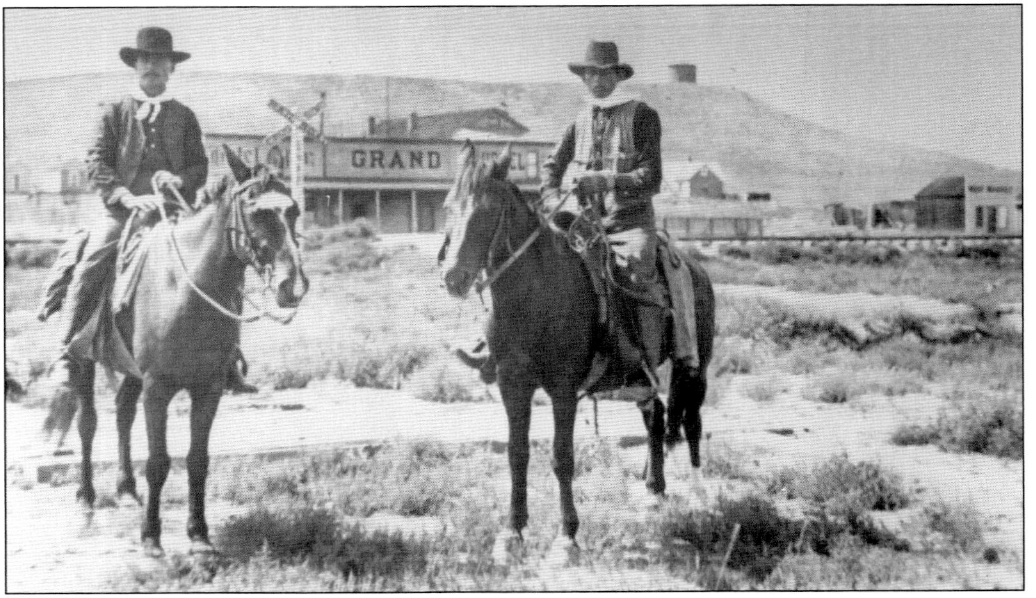

Martin Bakovc's 20-room Grand Hotel—seen in the distance—was described as a first-class hotel when it opened in August 1908. It was built on the site of and incorporated the former Cimarron Café and Hunter Rooming House owned in part by Edward Troutman. The hotel featured a large dining room, modern kitchen, and a separate bar room, "thus making it much better for ladies who are guests of the hotel." (Rosso family.)

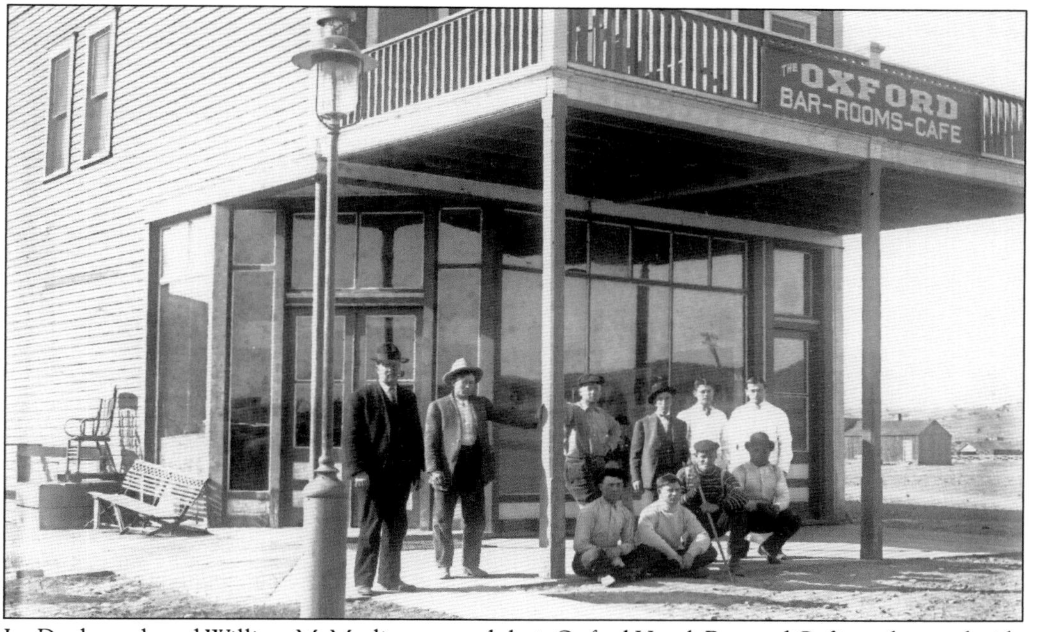

Ira Duckworth and William M. Marling opened their Oxford Hotel, Bar, and Café on the south side of the railroad track near South Collinson Avenue on April 27, 1907. There were 10 guest rooms and a bath upstairs, the saloon featured a 16-foot bar upon which fine wines and malt liquors were dispensed, and "the silverware and glass are the same used on the Harvey system." This image is from a five-by-seven-inch glass-plate negative. (Audrey Alpers Collection, The Old Mill.)

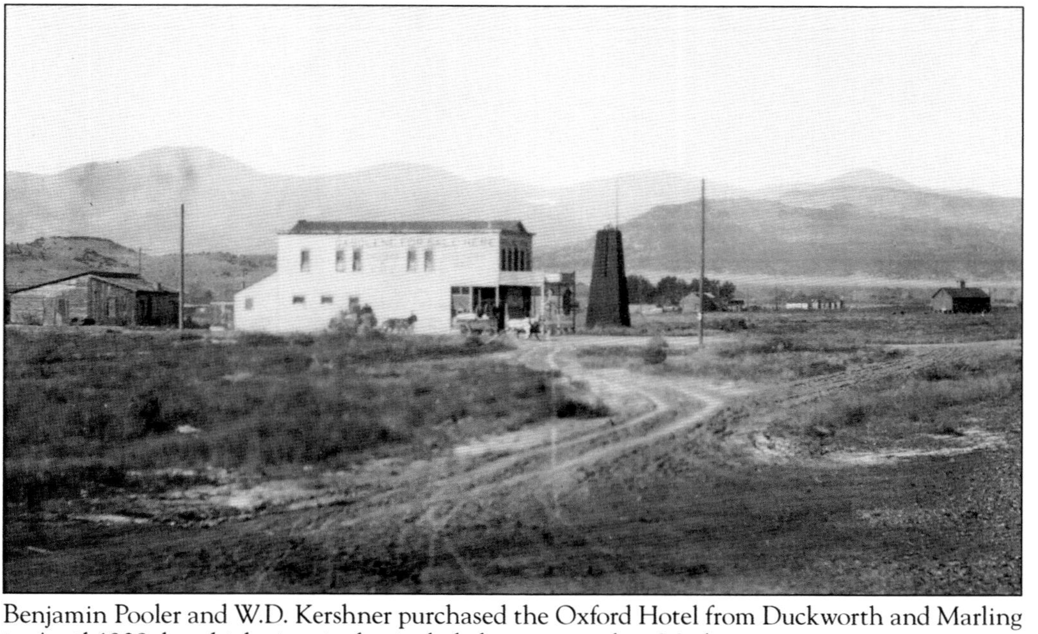

Benjamin Pooler and W.D. Kershner purchased the Oxford Hotel from Duckworth and Marling in April 1908, by which time it also included a meat market. Marling was preparing to move to Tennessee, and Duckworth did not wish to remain in the business alone. This c. 1919 view shows a hose house topped by a bell immediately adjacent to the building, which boldly advertises the sale of gasoline. (Authors' collection.)

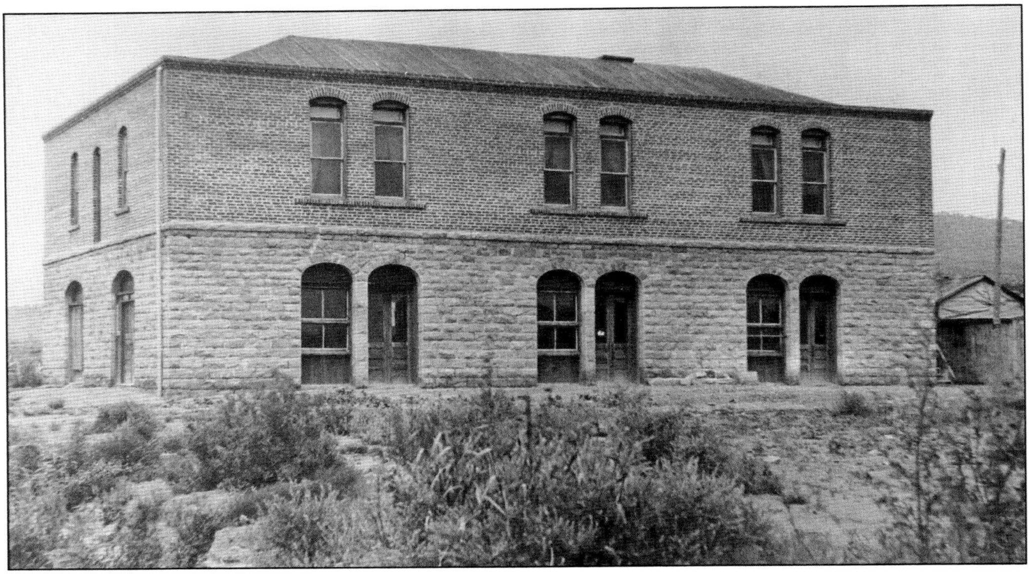

Narciso Federici built his stone-and-brick Cimarron Opera House south of Ninth Street in New Town. Seen here c. 1910, it was large enough to accommodate 250 people in the 50-by-78-foot interior. It was also known as the Athletic Hall, served as a movie theater, roller-skating rink, commercial laundry, and dance hall, and eventually was purchased by the Methodist church as a meeting hall. The second story was removed after the July 25, 1996, tornado. (Rosso family.)

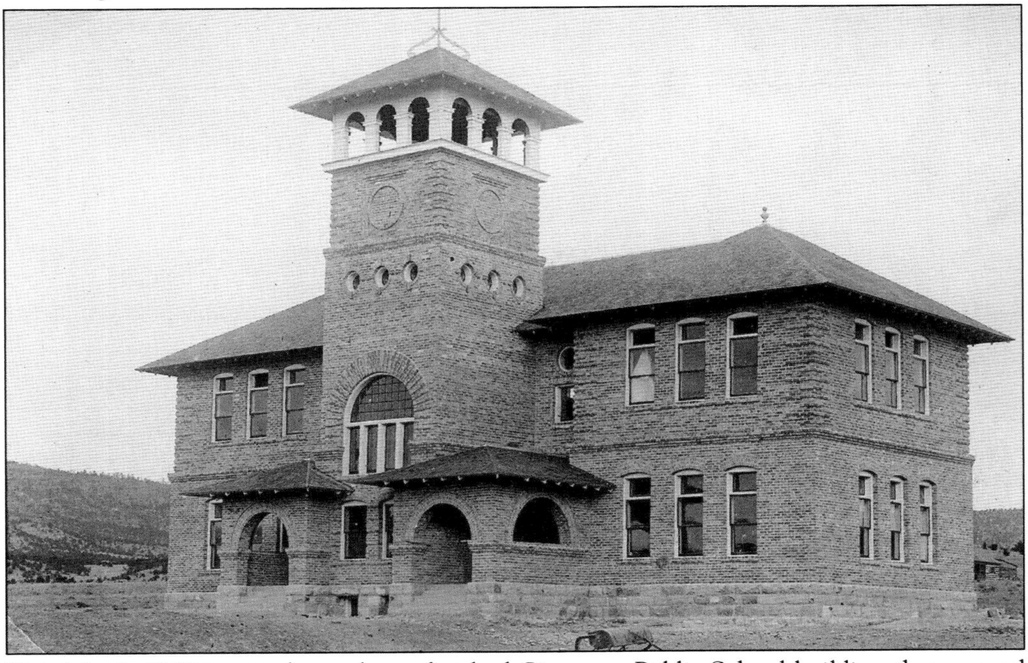

This March 1909 image shows the unfinished Cimarron Public School building that opened later that year. Interior work on the picturesque brick school was completed in 1911. A 12-hour windstorm and tornado on January 8, 1916 collapsed the west wing and the severely damaged the roof. An insurance policy paid $3,500 of the estimated $4,000 in damages, and plans were made to reconstruct the building with a shorter tower. (Troutman Studio, authors' collection)

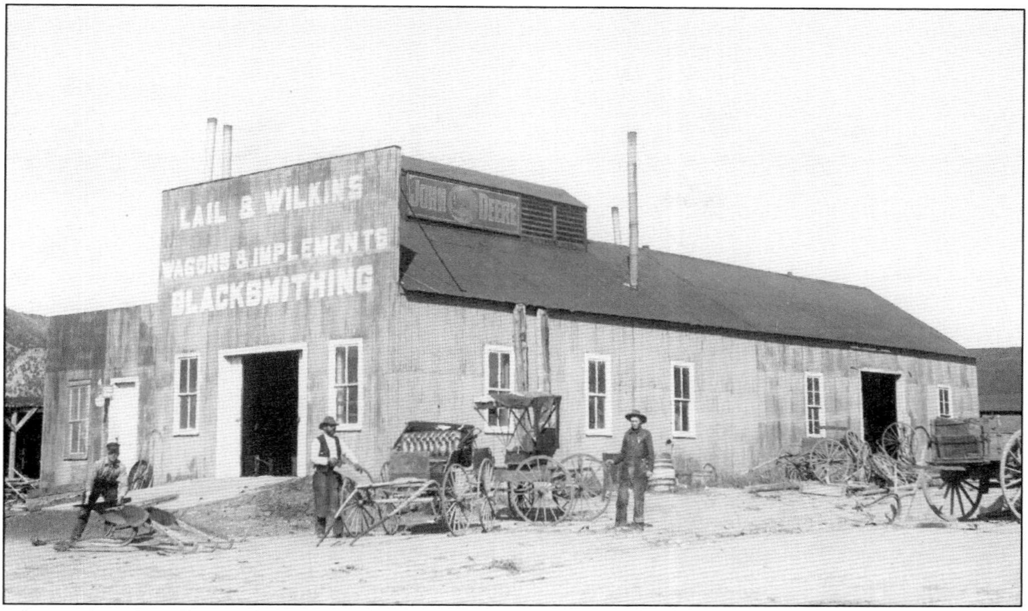

The Lail and Wilkins Blacksmith shop was located on the north side of Ninth Street downtown. In addition to wagons and John Deere products, James T. Lail and Norman Wilkins sold hay machinery, McCormick and Dain mowers, rakes, and binders. They offered a full range of equipment repair services. Lail had previously overseen the timber business of the St. Louis, Rocky Mountain & Pacific Railway. (The Old Mill.)

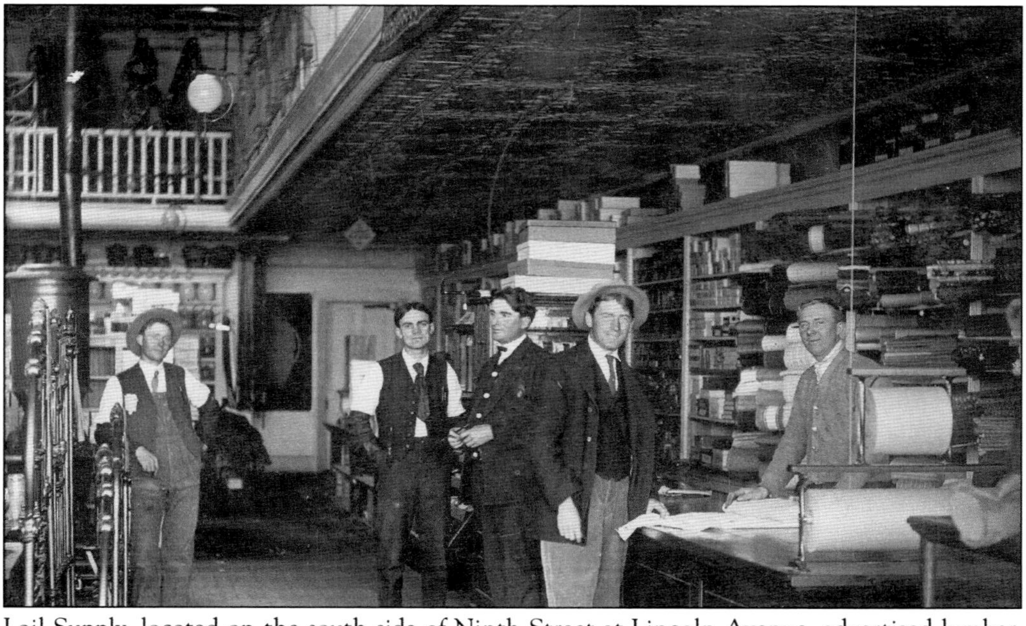

Lail Supply, located on the south side of Ninth Street at Lincoln Avenue, advertised lumber, hardware, and blacksmithing but by the late 1920s sold a little bit of everything—groceries, bed frames, fabric, chicken wire, razors, axle grease, furniture wax, and lumber. Third from left in this 1911 image is William B. Hickman, Cimarron's first mayor. The building later was used as a movie theater and was razed in the late 1980s. (Hickman family.)

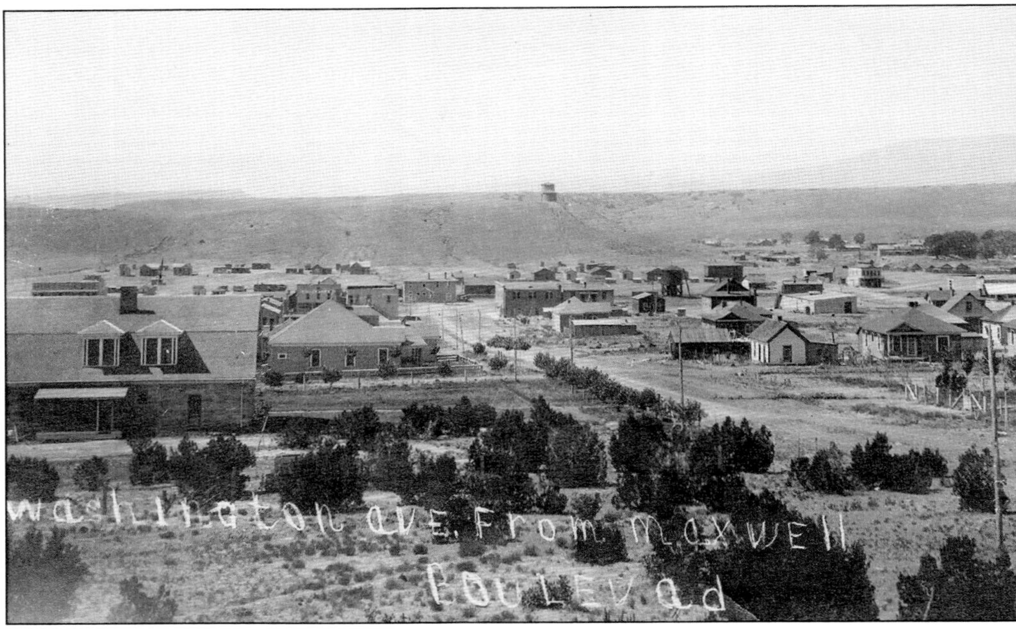

This early Troutman Studio view was taken above the intersection of Washington Avenue and Maxwell Boulevard and faces generally south. This early residential section featured a mix of stone, brick, and frame homes, many of which are extant, including the Kohlhausen home at left and that of Dr. Clarence R. Bass, who arrived from Elizabethtown in October 1907. Bass established his office and operating room adjacent to the St. James Hotel. (Authors' collection.)

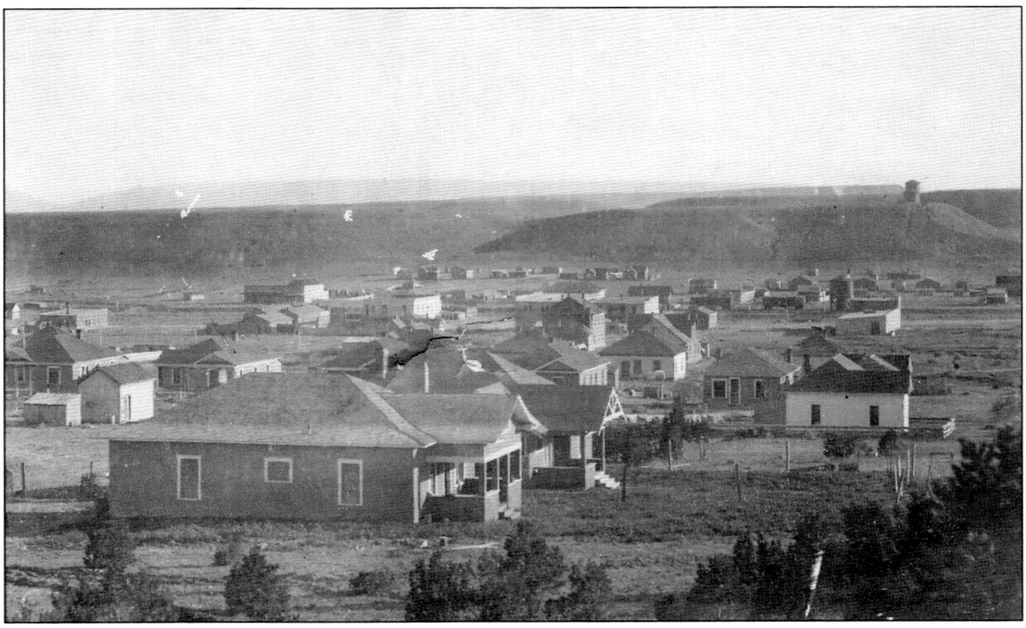

Similar to the previous photograph but taken a block farther west, this view shows residences along Lincoln Avenue. In the foreground is the home of Edward and Mary Troutman into which the family moved in 1922. The back of the two-story Swastika Hotel can be seen in the center of the photograph, with a few train cars in the distance. (Troutman Studio, authors' collection.)

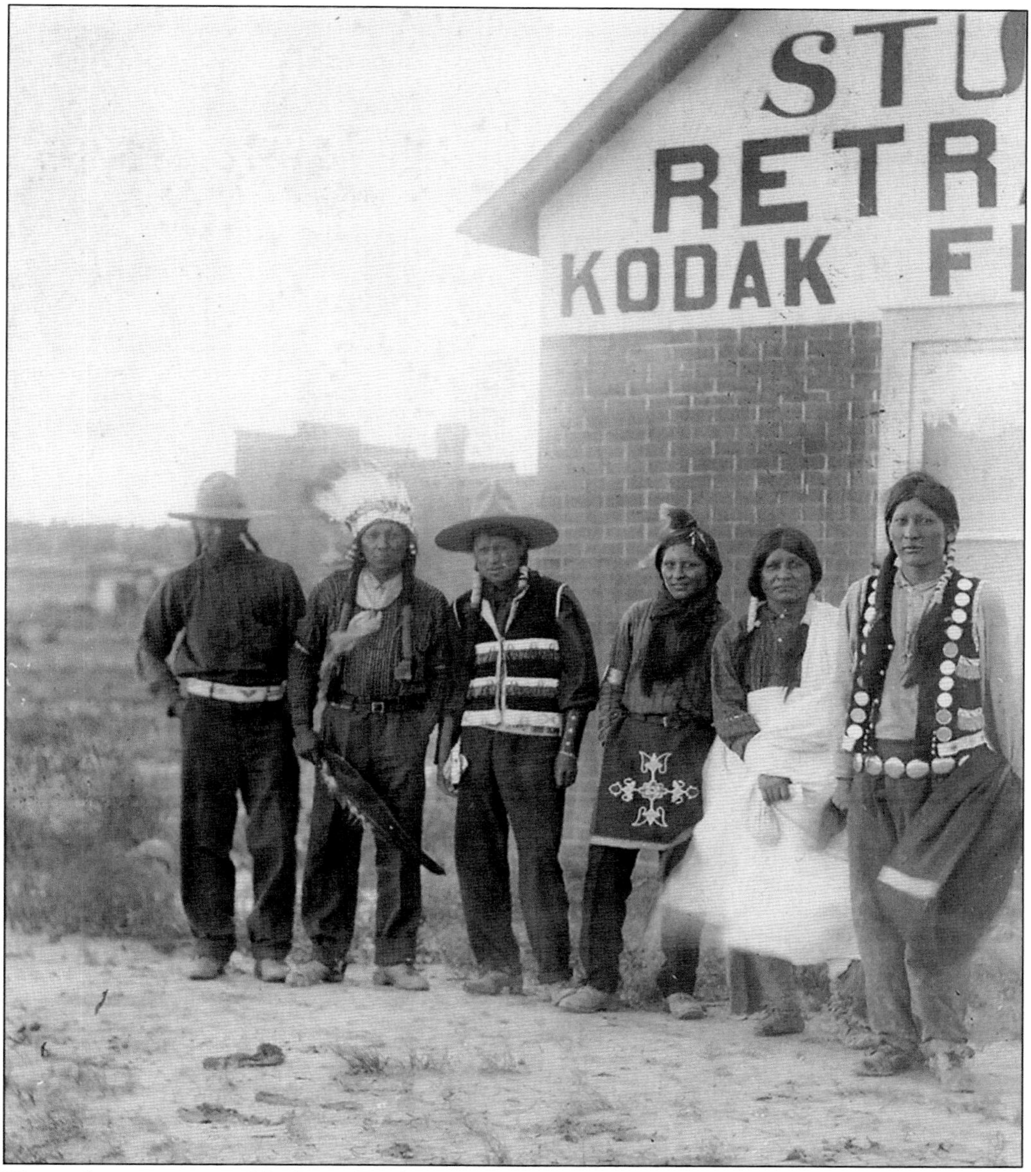

The earliest mention of St. Louis Rocky Mountain & Pacific Railway section boss Edward Alvin Troutman (1859–1933) in the *Cimarron News and Press* was in March 1907. He purchased the Cimarron Café in the Hunter Rooming House from "the Jacksons;" the rooming house itself was owned by Mr. and Mrs. Robert C. Hunter, a couple with two teenage daughters. By that August, Troutman was described as the former proprietor of the rooming house. He then purchased Lots 31 and 32, Block 35 from the Cimarron Townsite Company for $250 to build a new residence and continued to work for the railroad. Troutman is best remembered—along with his wife Mary Margaret Hoy Troutman (1865–1939)—for operating Troutman Studio. Mary was identified in the 1910 census as owner of the studio, and the two produced over 700 unique photographs and real-photo postcards depicting life in and around Cimarron. This postcard image depicts Taos Pueblo Indians outside the studio on July 6, 1911. The card was mailed by George Gumaer to his son Dolph in Port Jervis, New York. (Authors' collection.)

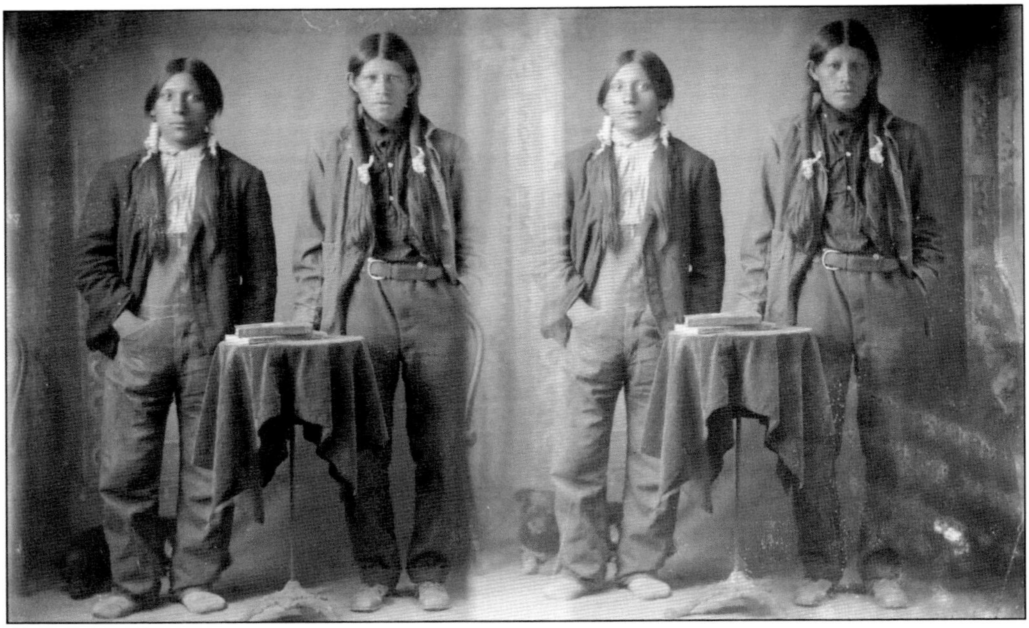

This single-camera stereograph was produced at Troutman Studio around 1911. Both subjects remained nearly motionless but were betrayed by the dog at the lower left, whose head is raised in the second image. Nevertheless, the stereo effect is striking, and this remains an intriguing example of the studio's techniques. The largest collection of Troutman Studio glass-plate negatives is held by the Palace of the Governors Photo Archives in Santa Fe. (Audrey Alpers Collection, The Old Mill.)

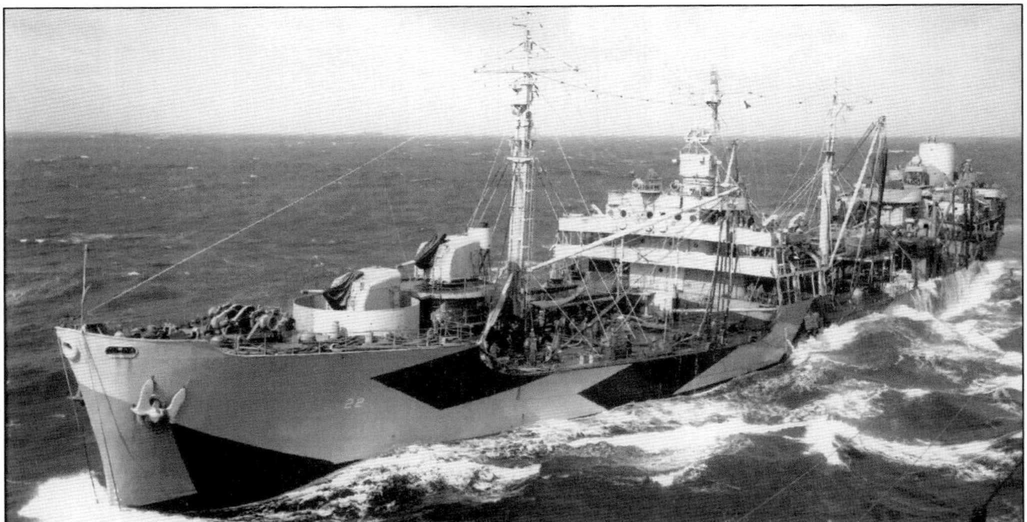

Launched on January 7, 1939, the USS *Cimarron* (AO-22) was a Cimarron-class oiler that saw duty during World War II and the Korean and Vietnam Wars and received a total of 21 battle stars for her service. During World War II, the crew developed the procedure for at-sea refueling of other naval vessels. At the time of her 1968 decommissioning, *Cimarron* was the longest-serving ship in the Navy. Several artifacts, including her bell and compass, are on view in Cimarron's schools. (National Archives.)

Six

Neighboring Communities

The land grant under Lucien B. Maxwell's control measured 1,714,765 acres—larger than the state of Delaware. Efficient management of the grant required that centers of operation be built to handle the varying businesses needed by settlers. As people congregated into towns, other services appeared. Baldy Town, French Henry, Elizabethtown, and Ute Park served prospectors near Baldy Mountain; communities such as Ring Place and Ponil Park were home to loggers; Miami and Rayado were thriving farming villages during the early 1900s; and Dawson's ranch would become a coal town with a population of more than 6,000. When gold played out, when the demand for lumber decreased, or when coal prices fell, a town's inhabitants would migrate in search of greener pastures. Many of these communities are now ghost towns—collections of wooden structures that are empty, windowless, and weathered—but all have their history and spectacular mountain vistas.

Settlement of the area was aided by two engineering feats that amazed those who participated in creating them as well as those who came later, and both involved the transport of water. When gold was discovered on Baldy Mountain during the winter of 1866–1867, it was soon evident that large amounts of water would be needed to mine the placer deposits. Maxwell and others constructed a 41-mile aqueduct to carry water from the Red River headwaters to the slopes of Baldy Mountain. At one point along its path, the "Big Ditch" spanned a canyon over 2,300 feet wide. Despite predictions, the Big Ditch proved to be unprofitable as most of the water was lost through evaporation or leakage.

The second major engineering accomplishment fared better. To limit flooding by the Cimarron River and provide water during times of drought, Charles Springer suggested that a dam be built at the river's headwaters. Construction began in 1916, and in 1918 the dam was completed, creating Eagle Nest Lake. At last, the wild Cimarron had been tamed. The concrete structure was impressive: 124 feet high and holding back 12,000 acre-feet of water. Today, the lakeshore town of Eagle Nest is a vacation resort for tourists and fishermen.

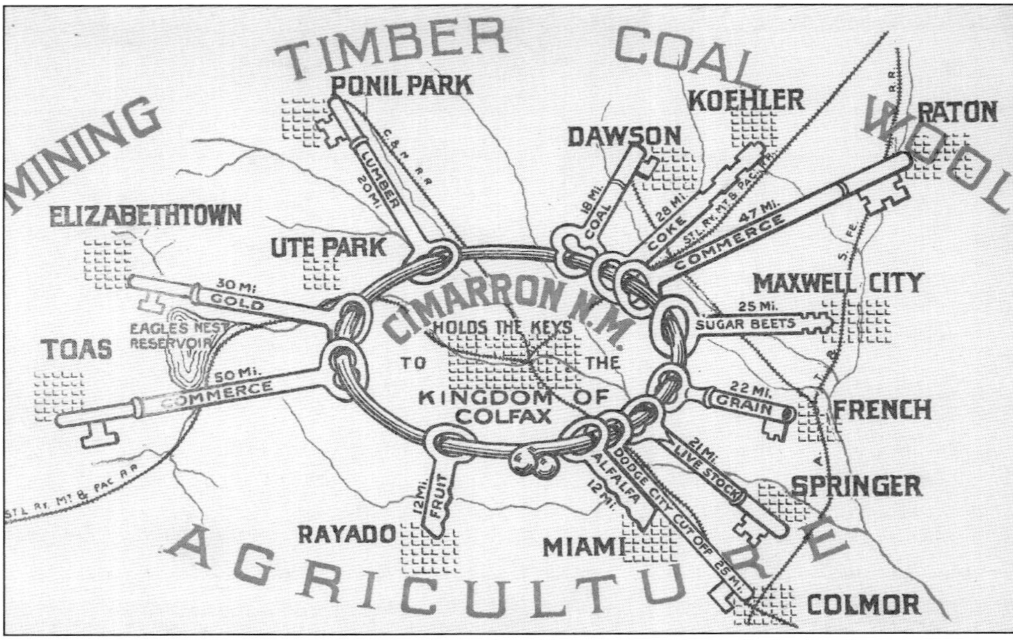

"Cimarron Holds the Keys to the Kingdom of Colfax." So proclaimed the local newspaper and this postcard a century ago, as an exclamation of civic pride and to emphasize Cimarron's location within "the richest County in point of natural resources in the United States." With gold mining, coal and coke, timber, sugar beets, fruit, wheat, alfalfa, wool, livestock, railroad service, and water, Cimarron was in the midst of it all. (Authors' collection.)

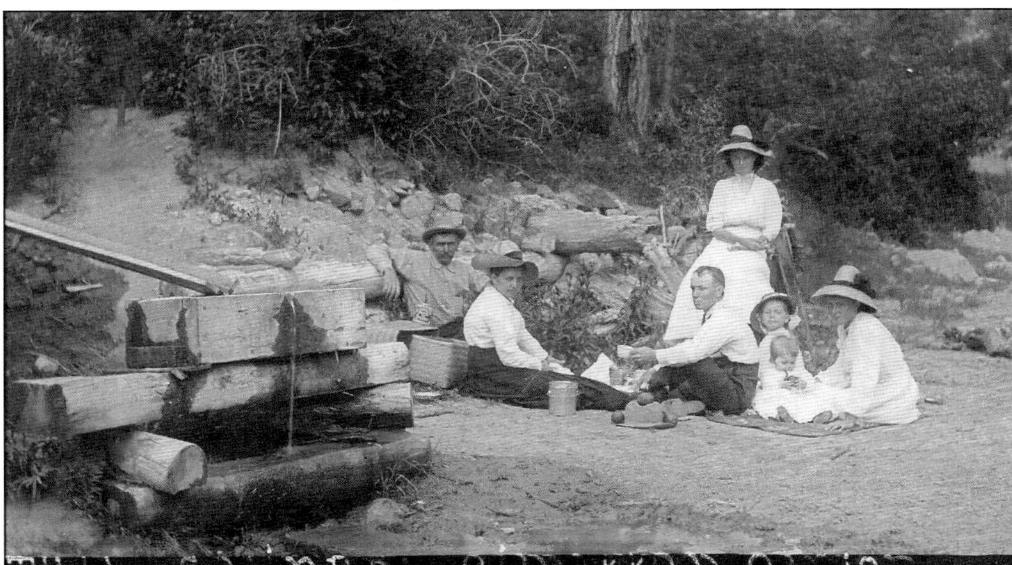

These picnickers enjoy the cool, clear water at Tub Springs on the road to Ute Park, now within Philmont. Gretchen Sammis recounted in 2009: "It was there in Cimarron Canyon and even after the road was rebuilt the water would be coming down. It was called Tub Springs because at one time there was a watering tub there for horses." This Troutman Studio postcard was sold by Cimarron Drug and Stationery Company. (Authors' collection.)

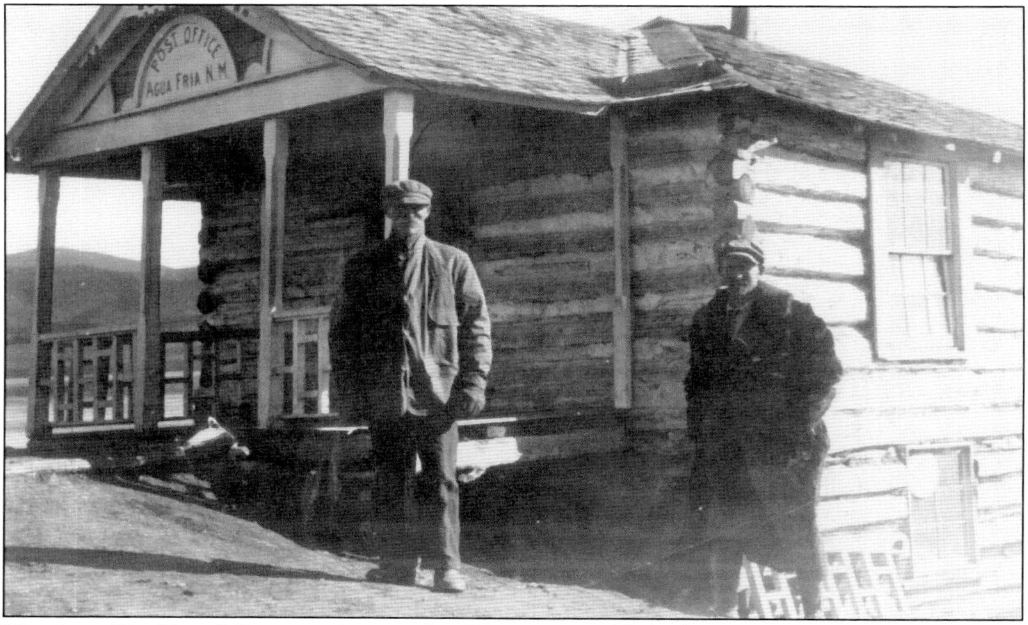

The Agua Fria Post Office, seen here in the 1920s, was established in 1919 in the small community of the same name at the south end of the Moreno Valley near the intersection of US Highway 64 and State Road 434. Benjamin F. Emerson served as postmaster for nearly three years. The last postmaster was Minnie Riley, who served from 1925 through December 1929, when the post office was closed. (Hickman family.)

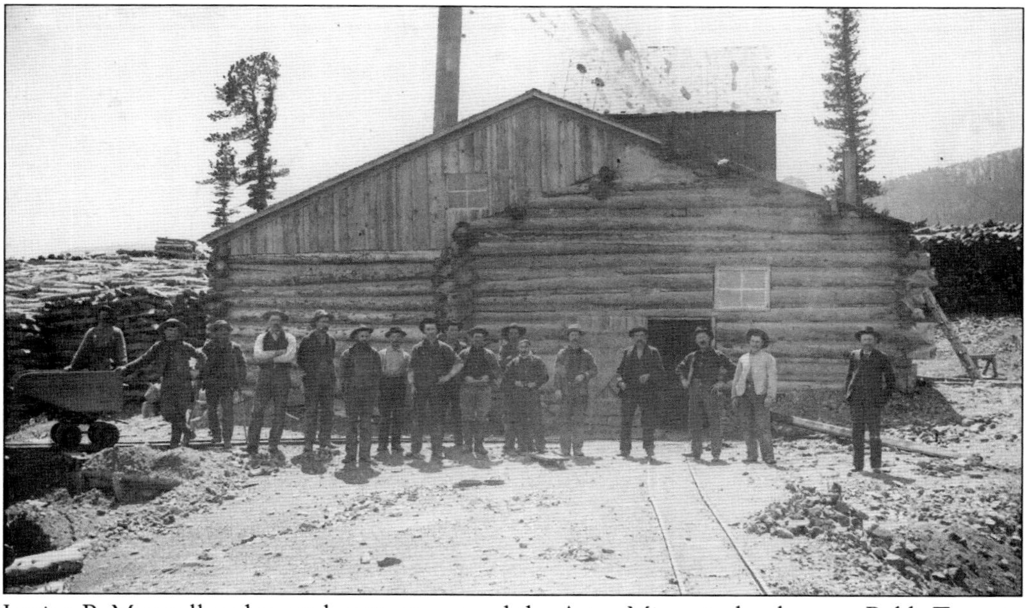

Lucien B. Maxwell and several partners opened the Aztec Mine at what became Baldy Town in 1868. Modern equipment helped the mine produce over $100,000 in gold the first year. A year later, most mining ceased. The Aztec was mined with some success in the mid-1890s and during and after 1909. This image is believed to date from 1894; note the stacks of mine timbers. (The Old Mill.)

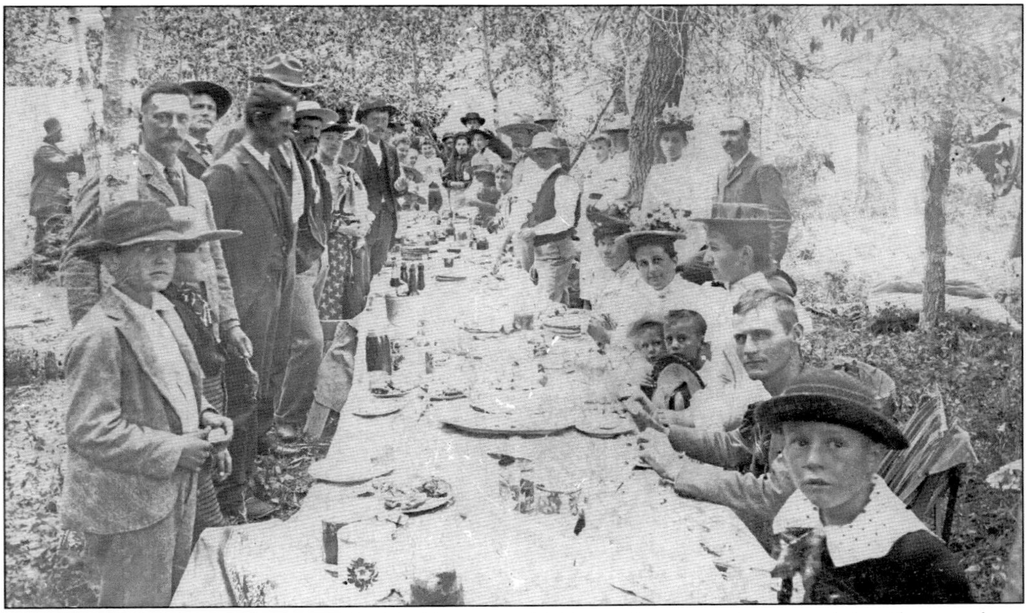

July 4, 1896, brought scores of Baldy Town and Elizabethtown miners and family members together on land owned by the Maxwell Land Grant at the mouth of the lower Cimarron Canyon. According to Fred Lambert, dance music was furnished by fiddler Hugh Strivens. The Lambert family owned an "old cow ranch just across the creek" close to the Railey and Lon Service ranches. (The Old Mill.)

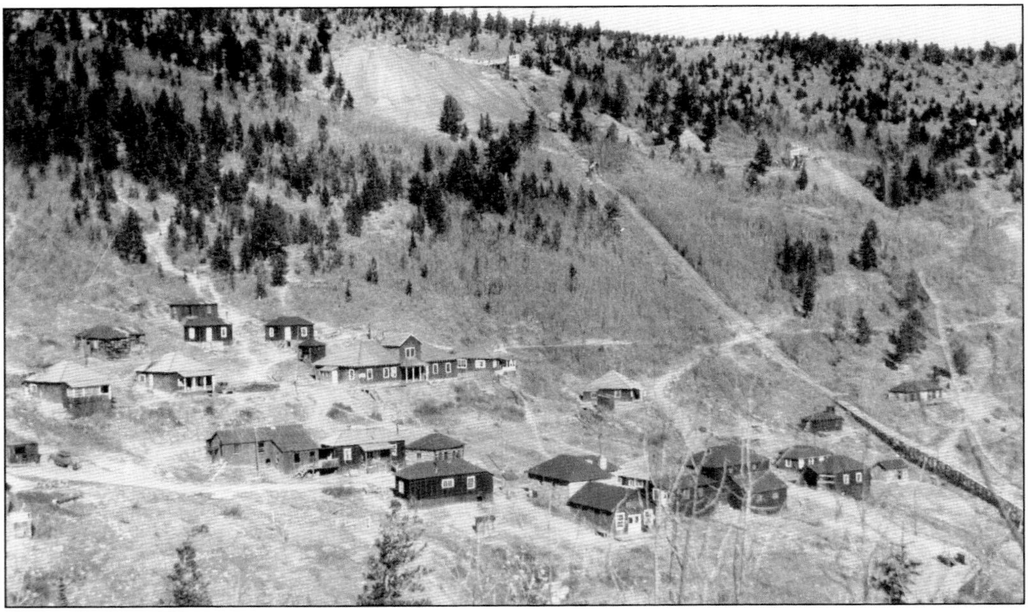

Following the closure of the Aztec Mine, Baldy Town became a virtual ghost town. The post office established in 1888 closed in 1926, and homes were removed between 1942 and 1946. The large hotel may be seen in the center of this 1950s photograph, with the town store directly down the hill; at right is the Mine No. 4 tramway. Baldy Camp attends to Scouts on their hike to the mountain's 12,441-foot summit. (Philmont Scout Ranch.)

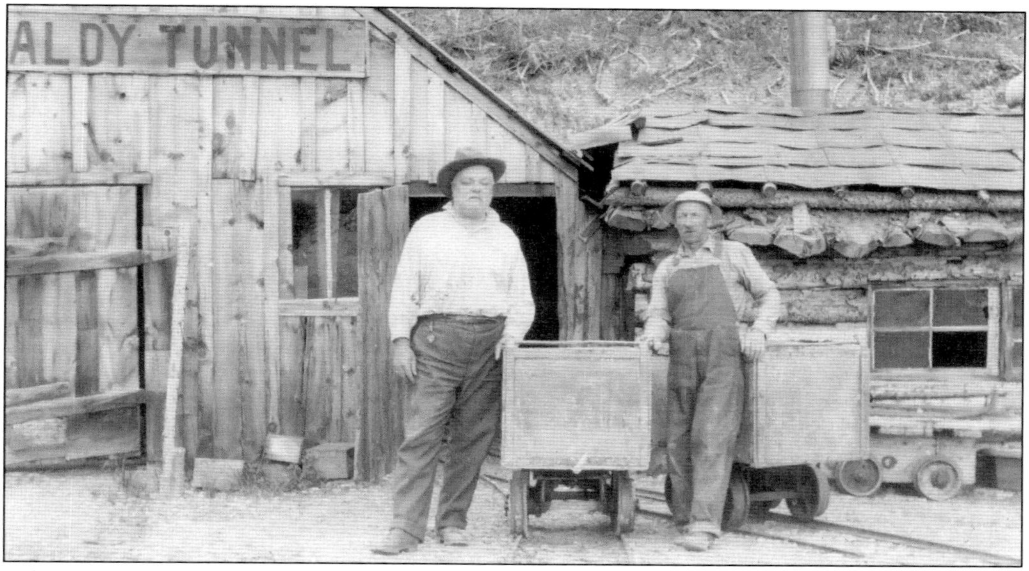

When William P. McIntyre (right) came to Moreno Valley in 1899 and witnessed the placer mines on Baldy Mountain, he decided to drive a tunnel into the heart of the mountain to claim the mother lode. Bill and brother Alex incorporated the Gold and Copper Deep Tunnel Mining and Milling Company. Two tunnels, one from each side of the mountain, were finally joined (within inches) in 1936, but no mother lode was discovered. The man at left is unidentified. (Hickman family.)

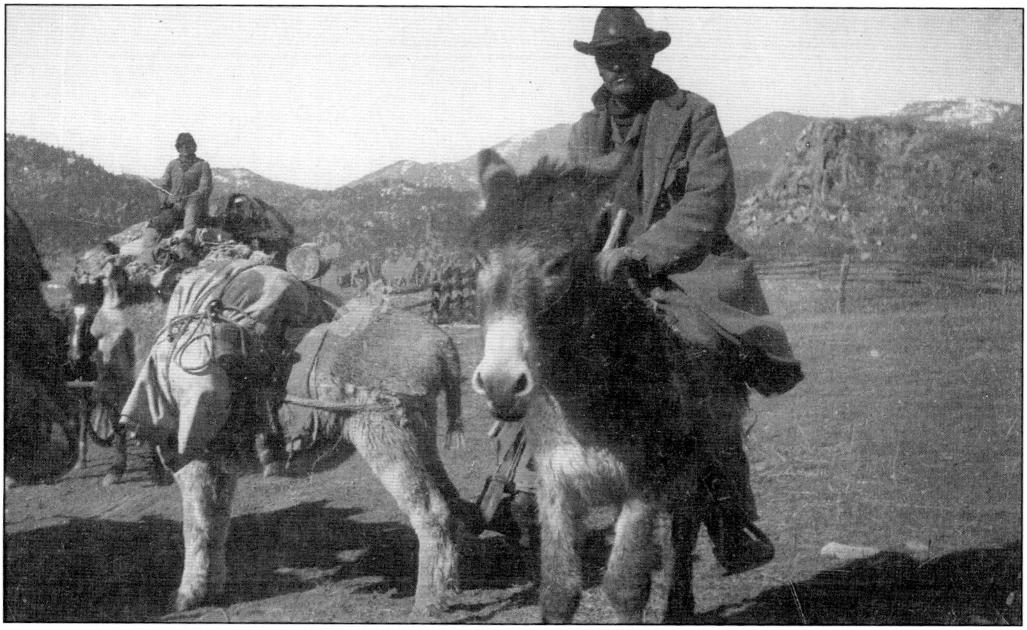

The promise of riches sparked by the Elizabethtown and Baldy gold rushes attracted thousands of miners from all walks of life. This well-equipped miner from Denver pauses to have his photograph taken in Ute Park in 1900. Elias Brevort reported in *New Mexico: Her Natural Resources and Attractions* (1874) that "gold is known to exist in over fifty different localities in the Territory" —quite appealing to prospectors. (Authors' collection.)

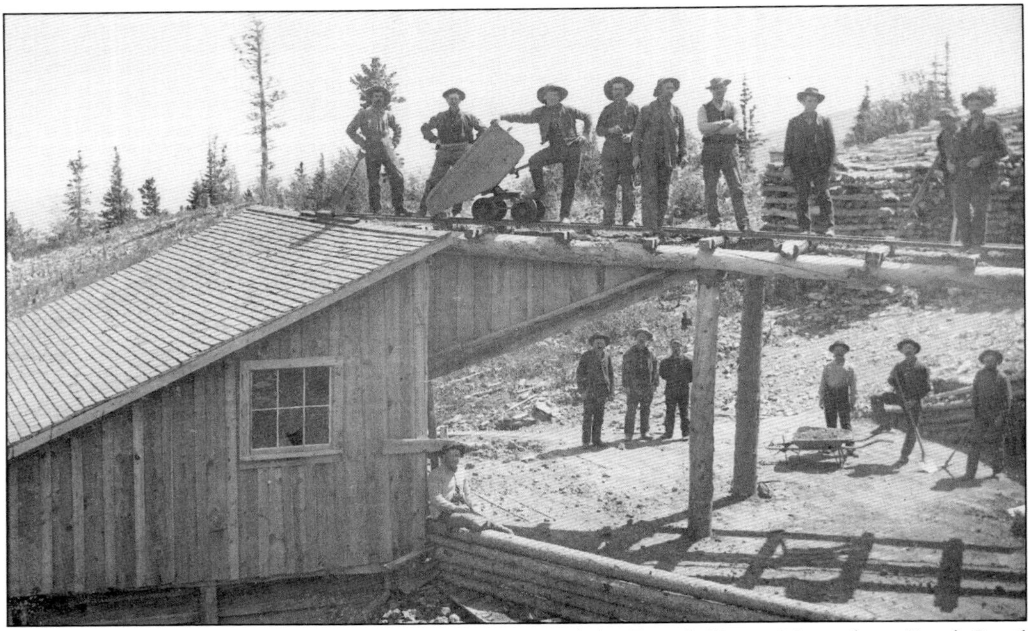

In 1869, Henry Buruel and fellow French miners opened the French Henry Mine along South Ponil Creek. The mine operated a 60-foot vertical shaft but found the cost of milling ore prohibitive and closed operations. The mine was reopened in 1894 by the Claude Mining and Milling Company, which constructed what today houses a small museum of mining artifacts at Philmont's French Henry staffed camp. (J.I. Phillips, The Old Mill.)

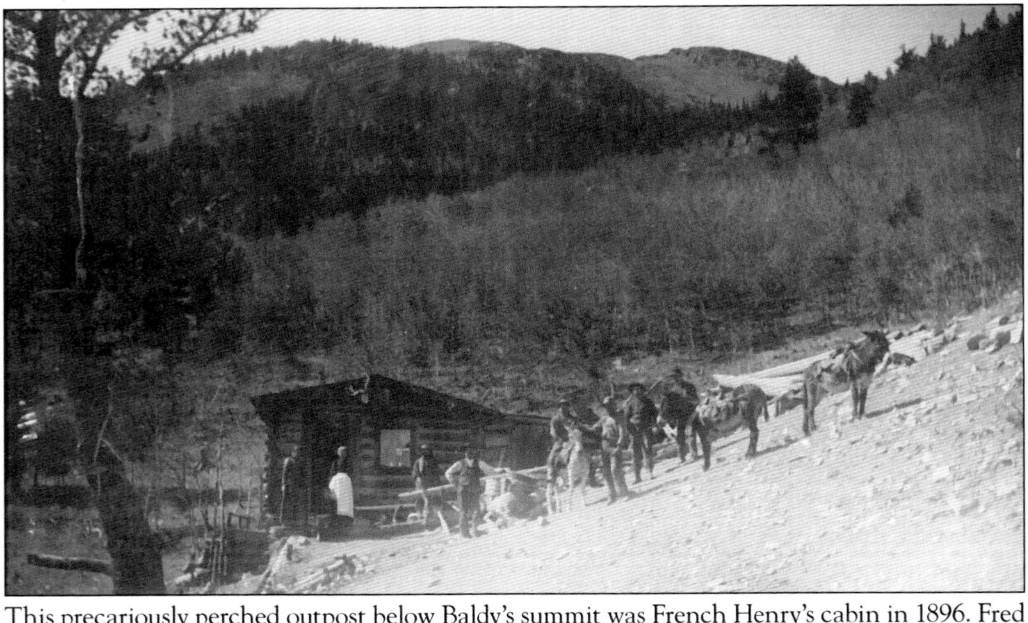

This precariously perched outpost below Baldy's summit was French Henry's cabin in 1896. Fred Lambert recalled, "This is where an old miner lived who tried to come down the side of Baldy Mountain sitting in a scoop-shovel . . . [He] didn't figure on the heat . . . from the fast-moving shovel bottom coming in contact with the loose rocks and gravel. As he neared his cabin he let go of the handle, his trousers on fire [and] made a dash for a nearby spring." (The Old Mill.)

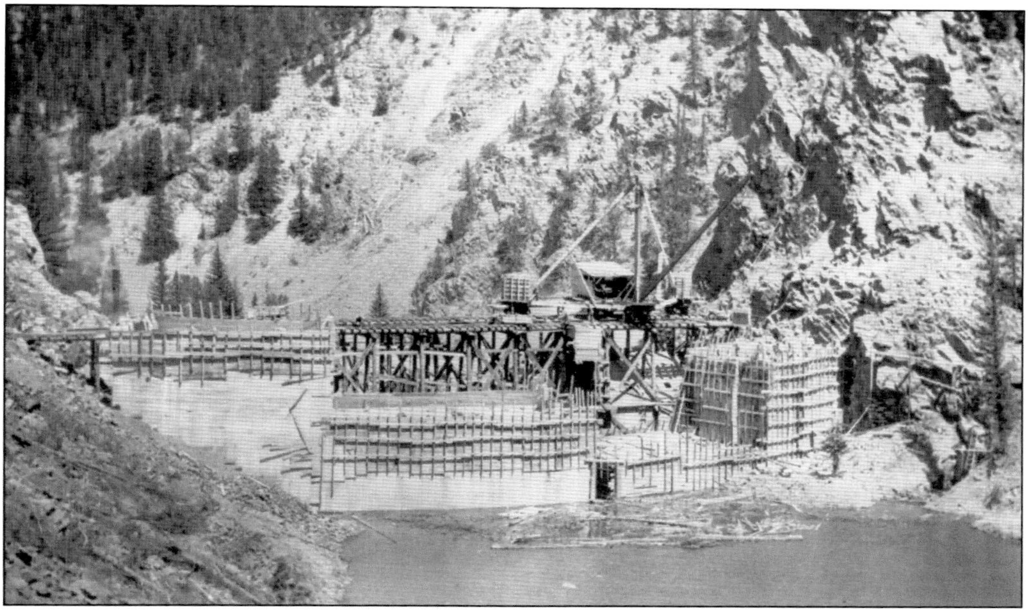

Charles Springer completed this dam in 1918 to control the downstream flow of the Cimarron River, in turn creating the reservoir behind it known as Eagle Nest Lake and flooding thousands of acres of ranch land. Litigation over the rights to this land delayed construction for over a decade. Creation of the lake led to the small resort community of Eagle Nest that fishermen and families now enjoy year-round. (The Old Mill.)

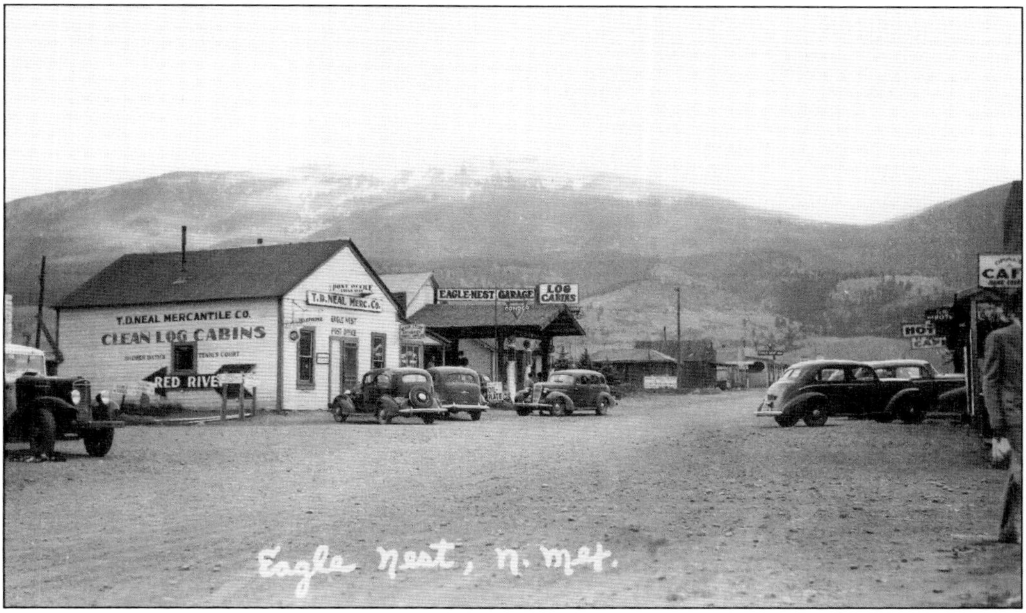

Originally named Therma after the daughter of the first local postal inspector, the name was changed in 1935 to Eagle Nest, after the area's numerous golden eagles. Postal inspectors once had the authority to change the name of a town, and in New Mexico did so with regularity. Today, the community serves tourists who fish the lake and hike the mountains in the summer and ski the neighboring resorts in the winter. (Authors' collection.)

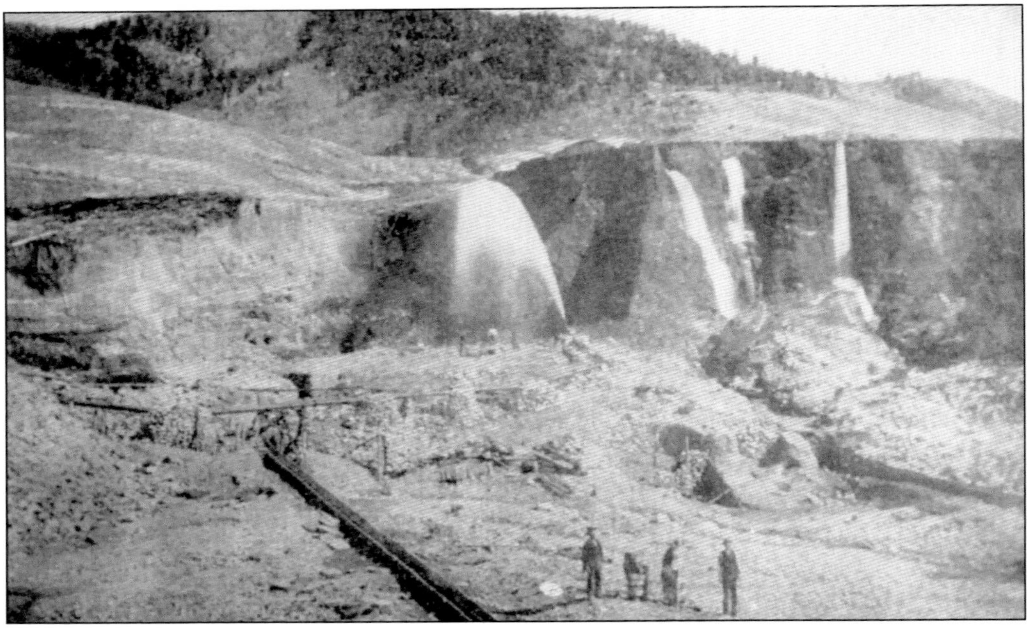

Hydraulic mining was fast, effective, and destructive and required the large quantity of water promised by the Big Ditch. This c. 1870s view in Moreno Valley demonstrates the impact this method had as entire hillsides were washed away through sluice boxes in the search for gold. Matthew Lynch was the last Big Ditch owner to demonstrate some success, but after 1880 the effort declined. (Philmont Scout Ranch.)

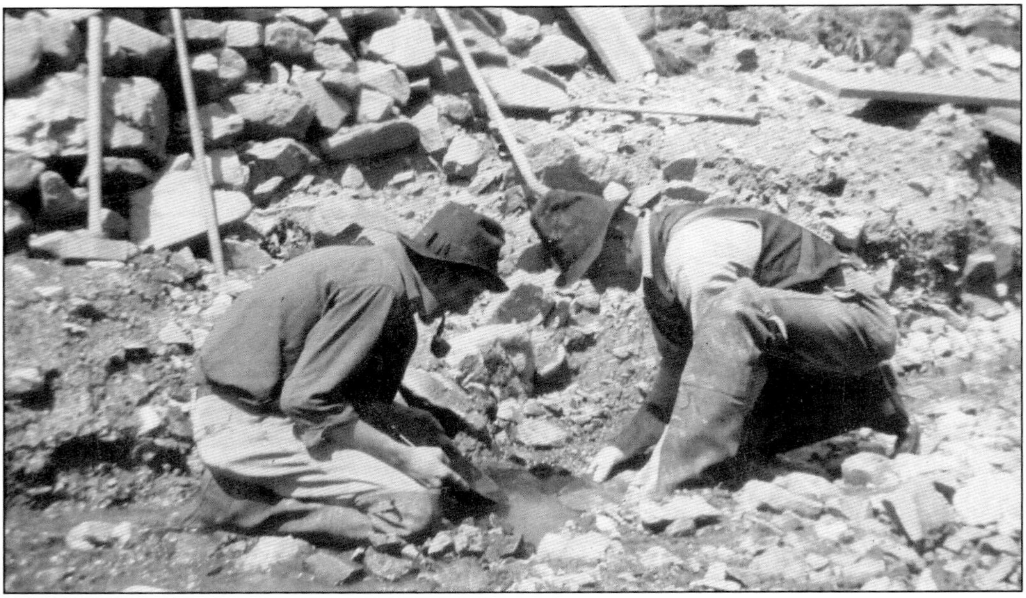

These Elizabethtown miners use shallow mining pans to sift through fine particles of gravel; gold was heavier than the raw material and would settle to the pan bottom as the miners worked. Pans like these were used to sample for promising spots where heavier equipment could make shorter work of the search. Philmont participants panned for gold at Cypher's Mine and at French Henry. (Hickman family.)

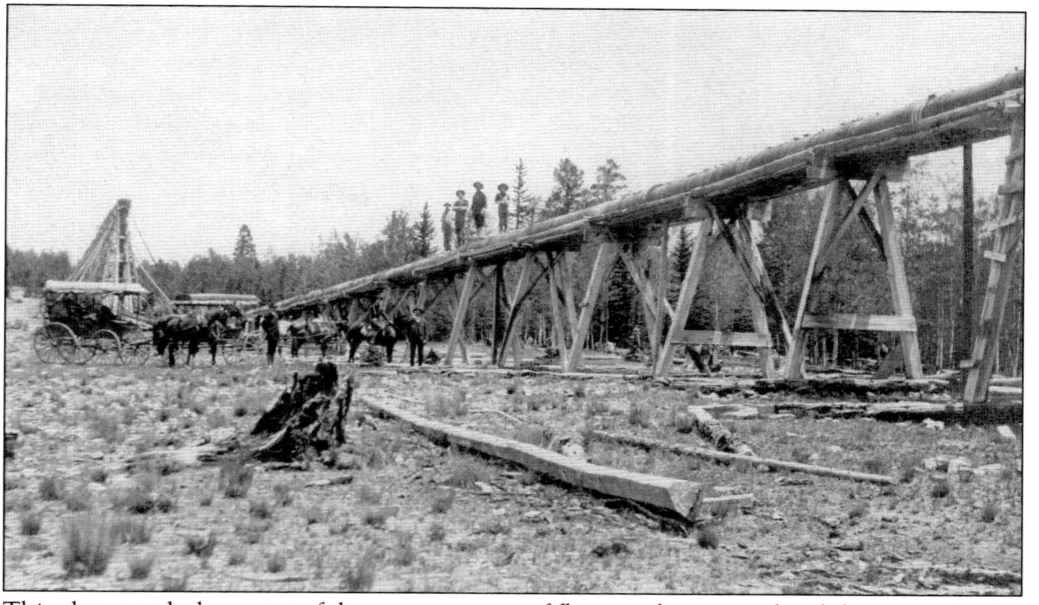

This photograph shows one of the upper sections of flume and supports that fed water to the Big Ditch in Moreno Valley. Flume widths varied between 2.5 feet and 7 feet, with a drop of 1 to 4 feet per mile. Eight miles of branch flumes near Red River Pass funneled water from Horseshoe, Lost, and Middle Fork Lakes to yield a flow rate of nearly eight million gallons per day at the bottom. (Raton Museum.)

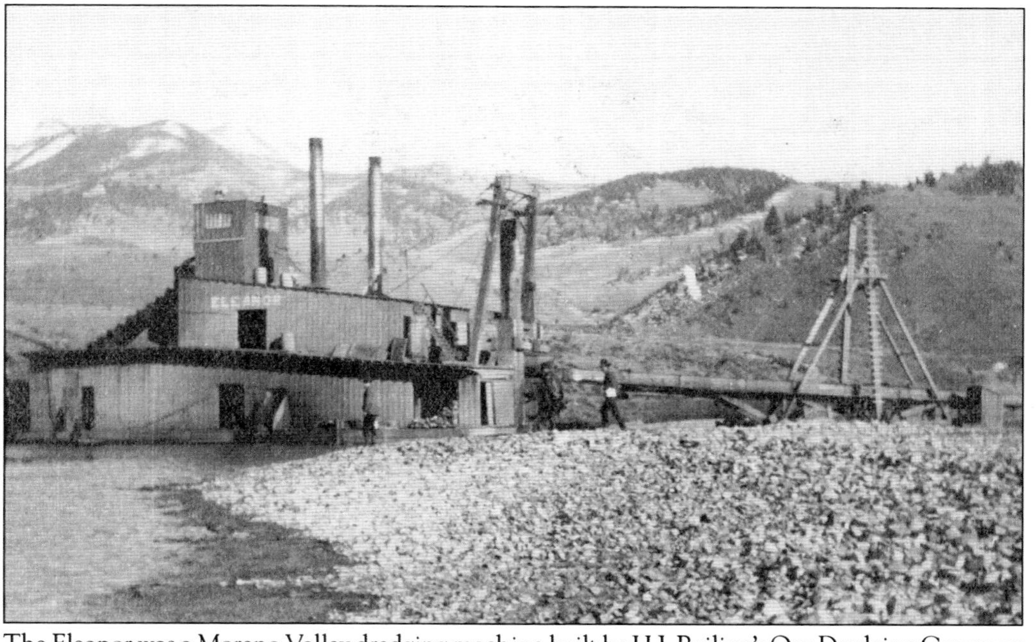

The Eleanor was a Moreno Valley dredging machine built by H.J. Reiling's Oro Dredging Company to churn through vast quantities of gravel in search of gold. Equipped with two 21,000-pound boilers, the Eleanor was christened in August 1901 and in four years produced $200,000 worth of gold. It was sold to the Maxwell Land Grant Company in 1906 and eventually sank into the soil. (Authors' collection.)

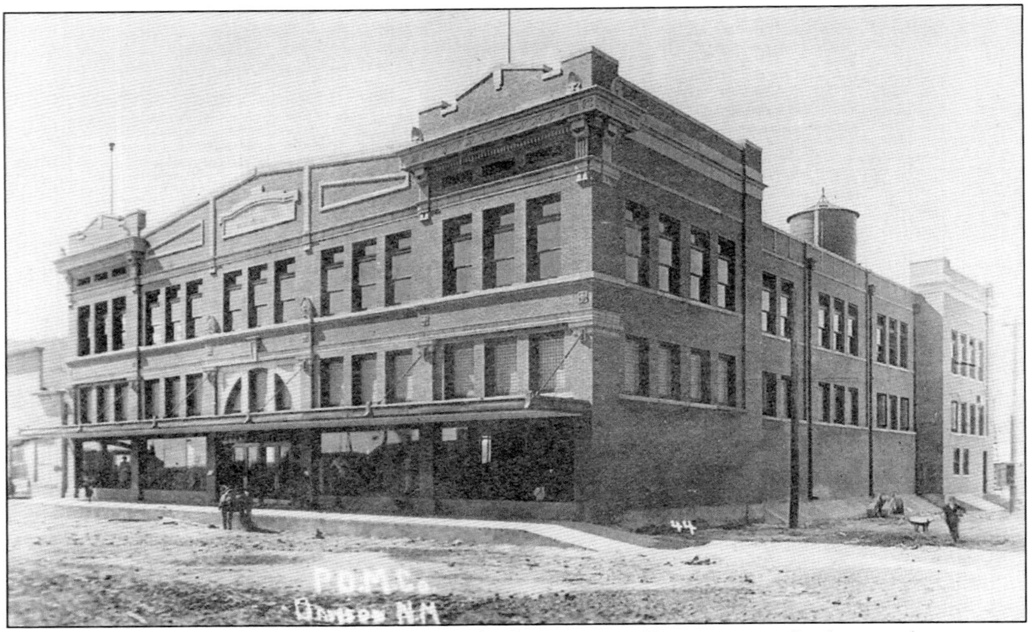

The stately redbrick Phelps Dodge Mercantile Company in Dawson was the largest department store in New Mexico when it was constructed in 1913. By 1919, there were 60 employees at this and three local branches. The store sold everything "from mousetraps to tractors," including clothing, groceries, and furniture, and an ice plant in the basement produced 5,000 pounds daily. Cash and scrip were accepted. (Authors' collection.)

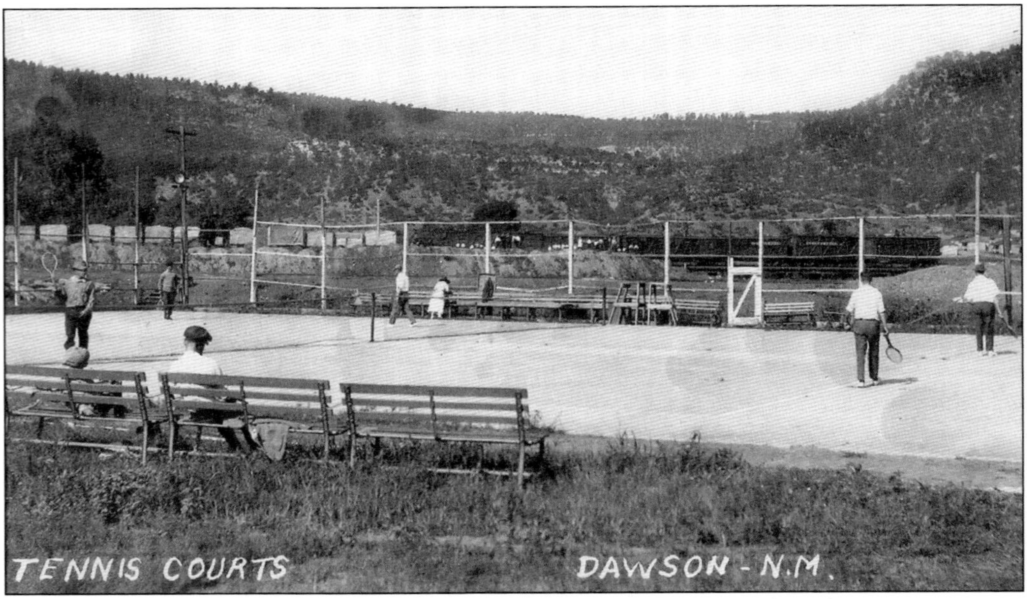

Residents of Dawson were provided access to modern leisure services such as these tennis courts. A $40,000 theater managed by E.R. Byers opened on August 25, 1907, with a production by the Wolfe Stock Company, which had earlier appeared in Hugo Seaburg's Coliseum Garden Theatre in Raton. The Dawson theater also showed motion pictures and served as a community gathering spot. (Authors' collection.)

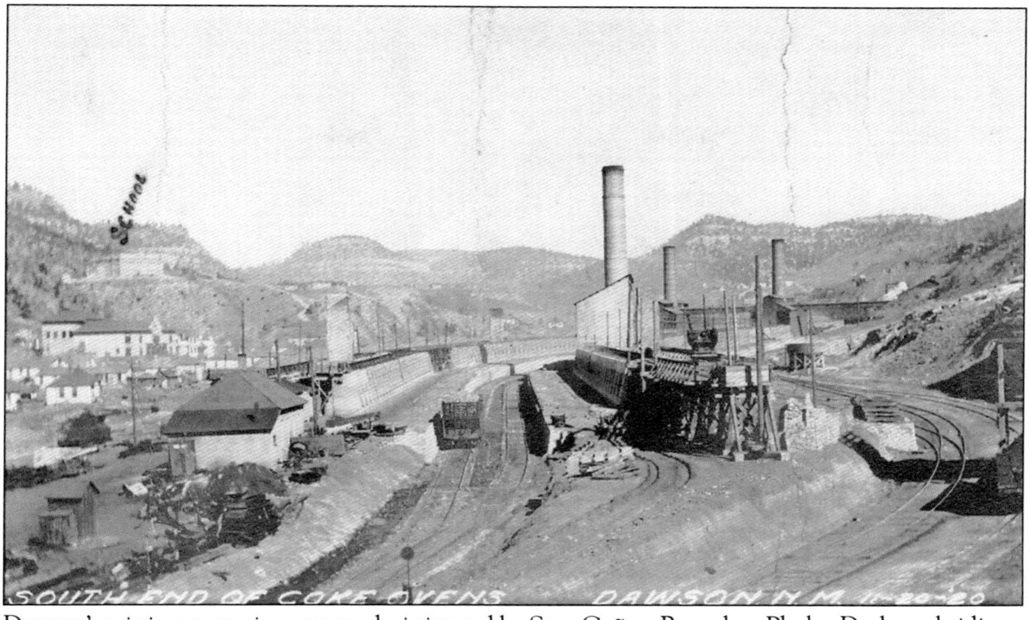

Dawson's mining operations were administered by Stag Cañon Branch, a Phelps Dodge subsidiary. Its products, coal and coke, were both used for home heating and industrial purposes. This November 1920 photograph shows the south end of the Dawson coke ovens, some of the 500 ovens that produced 600 tons of coke each day. Dawson's coke ovens were closed in 1926, and the mining effort focused on coal. (Authors' collection.)

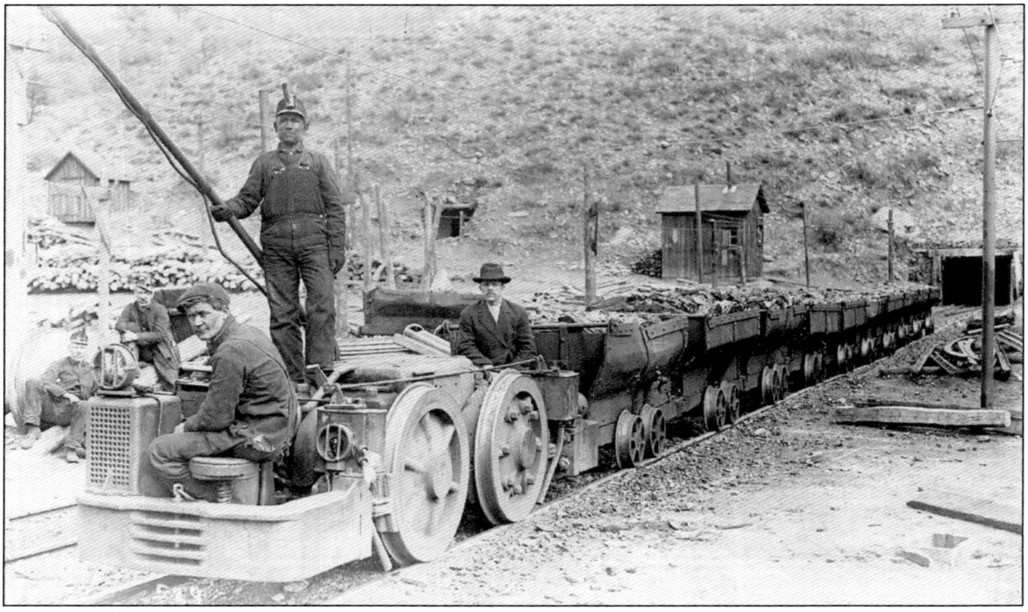

Mechanization in the 10 company mines brought shuttle cars to remove coal from underground. Tragic explosions sparked by coal dust in 1913 and 1923 took the lives of 263 and 120 miners, respectively, most of whom rest in the Dawson Cemetery. Only one mine remained after 1933, and when Phelps Dodge ceased operations and closed the town in April 1950, its residents relocated to Raton, Cimarron, and other nearby cities. (The Old Mill.)

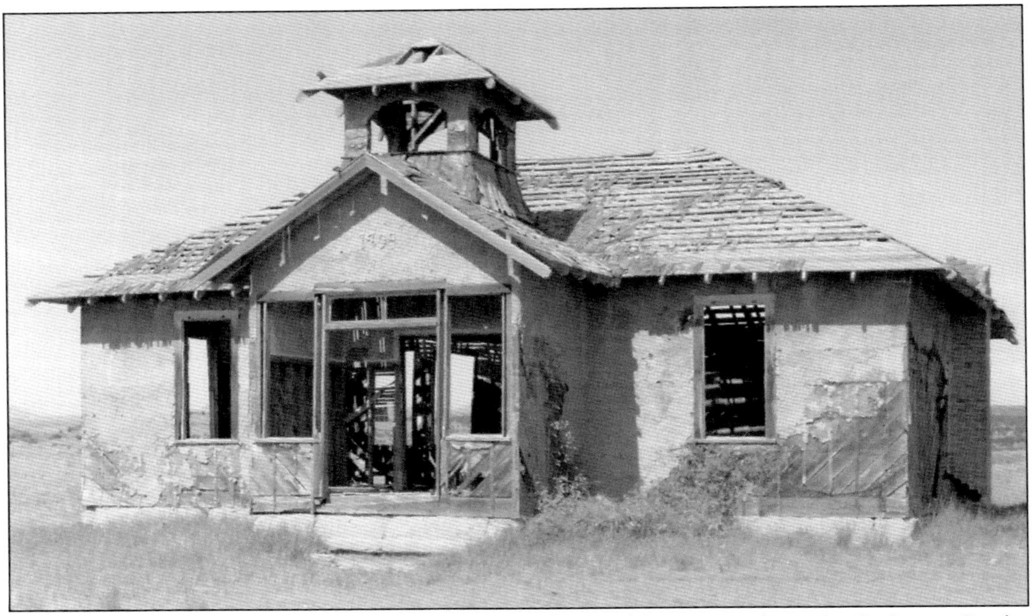

Colfax was established in 1908 about 16 miles northeast of Cimarron along the St. Louis, Rocky Mountain & Pacific Railway Company line. The New Mexico Land Sales Company offered 100 forty-acre area tracts, and the population grew slowly. By the 1940s, Colfax failed due to its proximity to Dawson, and by 1983 the 1909 schoolhouse was significantly dilapidated. Sadly, the last vestiges of Colfax were purposefully burned in 2011. (Authors' collection.)

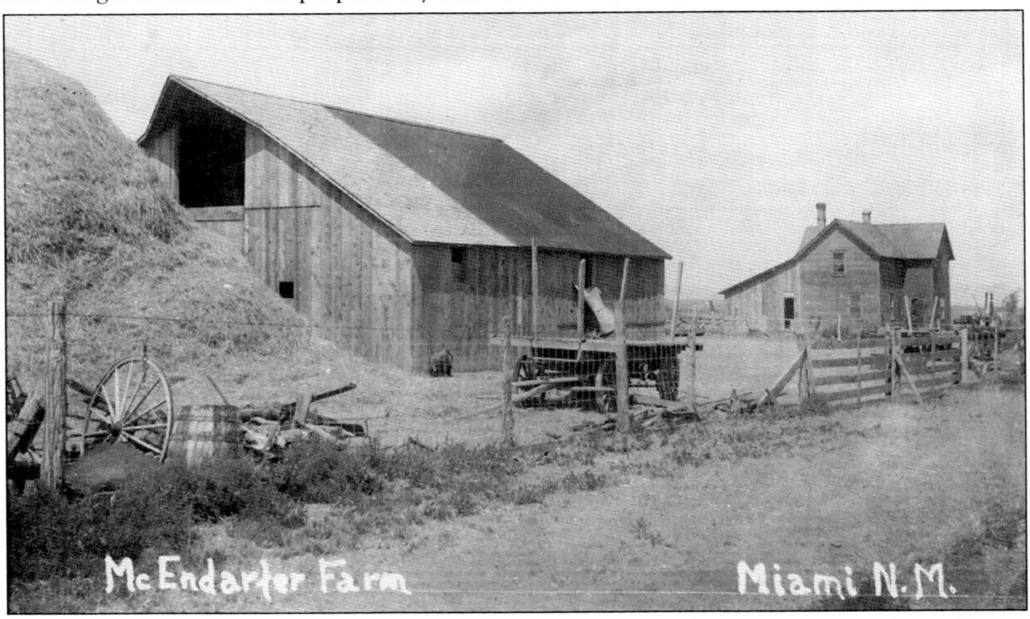

B.F. McEndarfer was a regular visitor to Cimarron for pleasure and in connection with his 80-acre Miami farm, seen here in 1912. McEndarfer recounted in 1914 that since arriving in the Miami Valley in 1909, his personal property and real estate had grown in value from $2,150 to $16,000. He raised oats, wheat, corn, and speltz. Miami once was home to a cheese factory, library, public school, mercantile, and planing mill. (McEndarfer family.)

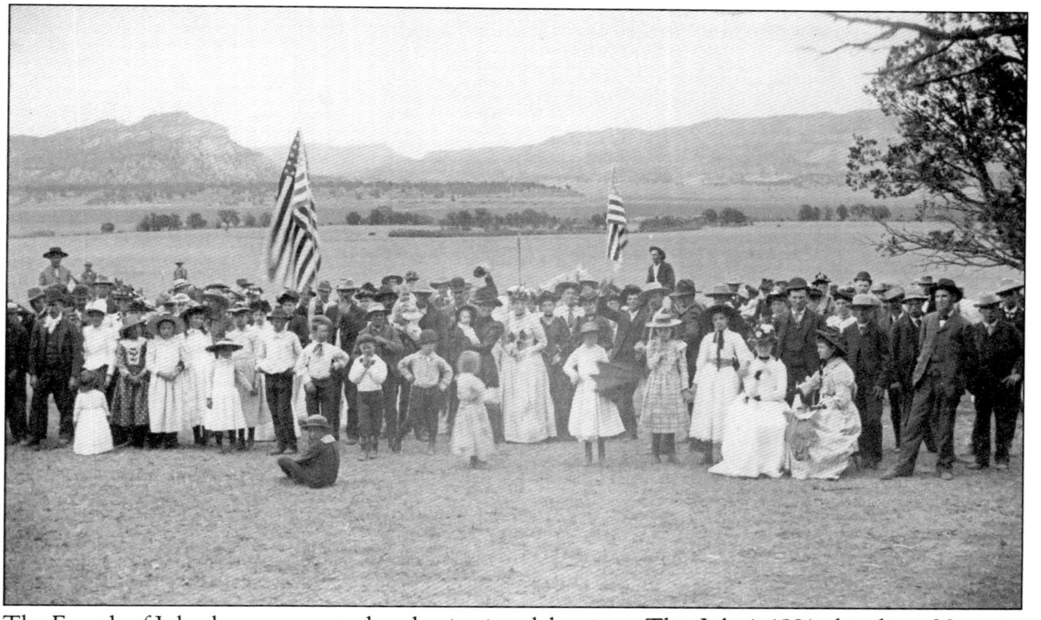

The Fourth of July always prompted enthusiastic celebrations. This July 4, 1891, shindig at Vermejo Park likely included a hearty feast, games and contests, and patriotic readings. Among the revelers are Zenas A. Curtis and Tom McBride, who later served as county treasurer. The Curtis Tool Company investors in 1916 included Zenas's daughter Henrietta "Nettie" Chase (1869–1927) of Vermejo Park. (The Old Mill.)

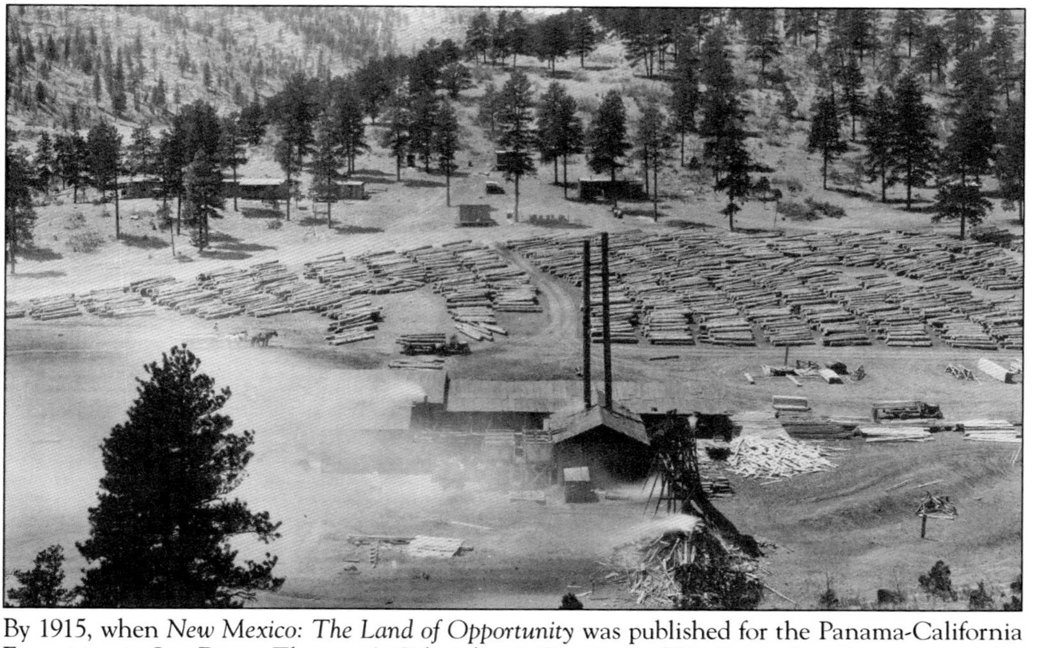

By 1915, when *New Mexico: The Land of Opportunity* was published for the Panama-California Exposition in San Diego, Thomas A. Schomberg's Continental Tie & Lumber Company was the primary lumber operation at Ponil Park, some 22 miles northwest of Cimarron. That year, the company boasted a monthly payroll of $10,000. Cut lumber was transported to the planing mill in Cimarron via subsidiary Cimarron & Northwestern Railway. (Raton Museum.)

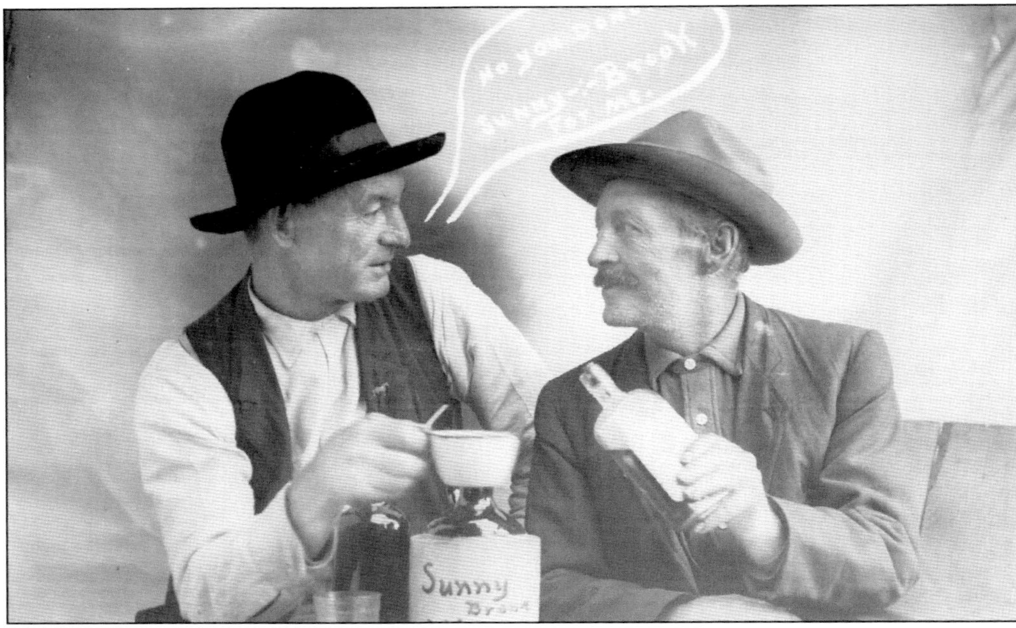

Comical photographs and exaggeration postcards grew in popularity as studios spread throughout the territory and photography became more accessible. This image, believed to be from Ring, shows two whiskey-drinking gentlemen, one of whom prefers Sunny Brook Whiskey: "No You Don't. Sunny Brook for me." Sunny Brook was advertised as a "pure food whiskey" that one "ought to use for your health each day." (The Old Mill.)

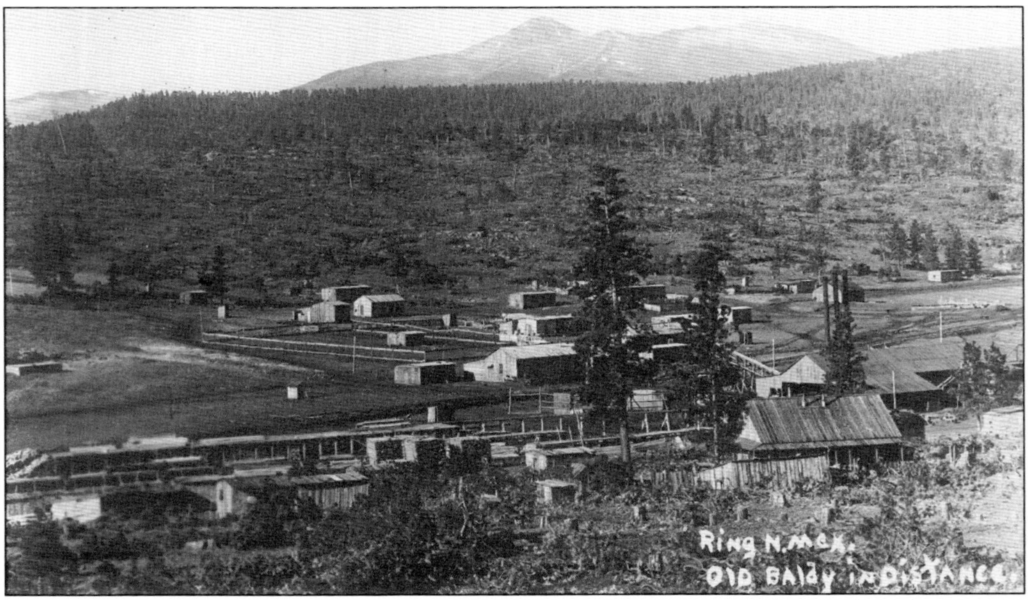

Ring was settled in 1890 by ranchers Timothy and Catherine Ring, who purchased 320 acres northwest of Ponil Park from the Maxwell Land Grant Company and whose house still exists. After 1906, a busy logging community was developed at this location, with timber processed on-site by independent operators for the Continental Tie & Lumber Company in Cimarron. This image looks southwest toward Baldy Mountain, which is visible in the distance. (The Old Mill.)

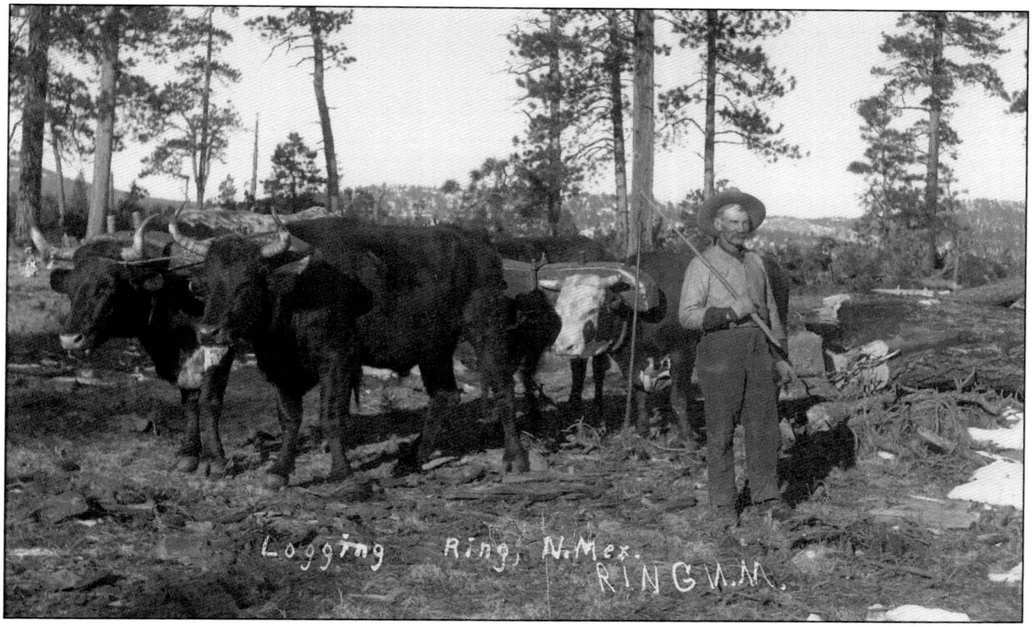

Logging in Ring and other communities was a prosperous but laborious undertaking. Teams of oxen did the heavy work needed to drag timber through the woods to nearby wagons, mills, or railcars. This Troutman Studio photograph captures one such team at momentary rest with a pipe-smoking driver; the glint of the sun is visible on the horns, yokes, whip handle, and log hook. (Authors' collection.)

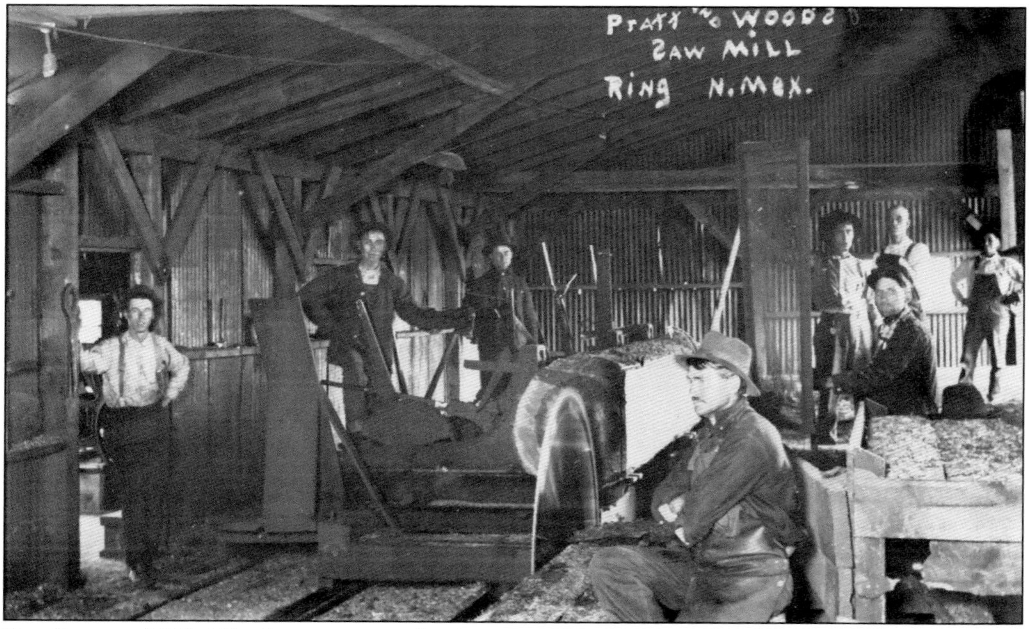

Bert Pratt and C.S. Wood were veteran lumbermen, having operated mills in Metcalf Canyon and Ponil Park, respectively, in 1908. Together, they operated this sawmill in Ring. The remnants of Ring are now within the boundary of the Valle Vidal Unit of the Carson National Forest, and it is nearby that Philmont developed the Ring Place staffed camp in 1991. (The Old Mill.)

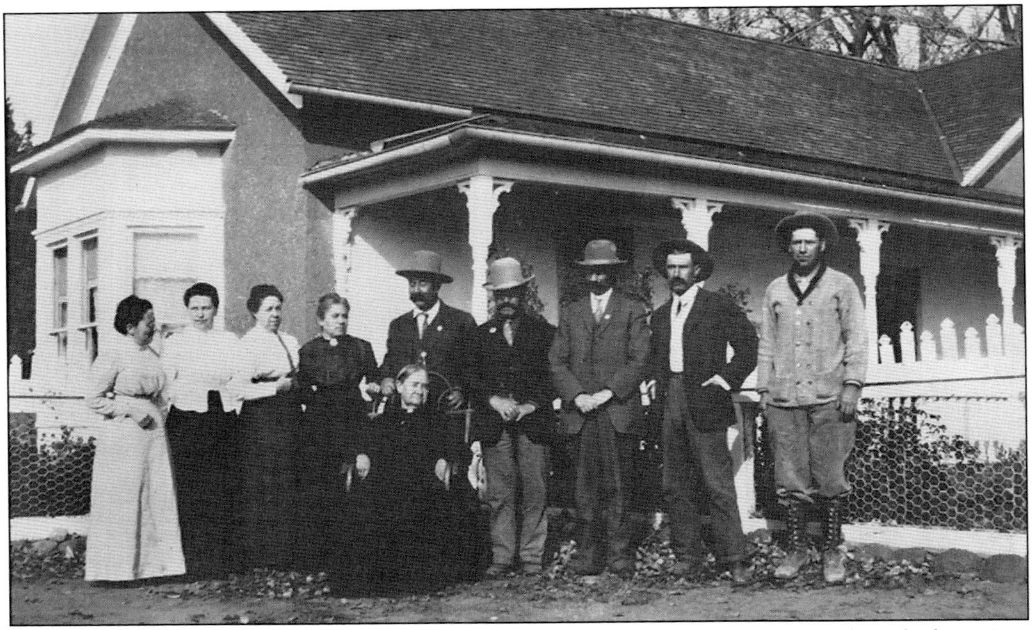

This handsome structure, modified after 1900 with a pitched roof and shown here before 1911, comprises a remnant of Lucien B. Maxwell's estate home at Rayado. Jesús Gil and Petra Beaubien Abreu (shown seated and surrounded by her family) ranched here beginning in 1864. Their sons formed the Rayado Land and Irrigation Company in 1907 before selling 30,000 acres four years later to the Rayado Colonization Company. (Philmont Scout Ranch.)

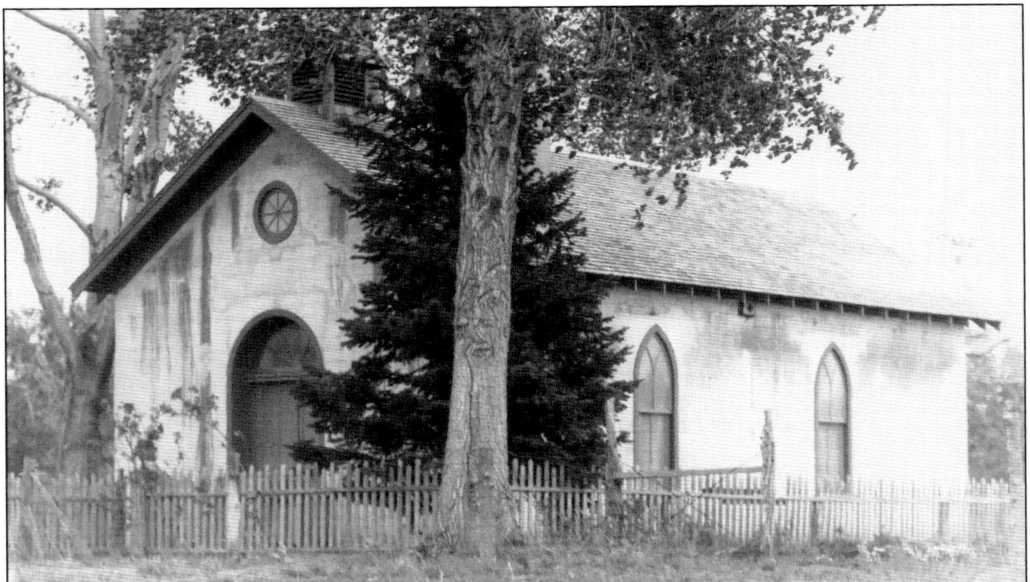

The Chapel of the Holy Child on the east side of State Road 21 in Rayado—on the old Santa Fe Trail—was constructed by Petra Abreu in honor of her recently deceased husband, Jesús Abreu, and opened in February 1904. Waite Phillips acquired extensive Rayado acreage in 1929. Rayado, then known as Carson-Maxwell, was used as a base camp beginning in 1947. (Philmont Scout Ranch.)

Seven

Ranching

Before Lucien B. Maxwell sold the grant in 1870, much land had already been parceled out to friends. In 1861, Maxwell had sold property to fellow trapper Peter Joseph. Richens L. "Uncle Dick" Wootton had acquired 2,500 acres of land over Raton Pass, where he had built a toll road in 1865. The Chase and Dawson Ranches date to 1868. When the grant was sold, Frank Springer, lawyer for the new owners, acquired land in return for his services and with his brother Charles created the CS Ranch.

Originally from Wisconsin, Manly and Theresa Chase moved first to Colorado during the gold rush and then down to northern New Mexico in 1867. The couple had met Maxwell some years earlier and arranged to buy land along the Vermejo River. In 1870, their son Mason was born, and the following year the family moved closer to Cimarron along Ponil Creek, building a house a short distance from where Kit Carson had put up a cabin 30 years earlier. Besides running cattle, horses, and sheep on his own land, Manly was also a joint partner in the Crow Creek and Horseshoe Ranches with John Dawson and others, and he raised a productive apple orchard known mockingly as Chase's Folly.

John Barkley Dawson grew up along the Missouri-Arkansas frontier. An early trip by wagon train to the California goldfields taught Dawson that there was more money to be made in selling beef to prospectors than in prospecting. In 1857, the family moved to West Texas, where John learned the business of ranching and the cattle drive. In 1866, it was Dawson who convinced ranching neighbors Charles Goodnight and Oliver Loving to blaze a different trail to the Colorado goldfields: west to the Pecos River, then north along the Sangre de Cristos, past Maxwell's ranch, and over Raton Pass into southern Colorado. Dawson soon bought 24,000 acres from Maxwell beside the Vermejo River, later discovering coal, and started the Dawson Fuel Company. In 1903, Dawson sold his property to the Phelps Dodge Corporation and moved to Colorado, discovered yet more coal, and left behind the thriving town that bore his name.

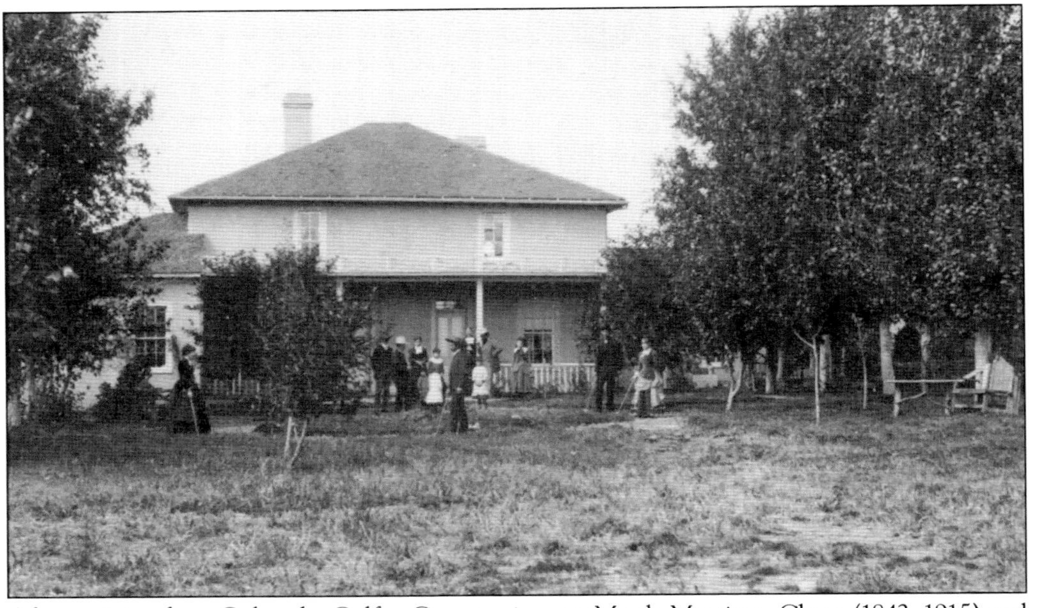

After arriving from Colorado, Colfax County pioneers Manly Mortimer Chase (1842–1915) and Theresa Wade Chase (1846–1900) purchased land from Lucien B. Maxwell to establish their Chase Ranch in the lower Ponil Canyon. In the center of this 1880s photograph, playing croquet, is former Civil War general Lew Wallace. Wallace is believed to have worked on his acclaimed 1880 novel *Ben-Hur* while visiting the Chase Ranch as New Mexico's governor. (The Old Mill.)

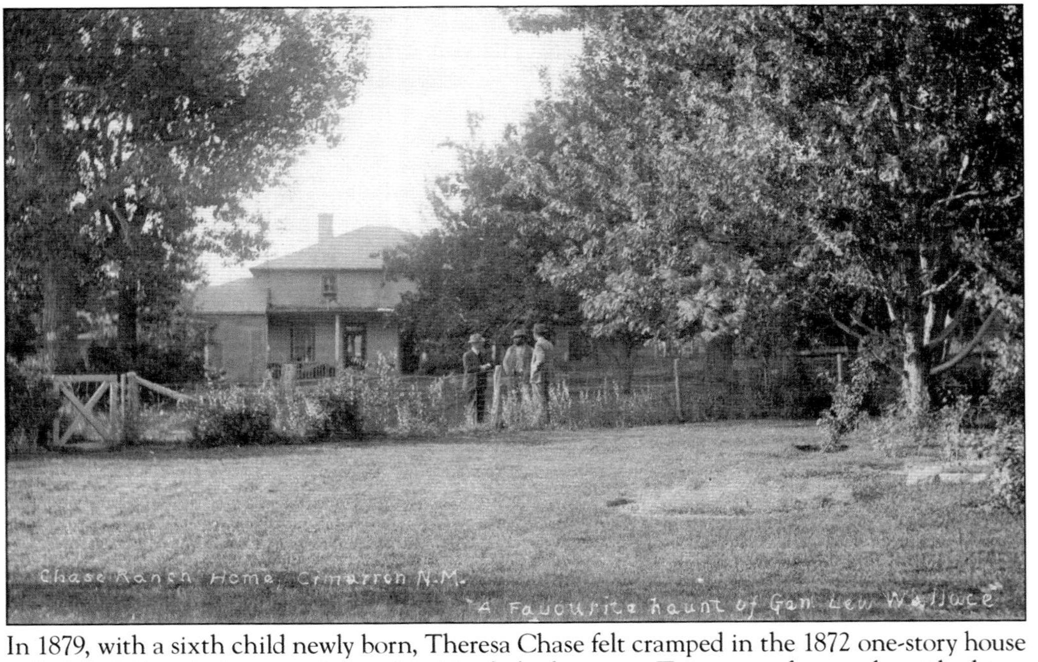

In 1879, with a sixth child newly born, Theresa Chase felt cramped in the 1872 one-story house called Oak Ranch. Just one hour after Manly had gone to Texas on a five-week cattle drive, Theresa rounded up all the ranch hands and told them to add a second story. Not to be outdone, Manly, stunned when he returned, immediately ordered that a larger kitchen, new dining room, and more bedrooms be added. (The Old Mill.)

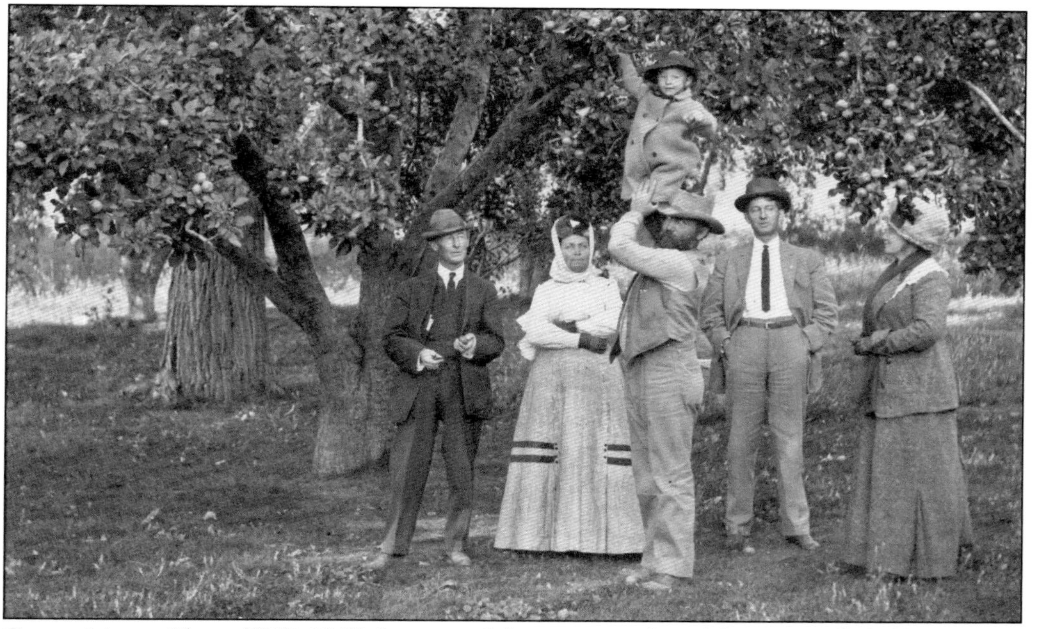

George Mason Chase (1870–1943), known as Mason, is seen here lifting a small child up to pick an apple in one of Chase's orchards. Mason's father, Manly, planted apple orchards on his land in the early 1870s and soon shipped enviable crops carrying the Chase name. After 1900, the elder Chase devoted considerable time to his orchards and won prizes at the 1908 Chicago World's Fair. (The Old Mill.)

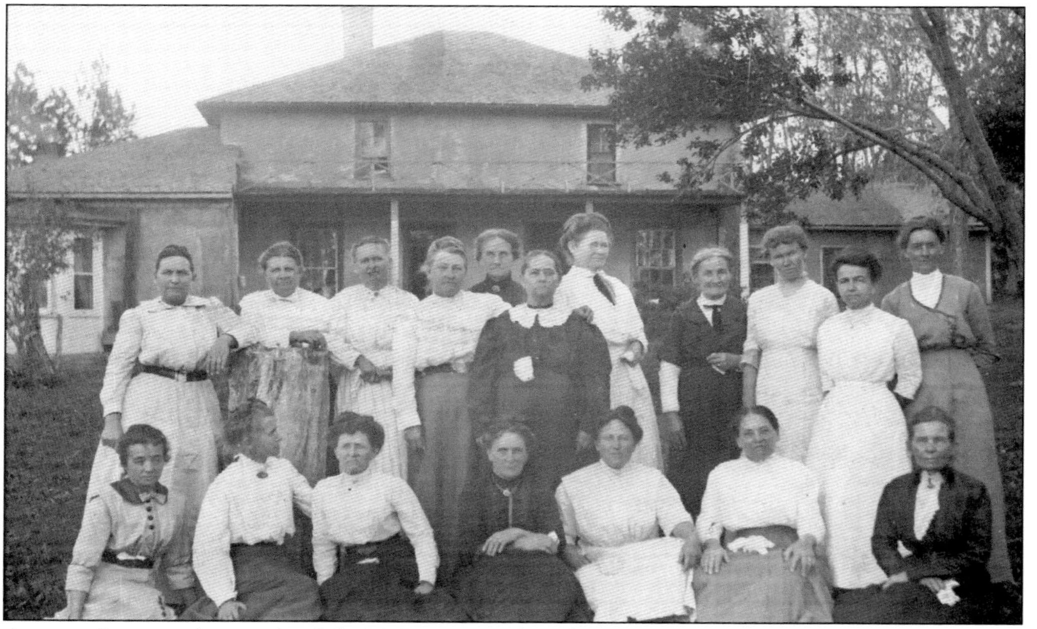

Among the attendees at this July 1912 party at the Chase Ranch are Mary Curtis, Mary Lodge, Jane Livingston, Mildred Vance, Margaret Whiteman, Alma Chandler, Gertrude Rupert, Barbara Cartwright, Hattie Crocker, Mary Lambert, and hostess Nettie Chase. Mary Troutman is standing at the far right in the second row. (The Old Mill.)

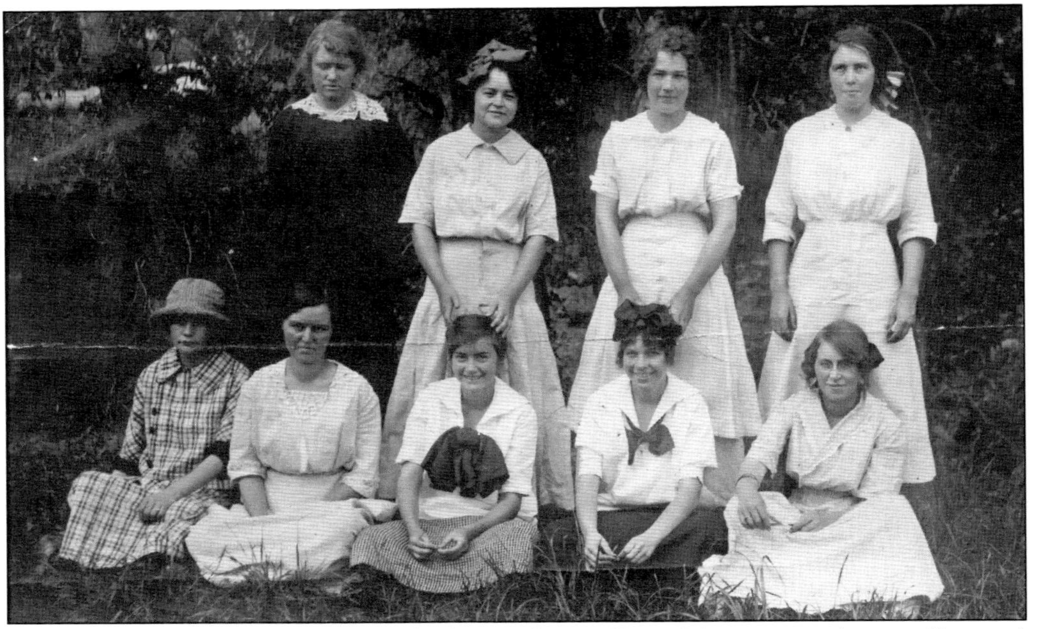

The Chase Ranch also was the site of this later gathering. Four of the guests are known: (first row) Vera Whiteman Besore (far left) and Alma Troutman (far right); (second row) Belle Cartwright (far left) and Julia Masten Ford (far right). Troutman (1891–1956), daughter of Edward and Mary Troutman, taught in the Cimarron School for many years and is buried in Cimarron's Mountain View Cemetery. (Arthur Johnson Memorial Library.)

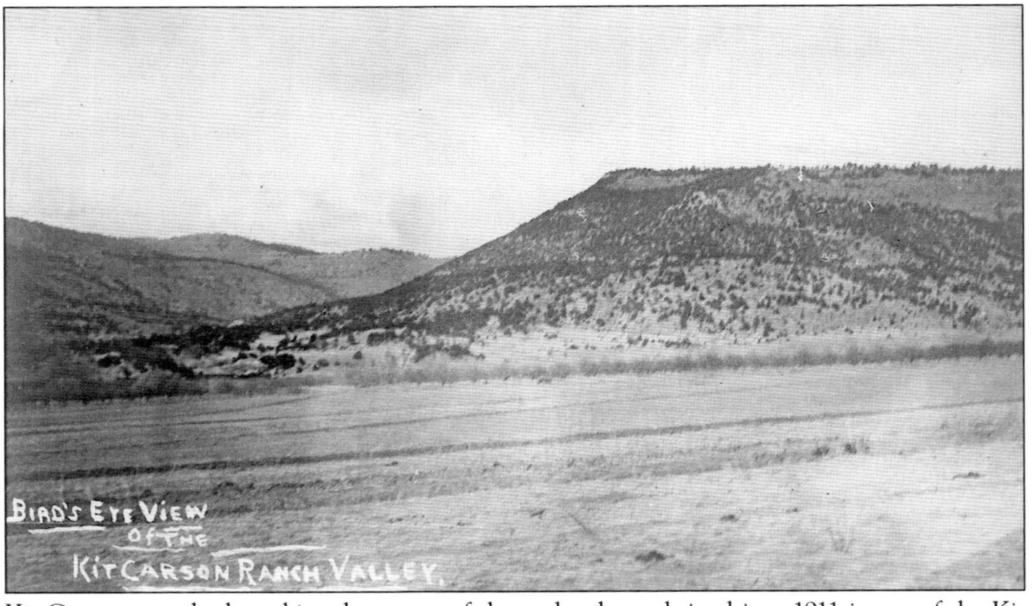

Kit Carson once had a cabin where part of the orchard stands in this c. 1911 image of the Kit Carson Ranch Valley. According to Gretchen Sammis, who presently owns and operates the famed Chase Ranch, "The canyon that goes west is Dean Canyon, which at the time was owned by the Chases. Mason Chase, however, lost it in a poker game." In the distance is Midnight Mesa, so called because "that's when all the action started." (Authors' collection.)

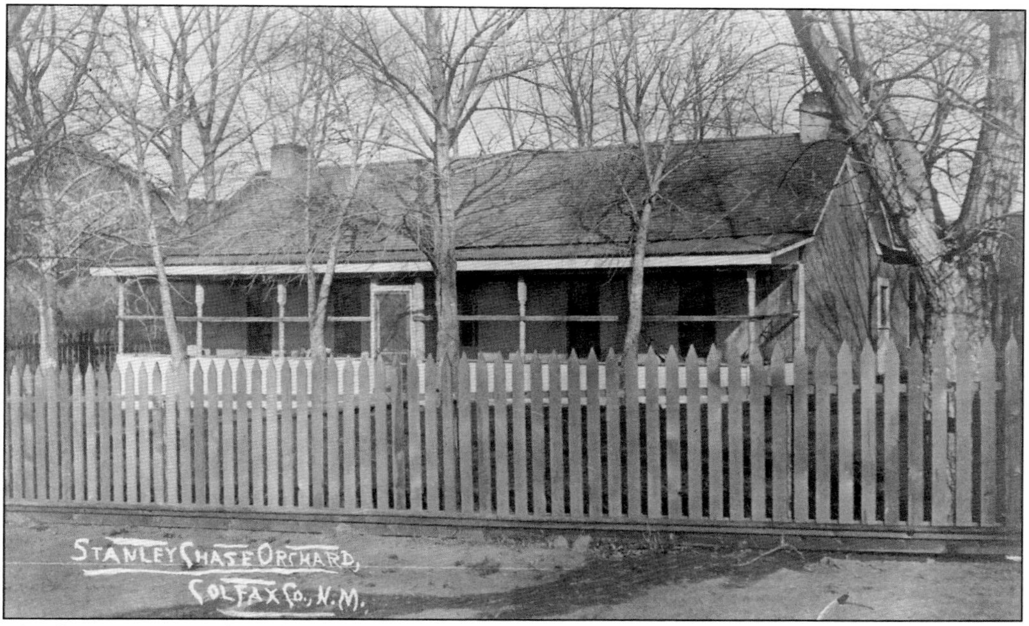

This house in an apple orchard sits on property once owned by Manly and Theresa Chase. Their son Stanley Mortimer Chase (1879–1954) was the grandfather of Gretchen Sammis. The house was torn down to make way for a new one that was never built. This photographic print was acquired by George Seward Gumaer in 1911. (Authors' collection.)

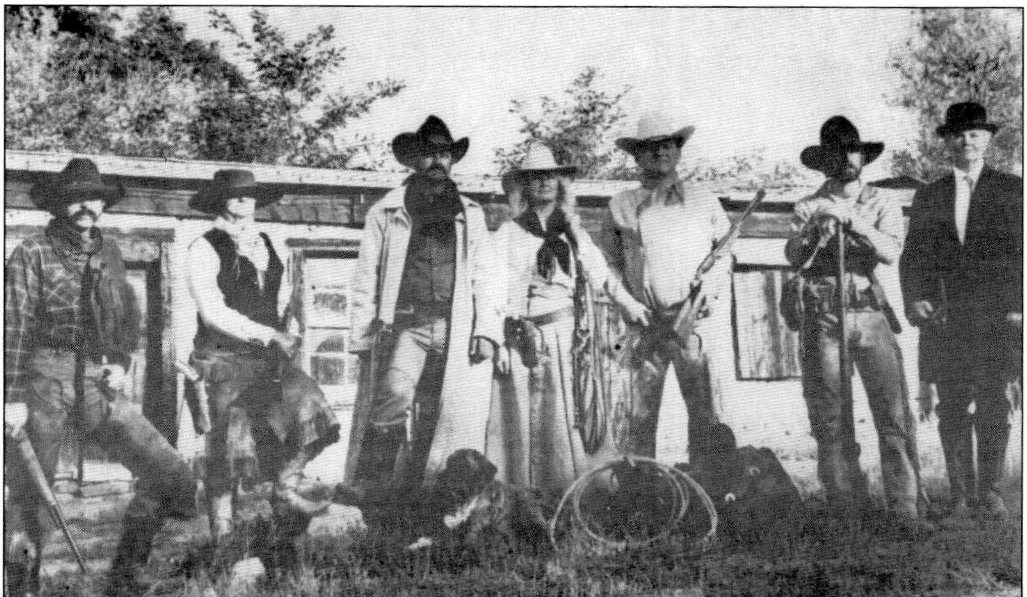

This undated photograph was taken at the Chase Ranch for Ferguson Western Store in Clayton. From left to right are Ramon Maez, Ruby Gobble of the Chase Ranch, Tom Ferguson, Peggy Ferguson, Donn Davies, Gary Loveland of the TO Ranch, and Gretchen Sammis, owner of the Chase Ranch. Sammis and Gobble were among those featured in *Hard Twist: Western Ranch Women* in 1995. (The Old Mill.)

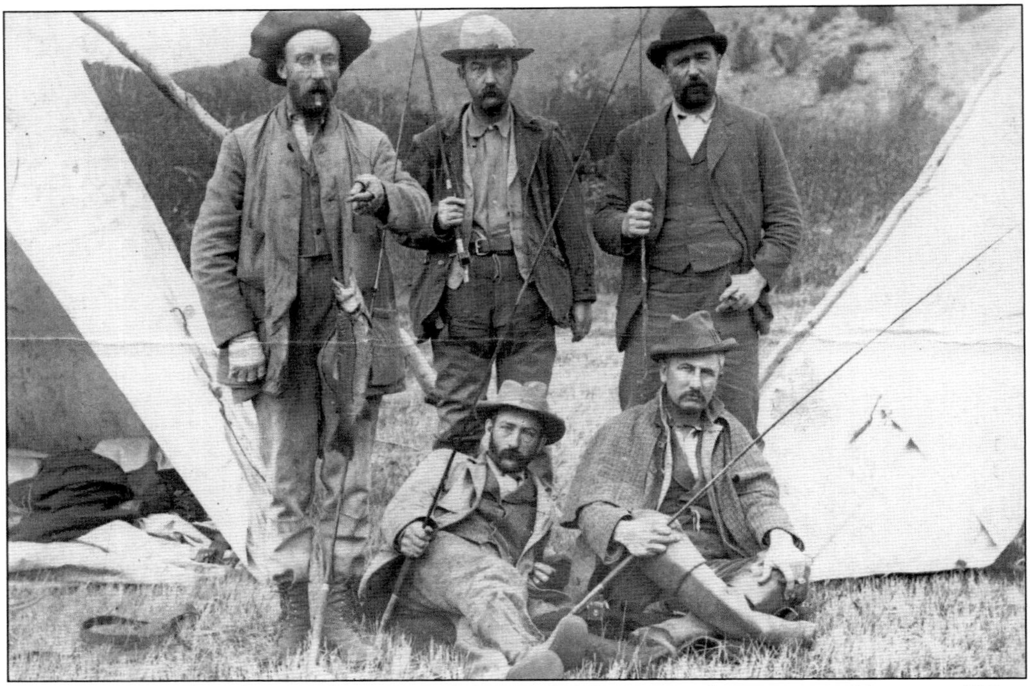

White River, Colorado, was the scene of this 1895 fishing expedition enjoyed by two of New Mexico's most influential men—Charles and Frank Springer. From left to right are (first row) Charles Springer and A.L. Hobbs of Raton; (second row) Captain Grierson, Frank Springer, and Hereford breeder H.M. Letts of Columbus Junction, Iowa, a business associate of Charles Springer. (Taos Historic Museums.)

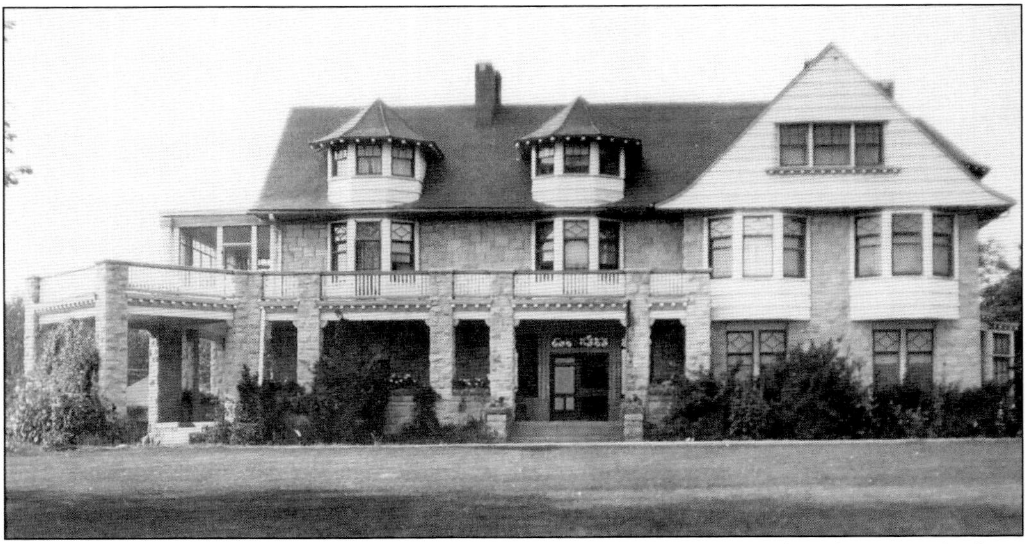

The striking three-story Charles Springer residence was built in 1904 on the Chase Ranch about two miles southeast of the Manly Chase home, on property Chase deeded to Springer for legal services rendered. Springer had married Mary Lorraine Chase (1877–1948) in 1899. Suspiciously, it burned to the ground on April 12, 1924, the same night the old Maxwell mansion in Cimarron was further damaged by fire. (Authors' collection.)

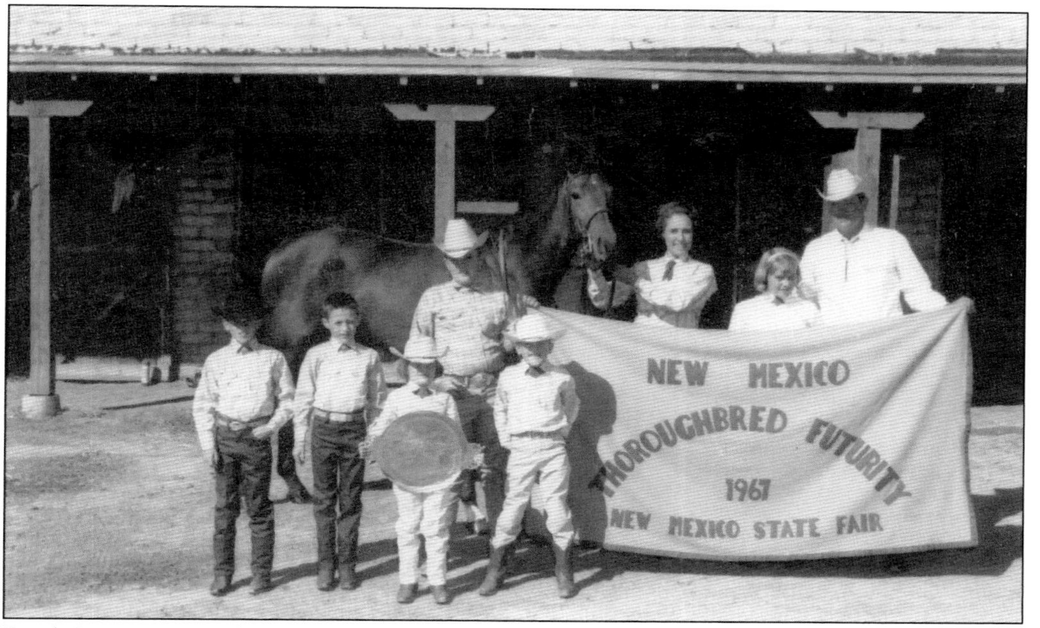

Frank Springer's grandson Les Davis (1919–2001) assumed management of the CS Ranch in 1947 and married Linda Mitchell six years later. Their children—Warren, Julia, Randolph, Kirk, Bruce, and Kim—all have played an important role on the CS. Thousands of youngsters met the Davis family through *Cimarron Kid*, Paul Conklin's 1973 book about Kirk. The Davis family owns and maintains The Old Mill museum. (The Old Mill.)

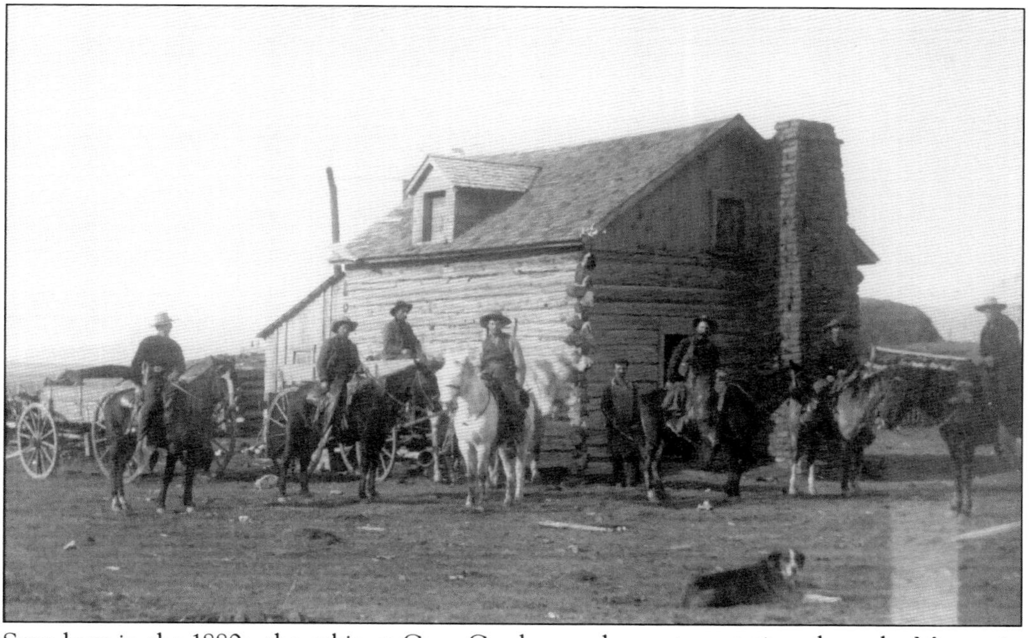

Seen here in the 1880s, the cabin at Crow Creek served as a stage station along the Mountain Branch of the Santa Fe Trail. The Crow Creek Ranch was acquired by and remains a division of the CS Ranch. For over 60 years, the Crow Creek was home to Earl Mayfield "Jiggs" Porter (1916–2005), who served as CS cow foreman from 1933 to 1999. (The Old Mill.)

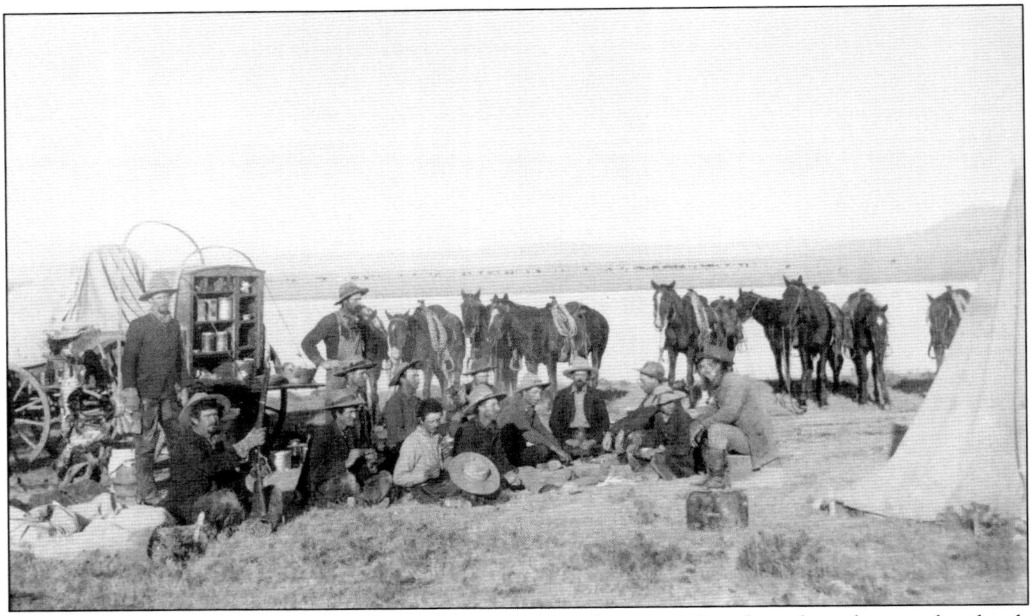

This c. 1900 image of the Wilson-Spencer ranch crew shows cowhands gathered around a chuck wagon while cattle dot the distant shore. A chuck wagon contained a well-stocked pantry and medicine chest and would meet the cowhands at a predetermined spot during a spring cattle roundup. Rease Stubblefield and Riley Littrell were identified in this image by Delbert Littrell Hughes in his 1971 book *Give Me Room!* (The Old Mill.)

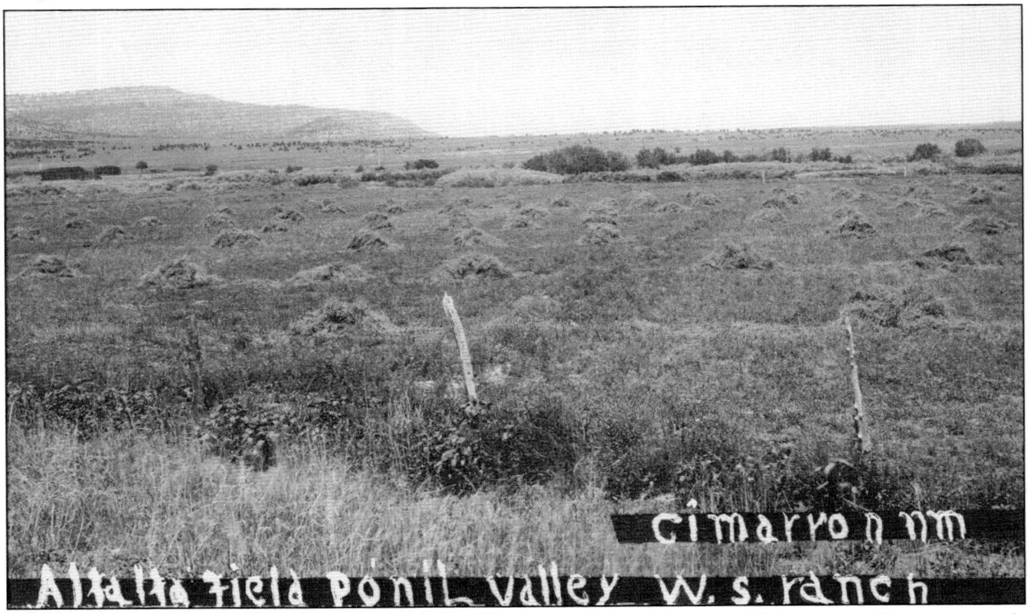

The 125,000-acre WS Ranch was established by Harold C. Wilson and Montague Stevens north of Cimarron in the 1880s. A 25,000-acre parcel became the French Tract before the WS was sold in 1945 to W.J. Gourley, who amassed 480,000 contiguous acres including the Vermejo Park Ranch. Vermejo Park was purchased by the Pennzoil Corporation in the 1970s and by Ted Turner in 1996. (Troutman Studio, The Old Mill.)

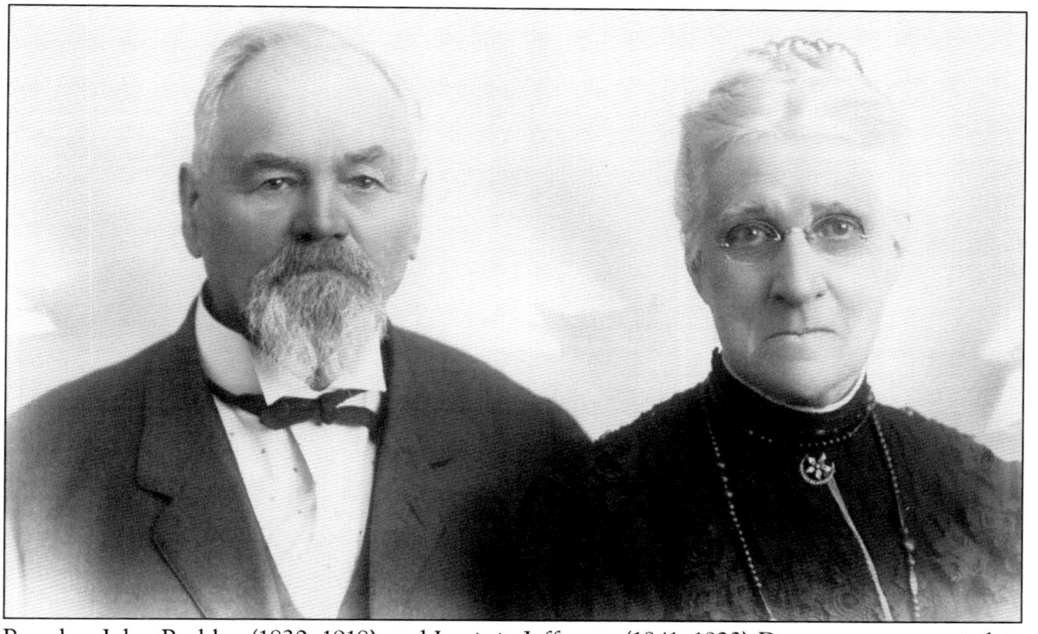

Rancher John Barkley (1830–1918) and Lavinia Jefferson (1841–1923) Dawson were married in 1873—his third, and her first. Over 45 years of marriage and six children followed. With Dawson's three older children, they forged a 24,000-acre empire along the Vermejo. Dawson sold his mineral rights in 1896 for $450,000, and the coal town of Dawson was established. Just over six years later, the Dawsons moved to Colorado. (Arthur Johnson Memorial Library.)

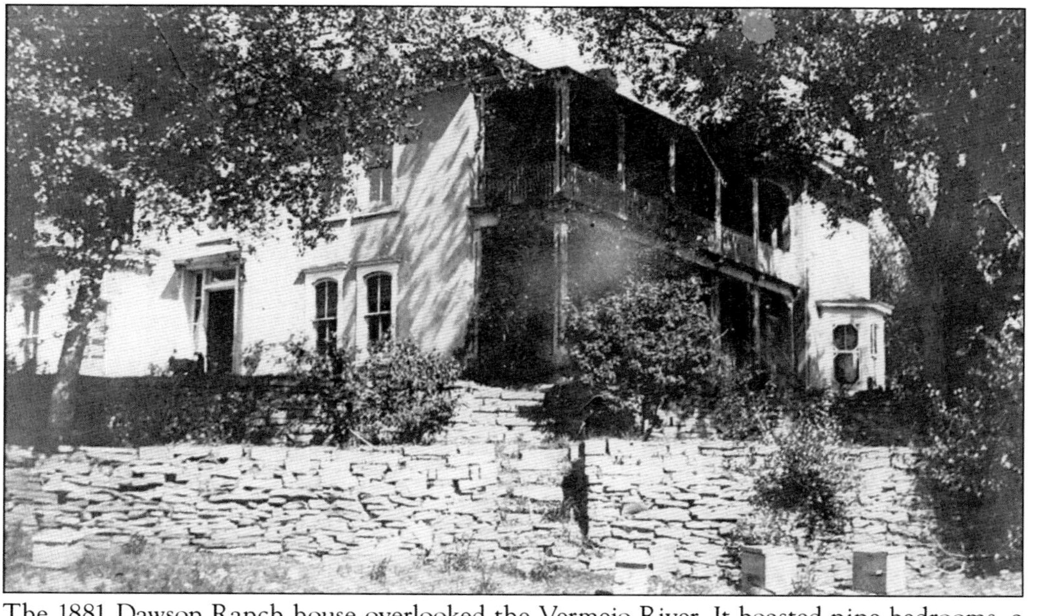

The 1881 Dawson Ranch house overlooked the Vermejo River. It boasted nine bedrooms, a dining room large enough for 50, and according to granddaughter Delphine Dawson Wilson "was surrounded by an 80-acre orchard growing some 45 varieties of apples, plus cherries, plums, pears, and peaches." Lavinia Dawson served as postmaster of Cimilorio in a first-floor office in the mansion. Note the beehives, undoubtedly used for pollination and honey. (The Old Mill.)

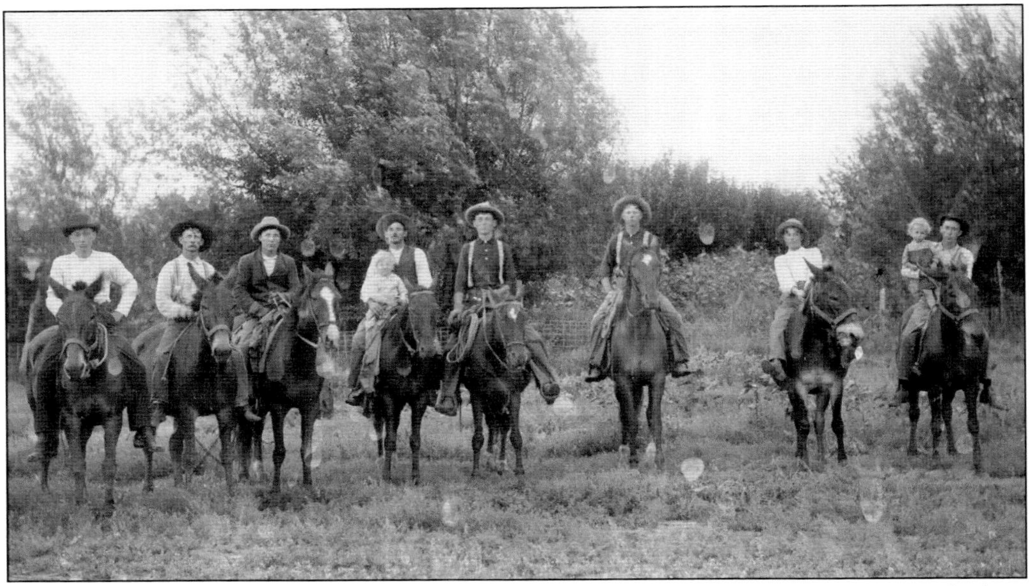

Northeastern New Mexican ranchers were not solitary businessmen. Chase, Dawson, and others often formed collaborations operating numerous companies, such as the Chase & Dawson Cattle Company, the Chase, Dawson & Maulding Cattle Company, and the Chase, Maulding & Dane Cattle Company. The Horseshoe Ranch was one such profitable business that Manly Chase and John Dawson ran during the 1880s, until Dawson sold his interest to Chase's relative, Ed Dane, in 1885. (The Old Mill.)

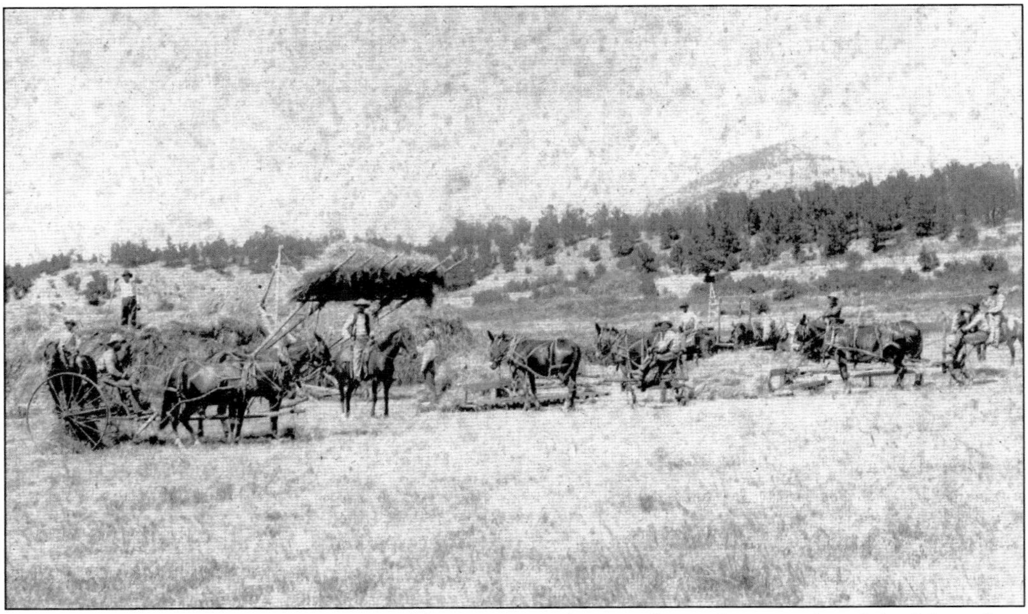

A ranch would be bought and then sold many times but, as these photographs of the Horseshoe Ranch in 1908 show, little would change in its operation. The cutting and moving of alfalfa for feed relied only on human and horsepower. It was not until companies like John Deere married the gasoline engine to the tractor in the early 20th century that ranching and farming grew into the huge industrial enterprises seen today. (The Old Mill.)

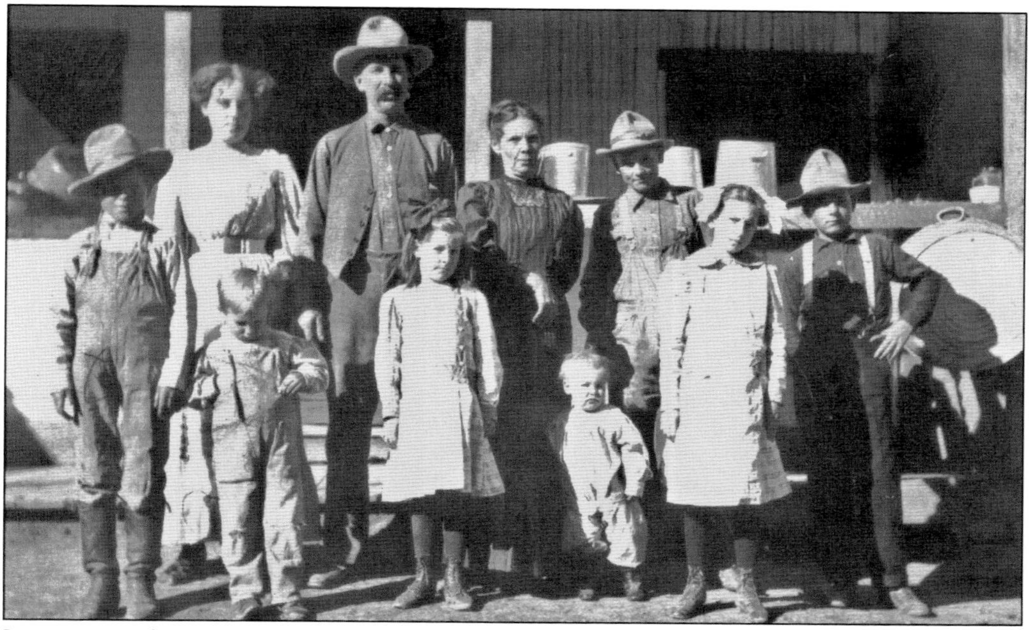

Immigrating from Germany in 1844, Mathias Heck spent time in California goldfields before joining the California Column during the Civil War and marching to New Mexico. In 1876, he bought a large tract of land along Cimarroncito Creek four miles south of Cimarron. The Heck Ranch and large family prospered with orchards and irrigated hay and alfalfa fields; by 1895, the property was valued at $1,950. (Arthur Johnson Memorial Library.)

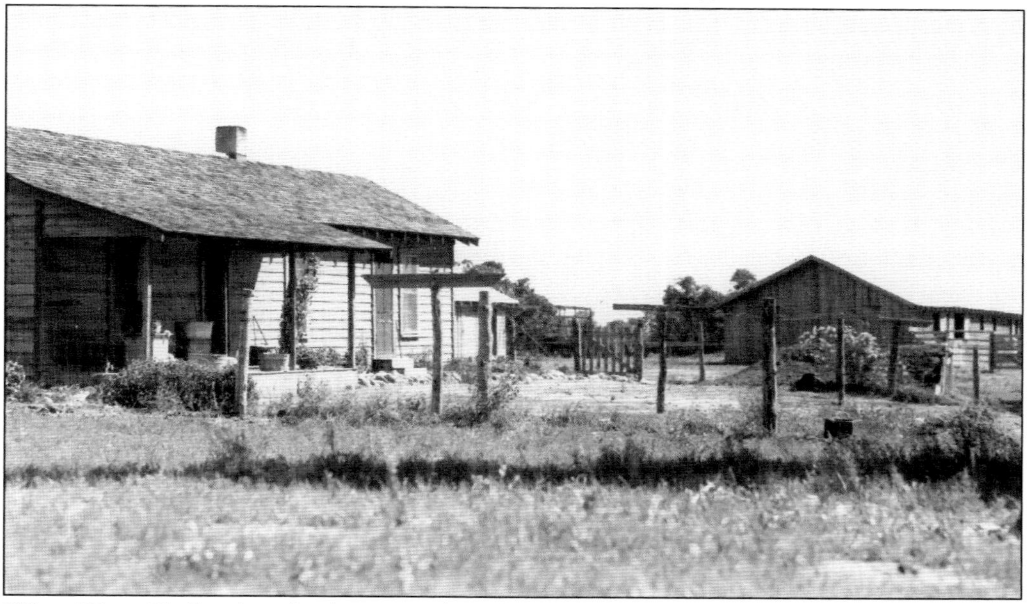

When Waite Phillips bought the original Heck Ranch in the 1920s, the Hecks bought land in Moreno Valley. Life on their Eagle Nest Ranch was cyclical: grow vegetables, pick cherries at Hickman's orchard in Cimarron, boil water for the laundry, and haul ice from the lake in winter. In 1943, the family purchased 11,000 acres west of Cimarron in Dean Canyon known as the Heck Place. (Philmont Scout Ranch.)

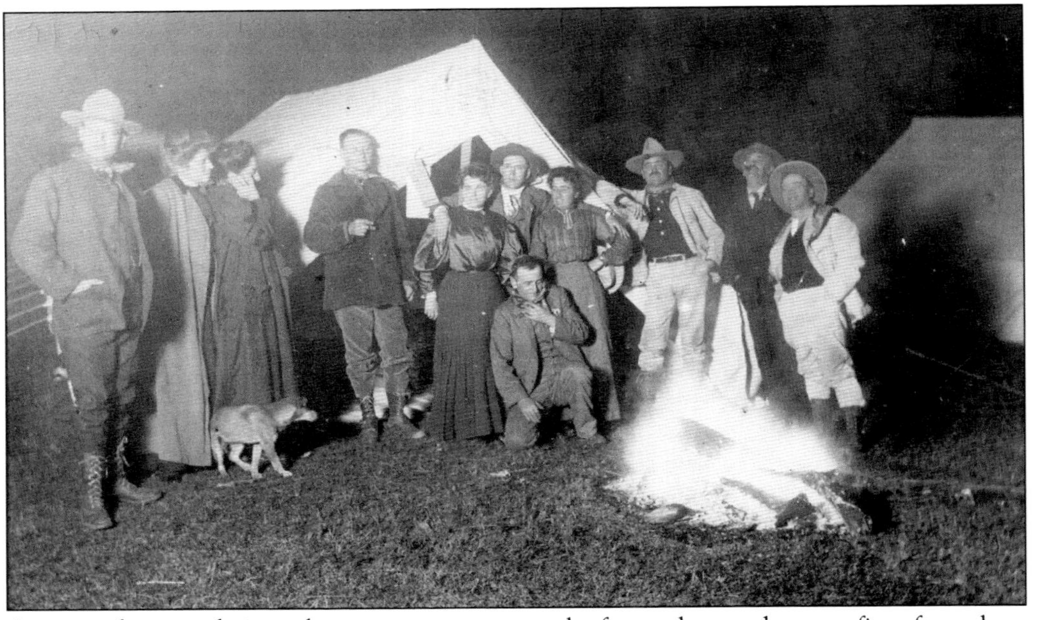

A sense of camaraderie and common purpose can be fostered around a campfire after a long day's work, and that certainly seems the case for these camping cowboys and their companions. The canvas tent in the background was made by Denver's Colorado Tent and Awning Company, which manufactured tents and other products for railroads. Neither the occasion nor the date was recorded. (The Old Mill.)

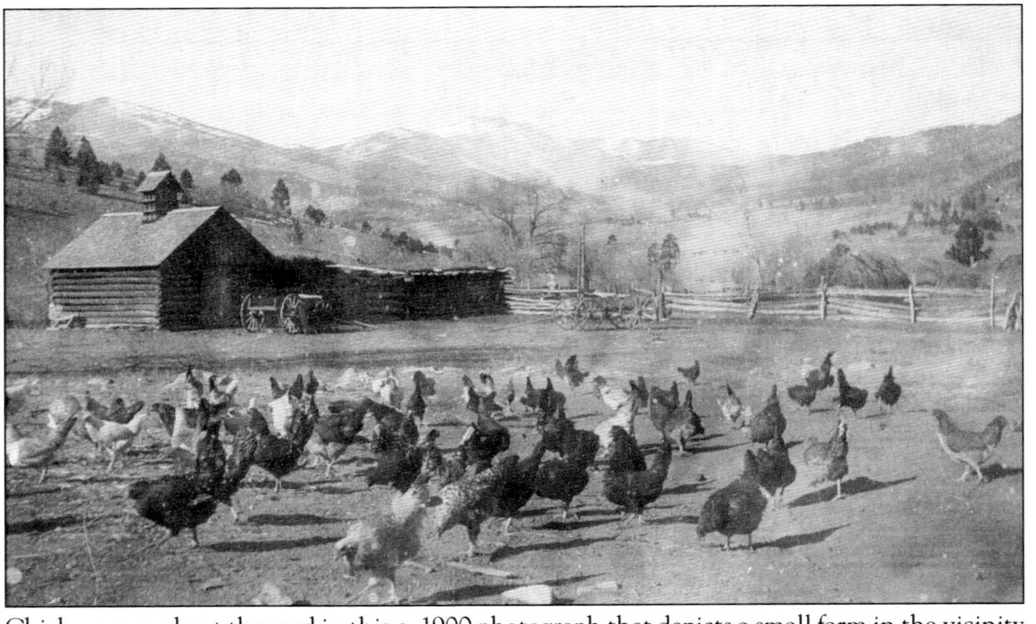

Chickens race about the yard in this c. 1900 photograph that depicts a small farm in the vicinity of Ute Park, with Baldy Mountain in the distance. According to *New Mexico: The Land of Opportunity*, "In 1890, New Mexico had 4,458 farms of more than three acres each; ten years later it had 11,834 such farms." The value of farm property in 1910 was estimated at $159.4 million. (Authors' collection.)

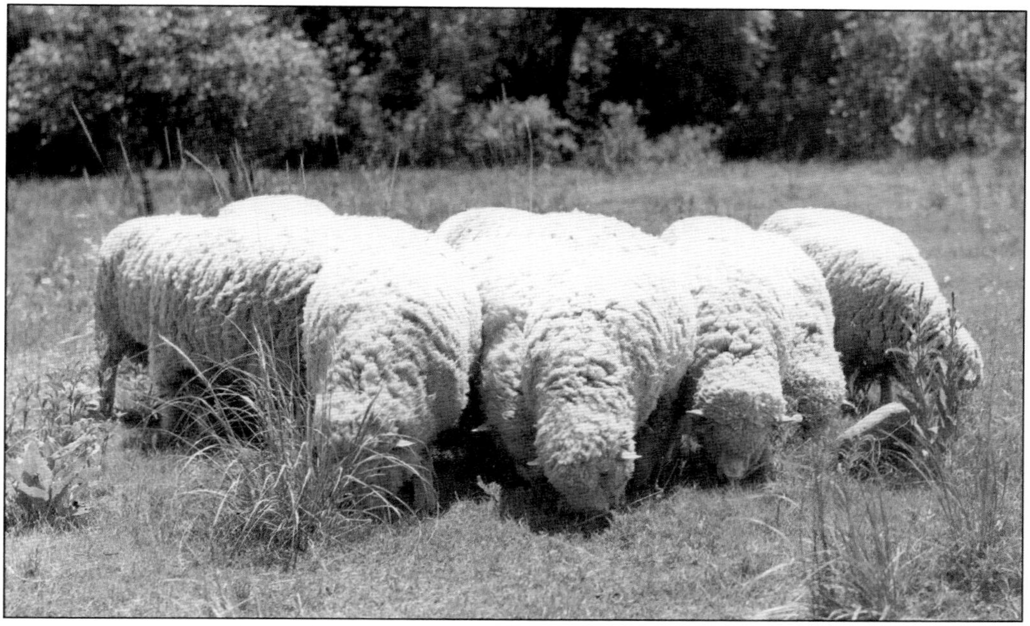

The sheep industry in New Mexico carried a significant economic impact. In 1915, approximately four million sheep wandered the range, and annual wool shipments exceeded 20 million pounds. Waite Phillips maintained a sheep headquarters at Rayado and donated his Philmont Ranch sheep to the Boy Scouts in 1941. They were sold in August 1943 so that the ranch operation could concentrate on horses and cattle. (Philmont Scout Ranch.)

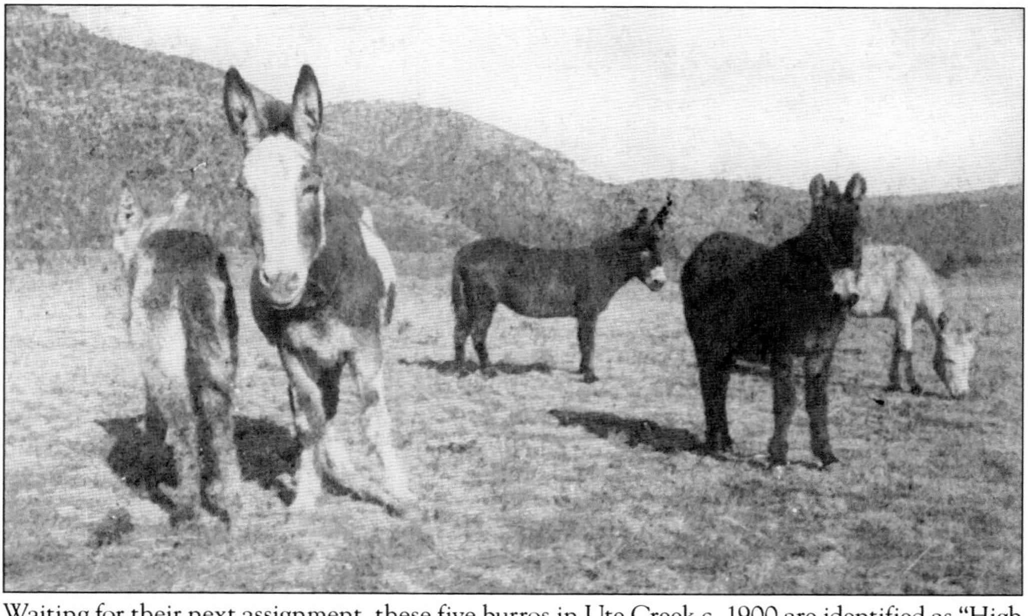

Waiting for their next assignment, these five burros in Ute Creek c. 1900 are identified as "High Eared Fur." Ute Creek was settled in about 1867, and a sense of permanence arrived when a post office opened the next year. The area was dotted with small farms and continued to serve as a stopping point in Cimarron Canyon. By the early 1900s, the community was renamed Ute Park. (Authors' collection.)

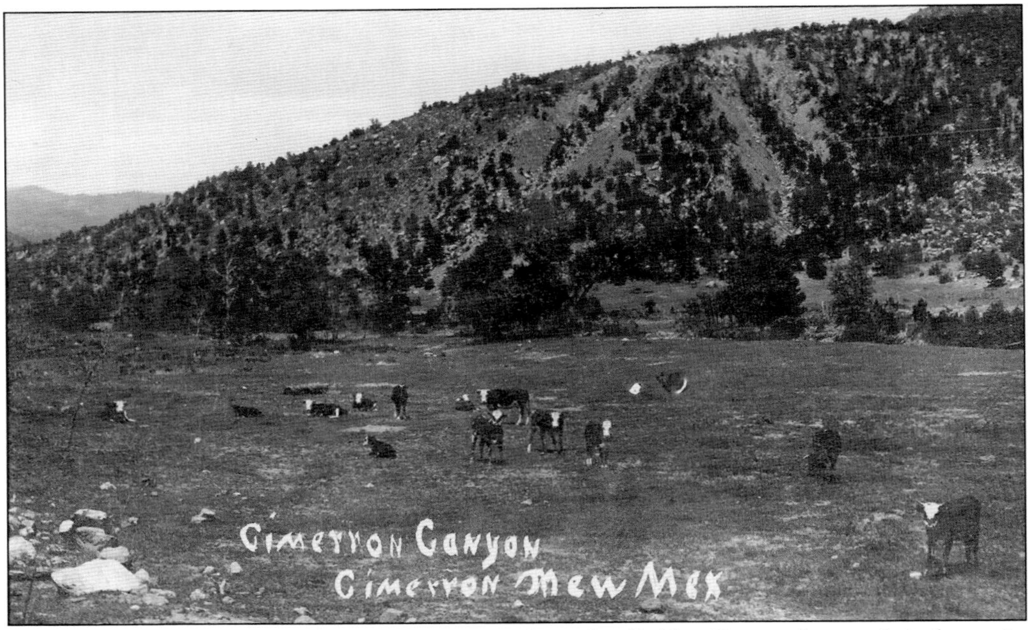

In 1880, Harry Whigham of Cimarron reported on the Colfax County livestock industry in *Report of the Commissioner of Immigration for Colfax County*. He estimated there were "75,000 head of cattle, 200,000 head of sheep, and 7,000 head of horses and brood mares" within Colfax and that a $6,950 capital investment could generate $17,052 of profit in five years. (Troutman Studio, authors' collection.)

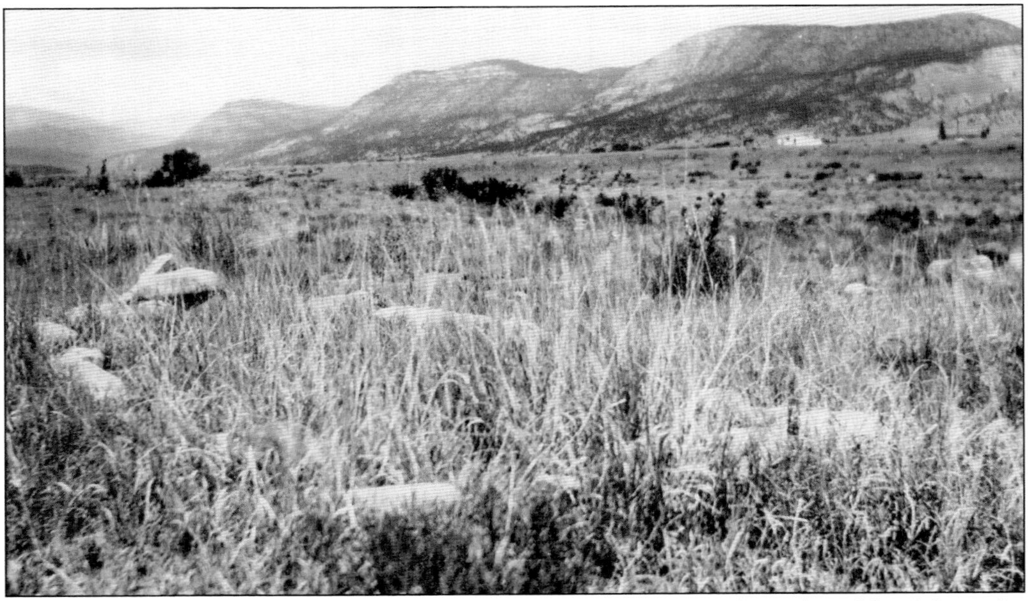

J.H. Nash was a Mississippi cattleman who came west in 1895 and purchased land from the Maxwell Land Grant Company. In 1901, Nash was helping saddle a horse when the horse spooked, wrapping a rope around Nash's leg and dragging him to his death. This site near Nash Gulch at the mouth of Cimarron Canyon marks his grave. The Lou Chandler house in the distance burned in the 1920s. (The Old Mill.)

Eight

Philmont

Waite Phillips grew up on a farm in Iowa where he learned to appreciate the beauty of nature. After spending three years traveling the West, Waite returned to Iowa to study business and soon joined two older brothers in the Oklahoma Territory oil industry. By 1925, the one-year-old Waite Phillips Oil Company was worth $25 million, and Phillips promptly sold. Since 1922, Phillips had been slowly acquiring considerable land in northeastern New Mexico, partly as an investment but also for recreational purposes. To his purchase of George Webster's Urraca Ranch, he added the Chandler, Heck, and Nash Ranches as well as land along Ponil and Rayado Creeks. The latter had once been owned by Jesús and Petra Abreu, relatives of Lucien B. Maxwell.

Phillips's holdings, now totaling over 300,000 acres, were first called the Hawkeye Ranch but were soon renamed Philmont. Phillips used his land for raising commercial cattle, sheep, and horses and for recreational hunting and fishing. Lodges along Cimarroncito and Rayado Creeks were built or renovated for extended stays in the backcountry. In 1925, Phillips began construction of a magnificent Mediterranean-style mansion, the Villa Philmonte.

Having obtained great wealth and able to live comfortably, Phillips now felt that his station in life demanded he share his possessions with others. On November 28, 1938, he and his wife Genevieve deeded 35,857 acres of land along Ponil Creek to the Boy Scouts of America "for the benefit of the members of the Boy Scout organization." This initial gift was called the Philturn Rockymountain Scoutcamp. Three years later, an additional gift of more than 91,000 contiguous acres was made, along with the spectacular Villa Philmonte. A separate purchase of 10,098 acres that included Baldy Mountain was made for the Boy Scouts of America by lumber executive Norton Clapp in 1962, with the Philmont Scout Ranch now comprising 137,493 acres. Each summer, over 23,000 campers and 5,000 participants to the Philmont Training Center enjoy the learning experiences that the ranch has to offer.

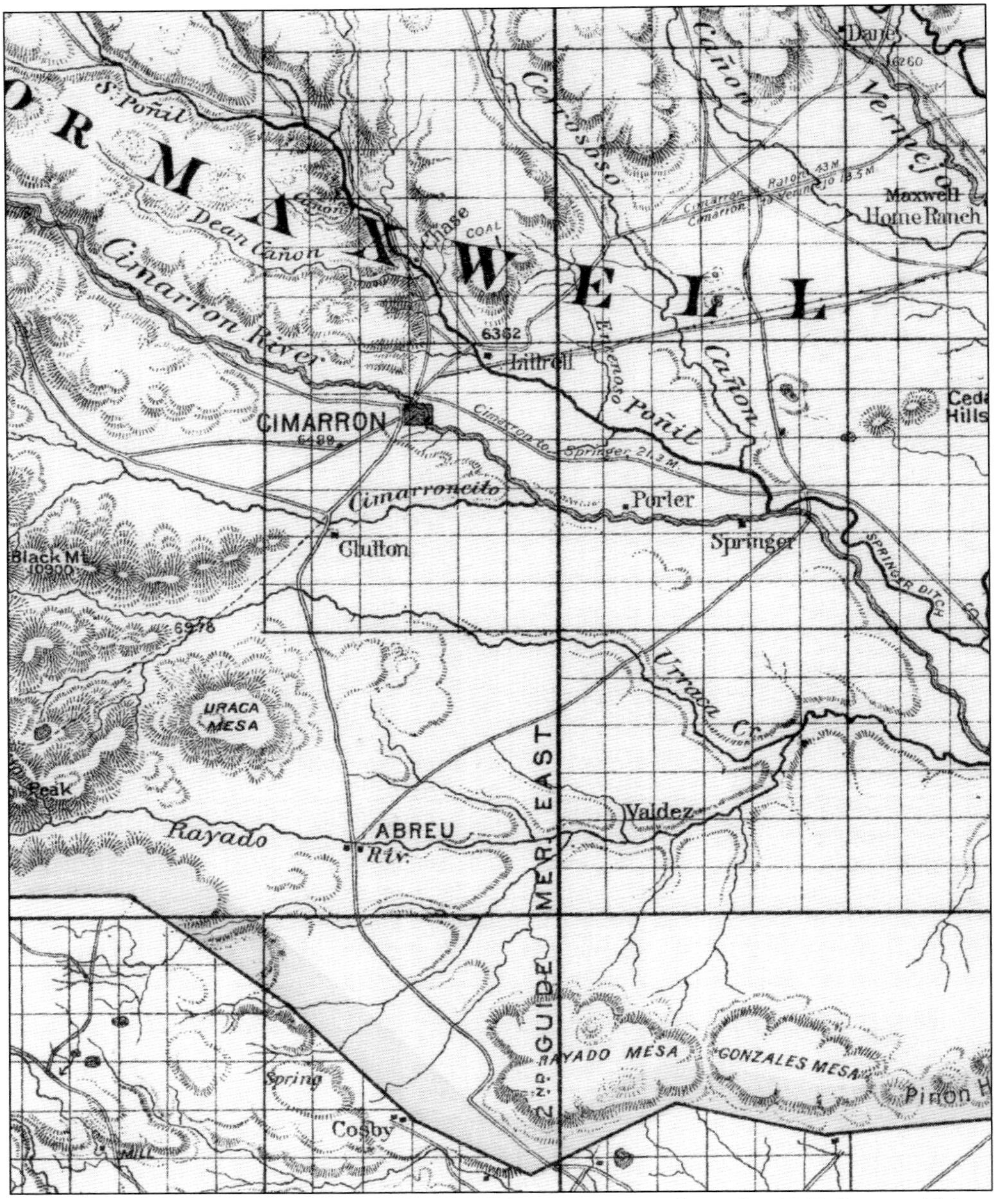

This excerpt showing Cimarron and the immediate vicinity is from the 1889 *Sectional Map of Colfax and Mora Counties, New Mexico*. It was drafted by Edward Rollandet—who also created the map on page 21—using Maxwell Land Grant Company surveys and other sources and shows the principal landowners of the day. Most had purchased tracts directly from Maxwell or from the Maxwell Land Grant Company: Mason M. Chase in the Ponil Canyon, the Littrell family spread northeast of Cimarron, land grant director Henry M. Porter to the east, Jesús Abreu at present-day Rayado, and the Urraca Ranch then owned by Englishman Francis Clutton and eventually purchased by George H. Webster Jr. The 1904 *Official Map of Colfax County New Mexico* by J.P. Brackett depicts several of these same properties and some changes: Clutton was replaced by McCormick, Littrell was replaced by French, the Heck land on the Cimarroncito Creek is marked, and the Springer name is more widespread. (Authors' collection.)

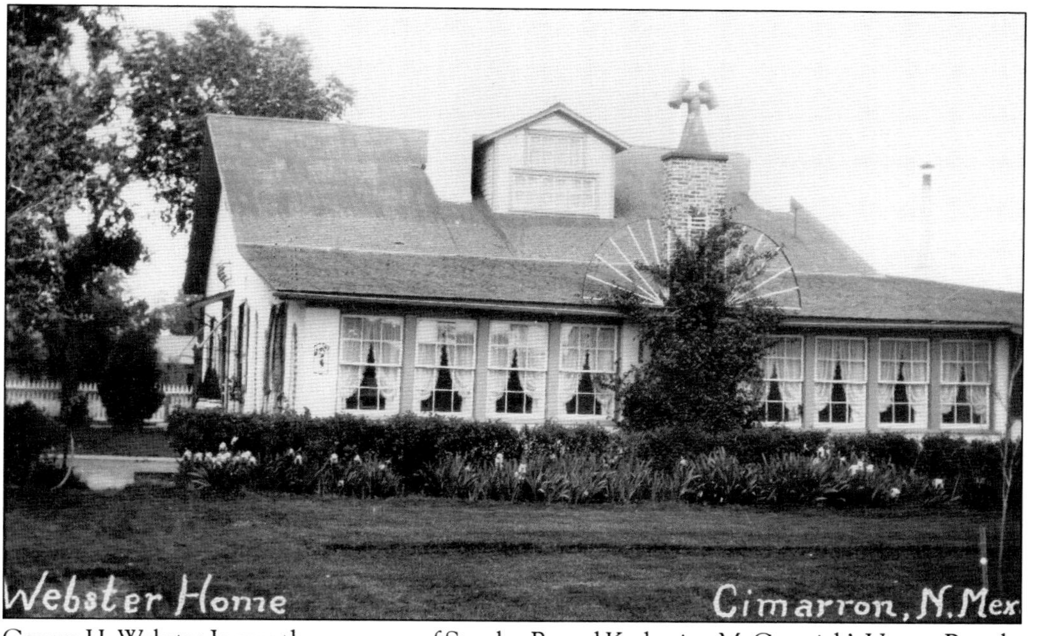

George H. Webster Jr. was the manager of Stanley R. and Katherine McCormick's Urraca Ranch, also known as the McCormick Ranch. When, in 1910, Stanley was unable to maintain the ranch for health reasons, it was sold to Webster. This was Webster's second home on the Urraca, constructed after his original home—the old Clutton place—was destroyed by fire in 1917. Today, it is home to Philmont's general manager. (Raton Museum.)

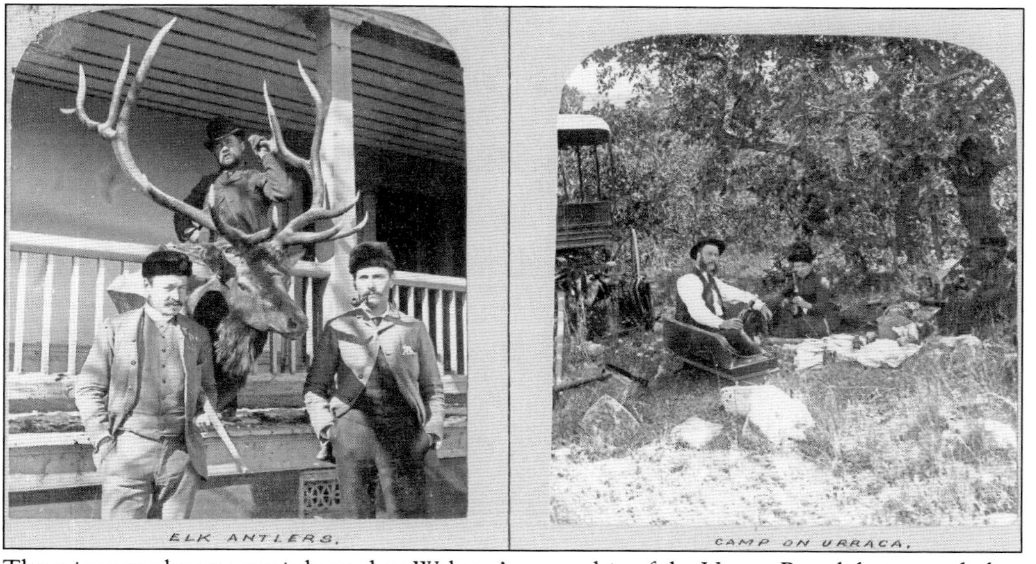

These images almost certainly predate Webster's ownership of the Urraca Ranch but nonetheless typify his recreational use of the land. The January 26, 1916, *Racine Journal-News* (Wisconsin) reported that Stuart Webster had donated a large elk head with a 12-point rack to the local Elks lodge. The elk had been killed on his brother George's well-stocked then 74,000-acre Urraca Ranch. (The Old Mill.)

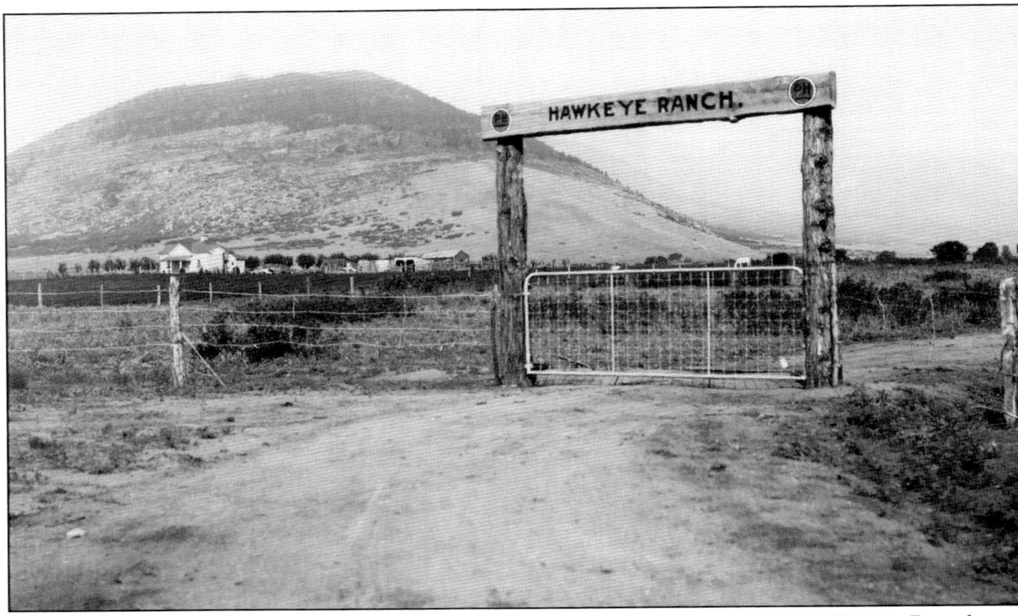

Waite and Genevieve Phillips purchased George H. Webster Jr.'s 80,000-acre Urraca Ranch and adjoining acreage in 1922 and 1923. Initially named Hawkeye Ranch—after Mr. Phillips's home state of Iowa—the ranch was renamed Philmont, derived from the name Phillips and the Spanish word for mountain, *monte*. By 1932, the ranch comprised some 300,000 acres. This gate carries the ranch name in the 1920s. (Philmont Scout Ranch.)

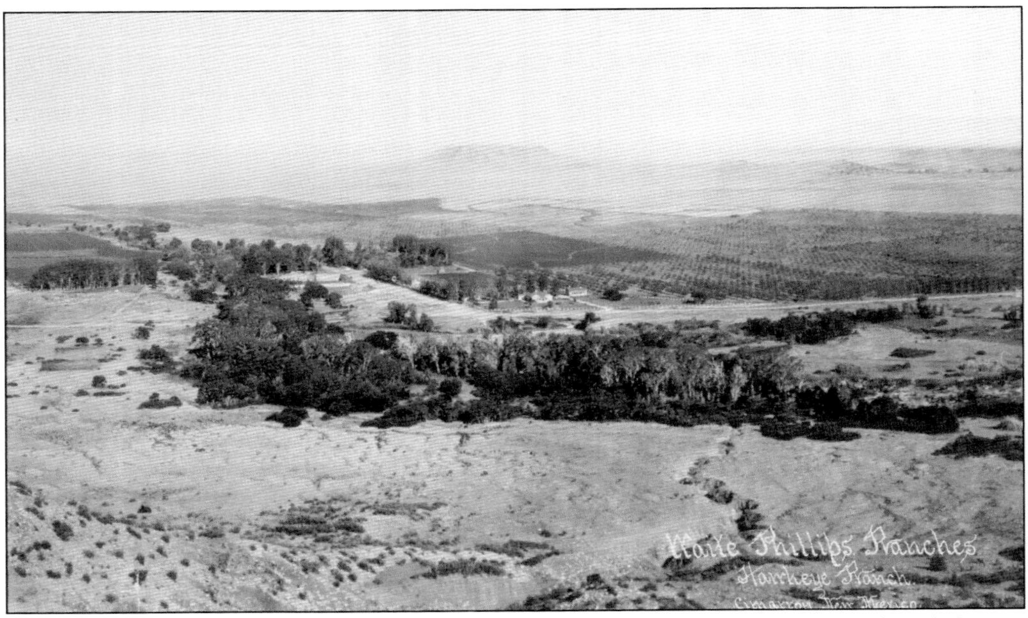

In the early 1920s, Waite Phillips's Hawkeye Ranch scarcely resembled modern-day Philmont, but the land is the same and other constants may be noted. The Phillips residence in the center of this image taken from atop Horse Ridge was close to what are now Philmont's administrative offices, with Coyote Mesa in the distance. This panoramic photograph extends onto page 109. (Philmont Scout Ranch.)

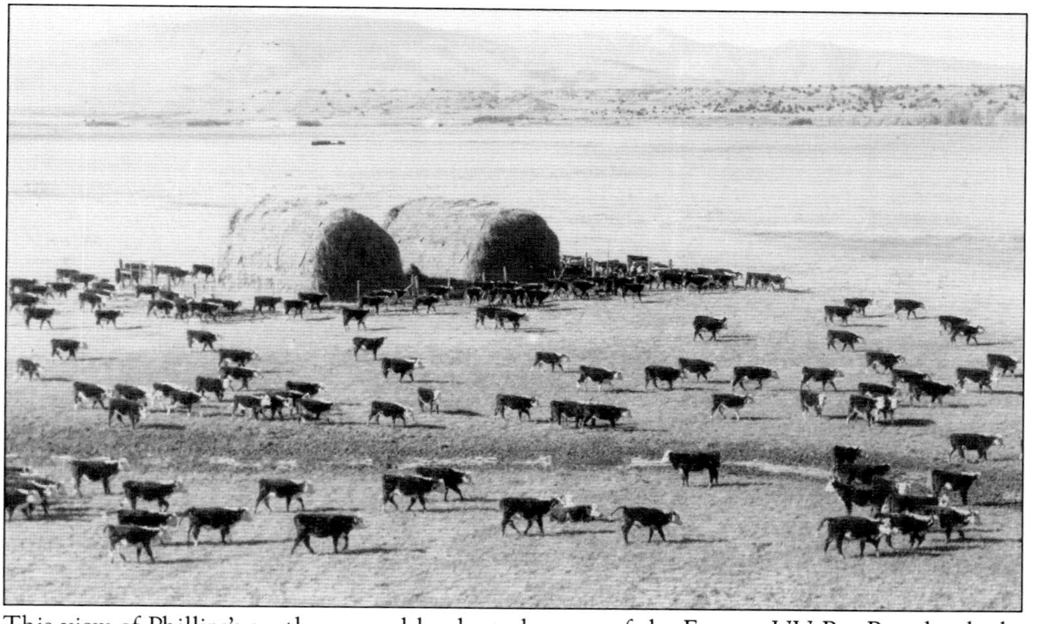

This view of Phillips's southern ranchland—today part of the Express UU Bar Ranch—looks toward the northwest, with Urraca Mesa in the distance and the Tooth of Time to its right. Remarkable views of the Tooth and the plain stretching north toward Colorado are visible from State Road 21 between Rayado and Miami. It is no wonder that the Phillipses and earlier settlers were attracted to this land. (Philmont Scout Ranch.)

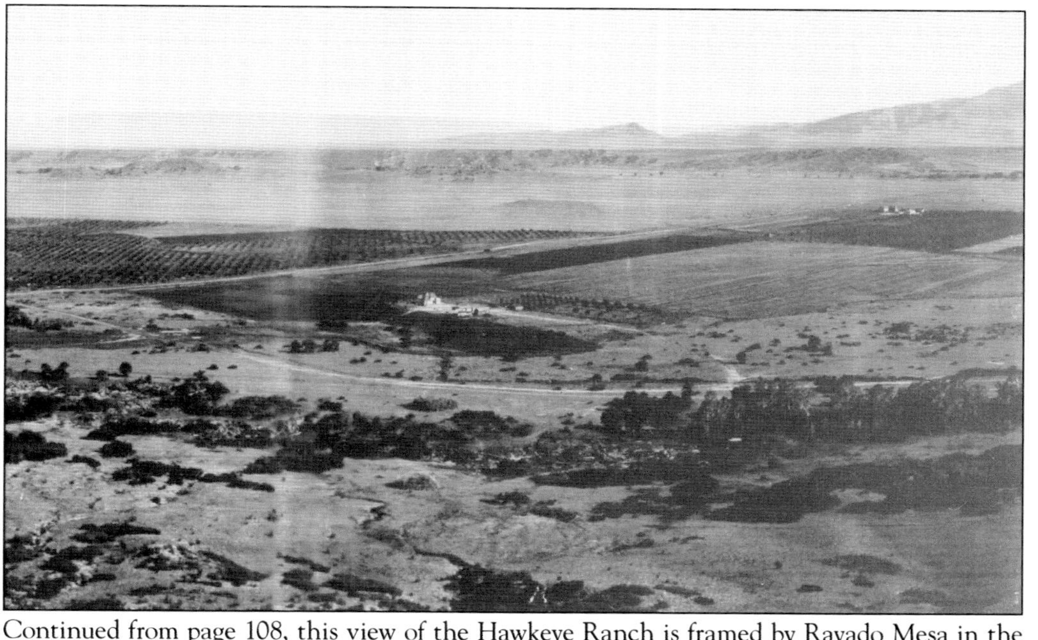

Continued from page 108, this view of the Hawkeye Ranch is framed by Rayado Mesa in the distance and Urraca Mesa at the right. Along the road to Rayado as it climbs toward Urraca Mesa is the crest known to mid-2000s Philmont staff members as "Cell Phone Hill," one of few spots where reliable service could then be found. Ironically, it is footsteps from prominent Santa Fe Trail swales. (Philmont Scout Ranch.)

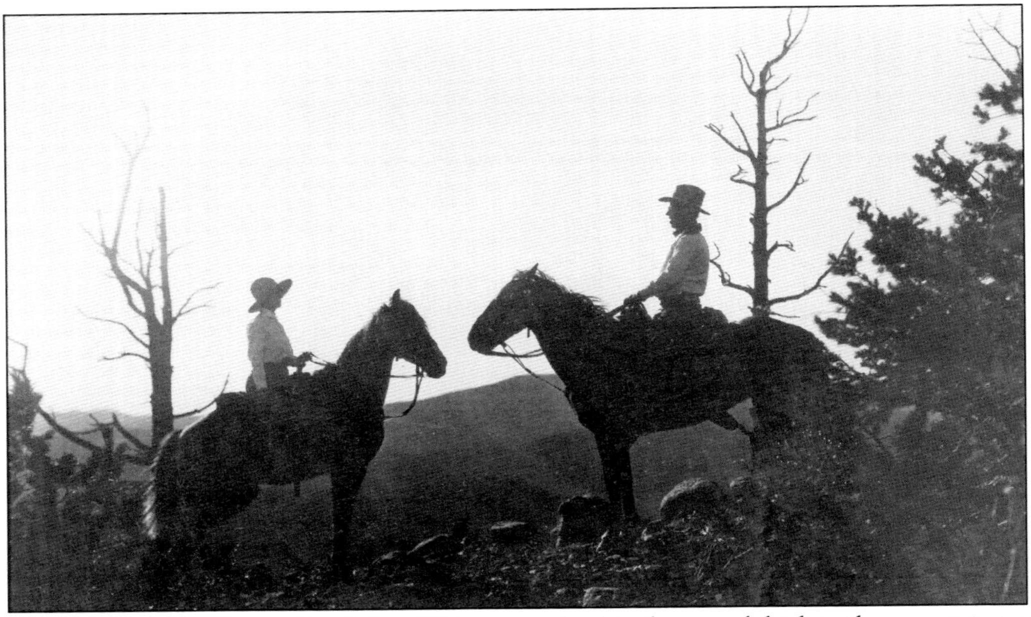

Elliott "Chope" Phillips and his father, Waite, pause for this photograph high in the mountainous terrain of the Philmont around 1930. Waite was deeply affected by the tragic loss of his twin Wiate in 1902 while the two young men were working their way through the West. His brother was never far from his thoughts, and his determination to succeed was propelled by the loss of Wiate. (Philmont Scout Ranch.)

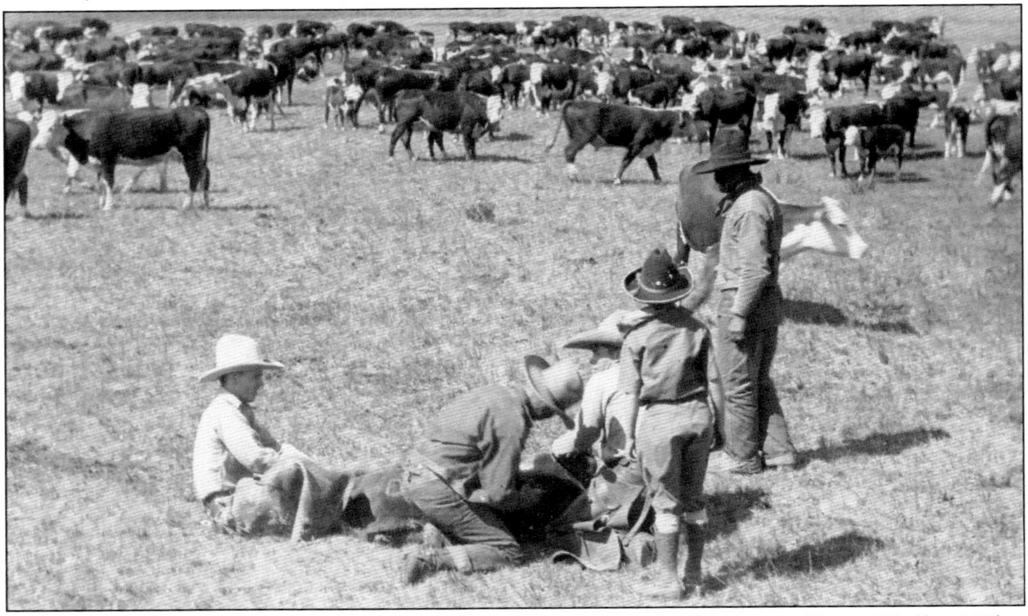

What a wonderful place the Philmont Ranch must have been for young Chope Phillips! This 1927 cattle branding at La Grulla Park high above Rayado Canyon offers as authentic a learning environment as ever existed for an aspiring cowboy. Phillips and his wife, Virginia, established the Phillips Ranch near Watrous in 1959 and ranched for many years before retiring to Amarillo, Texas. (Philmont Scout Ranch.)

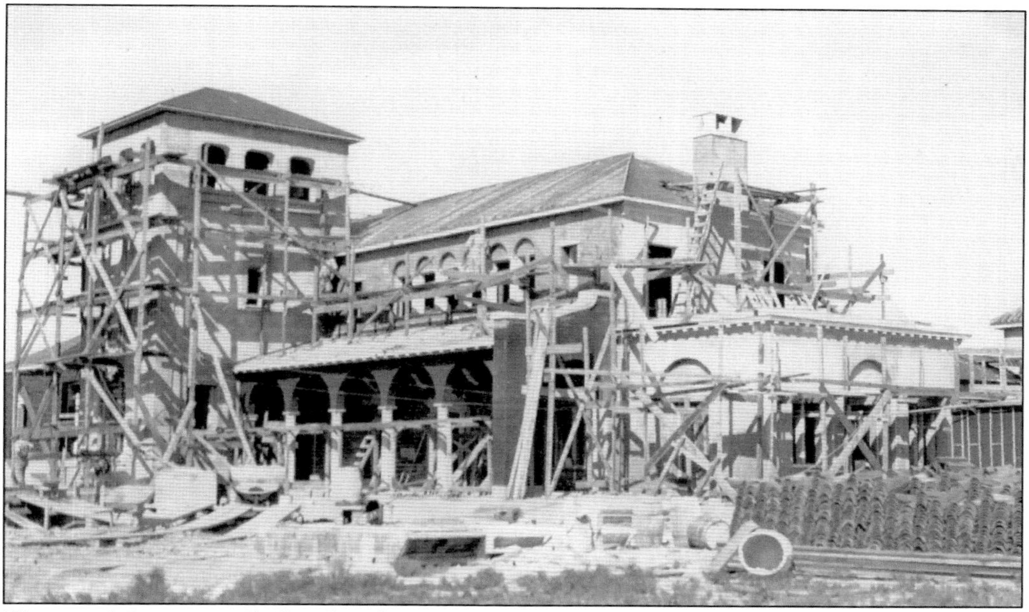

Waite and Genevieve Phillips hired Kansas City architect Edward Buehler Delk (1885–1956) to design the Spanish-Mediterranean Villa Philmonte (1925–1926) four miles south of Cimarron. Surrounded by an apple orchard, the villa served as their vacation residence until 1941, when they donated the home and an additional 91,538 acres to the Boy Scouts, increasing the size of Philmont Scout Ranch to 127,395 acres. (Philmont Scout Ranch.)

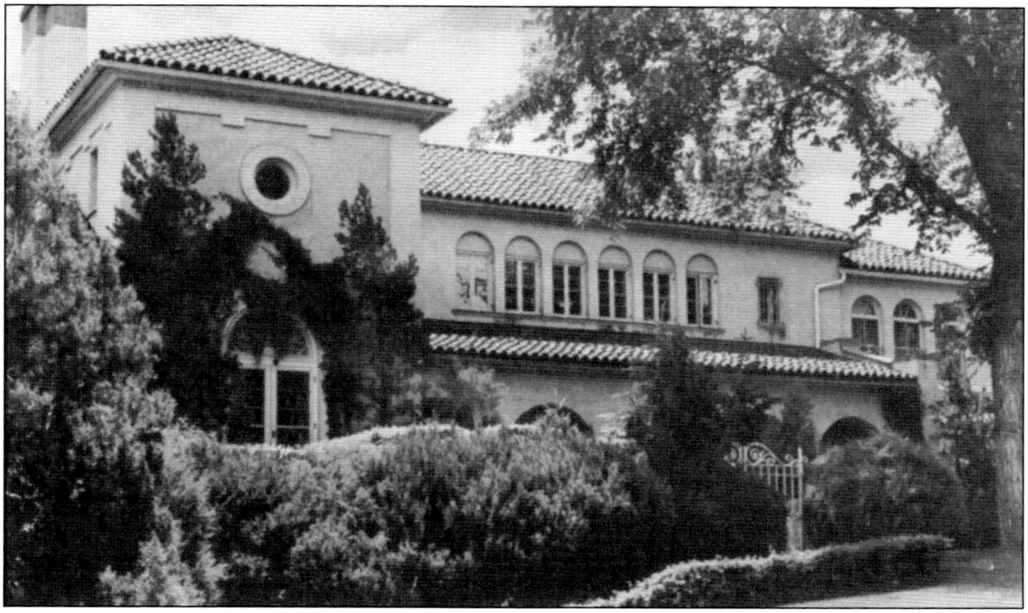

The Villa Philmonte was a sister structure of sorts to the Phillipses' palatial 72-room Villa Philbrook on 23 acres in Tulsa, also designed by Delk. Philbrook was their primary residence from 1927 until 1938, when it was donated to the city for use as an art museum. The Tulsa home is now known as the Philbrook Museum of Art—a showplace for its architecture, gardens, and art. (Authors' collection.)

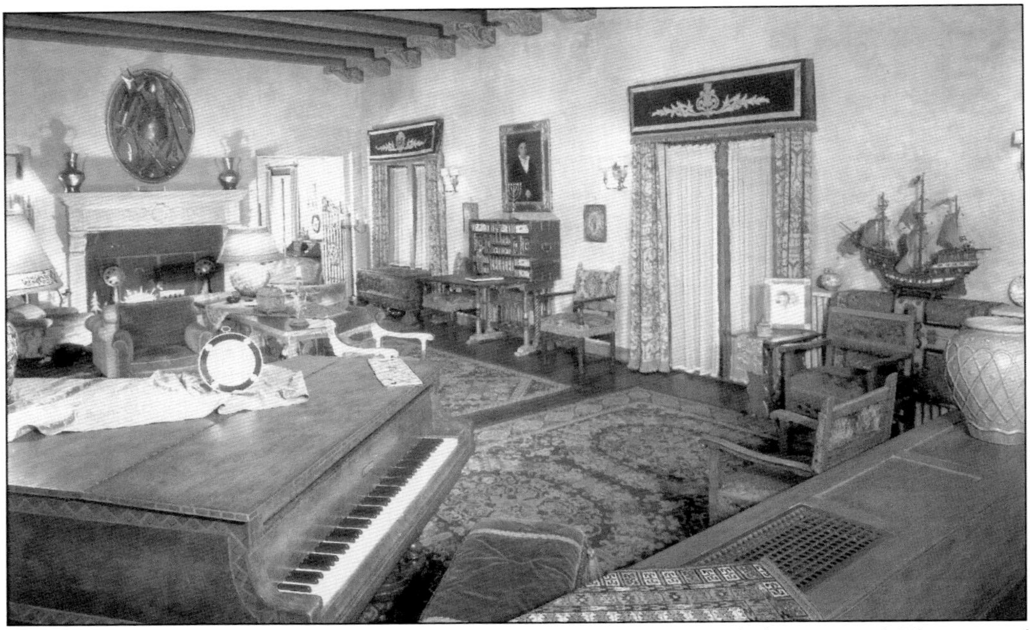

The Villa Philmonte is now maintained as a museum with tours provided year-round. This view of the formal living room dates from the 1930s, and care is taken to preserve the home as left by the family. Registered piano technician Dale Probst of Wichita Falls, Texas, completed a restoration of the 1927 Knabe B Grand player piano in 2011, including a complete rebuild of the player unit. (Philmont Scout Ranch.)

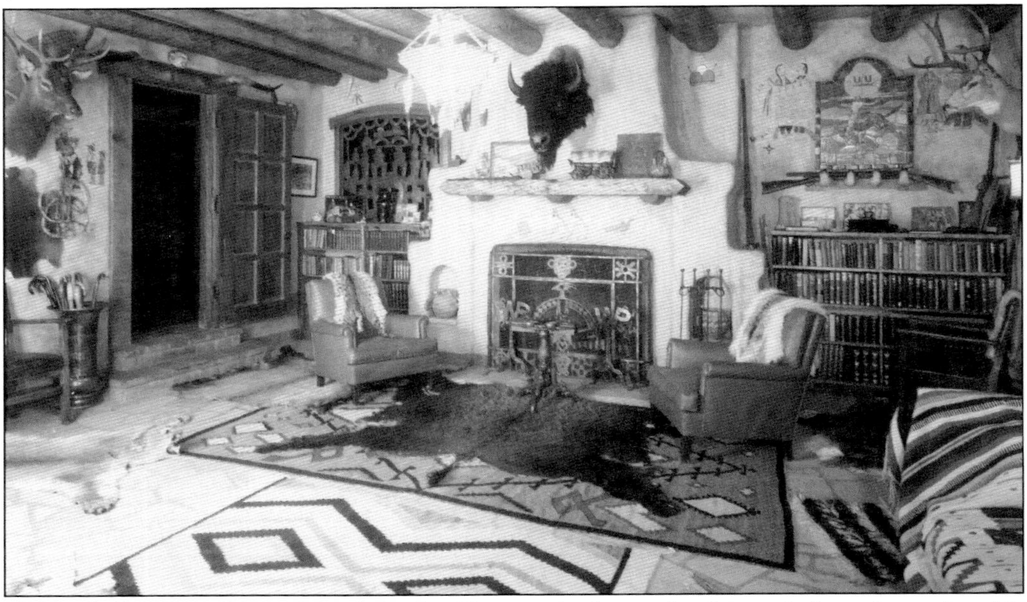

Waite Phillips's trophy room and ranch office on the lowest level is an informal, comfortable retreat as shown in this 1930s photograph. The walls are adorned with game indigenous to Philmont. Adjacent to this room is a Trapper's Closet equipped to support a foray into the woods. An entertainment room is on the same level across a hallway, which leads to the automobile court. (Philmont Scout Ranch.)

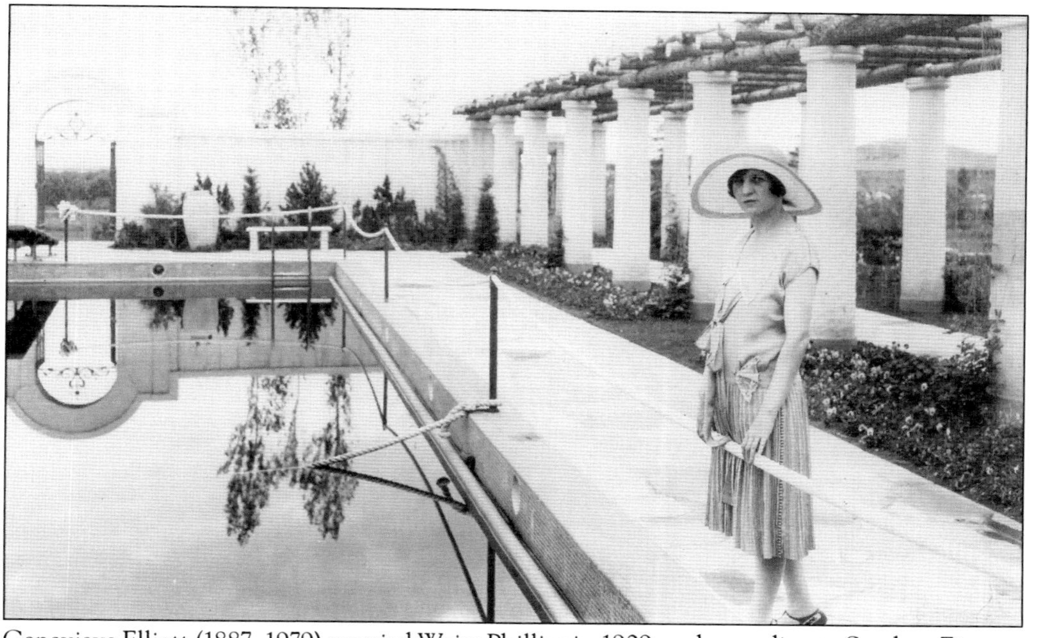

Genevieve Elliott (1887–1979) married Waite Phillips in 1909, and according to Stephen Zimmer and Nancy Klein in *Vision, Grace and Generosity: The Story of Waite and Genevieve Phillips and the Philmont Ranch*, Phillips "rarely made an important business decision without discussing it with her first." The villa pool was filled in during the 1950s. The mountain lion statue at the west end remains. (Philmont Scout Ranch.)

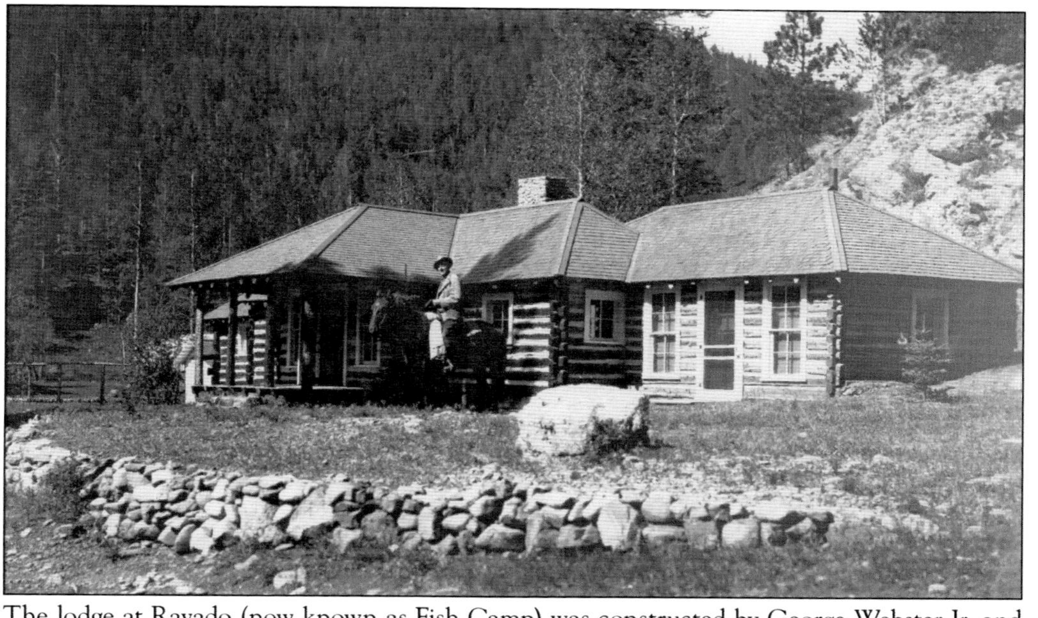

The lodge at Rayado (now known as Fish Camp) was constructed by George Webster Jr. and enlarged by Waite Phillips to include rooms for children Chope and Helen Jane. It was a favorite getaway spot at the confluence of the Rayado and Agua Fria Creeks and the site of the September 1973 establishment of the Philmont Staff Association. It remains a choice staffed camp destination. (Philmont Scout Ranch.)

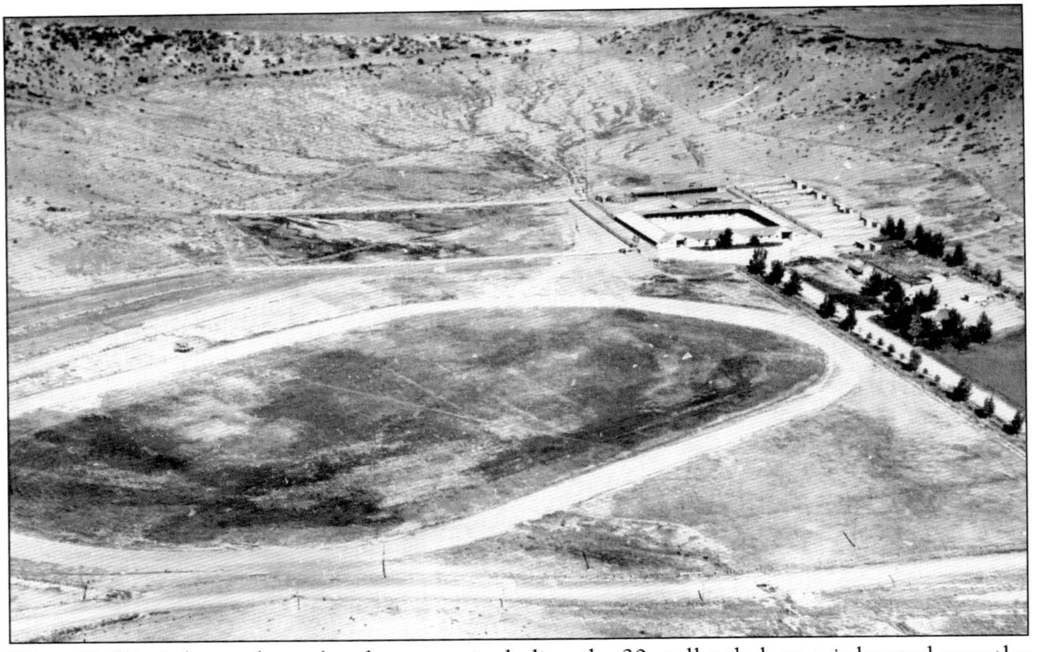

Waite Phillips's former horse headquarters, including the 30-stall polo barns, is located near the base of Horse Ridge near the Philmont administrative offices. The practice track is long-abandoned but its shape remains visible in modern aerial photographs. Bob Knox, who enjoyed a distinguished career at the Philmont and wrote *Growing Up to Cowboy*, spent his first working day in 1949 at the polo barns with Lawrence "Boss" Sanchez and Melvin Hall. (Philmont Scout Ranch.)

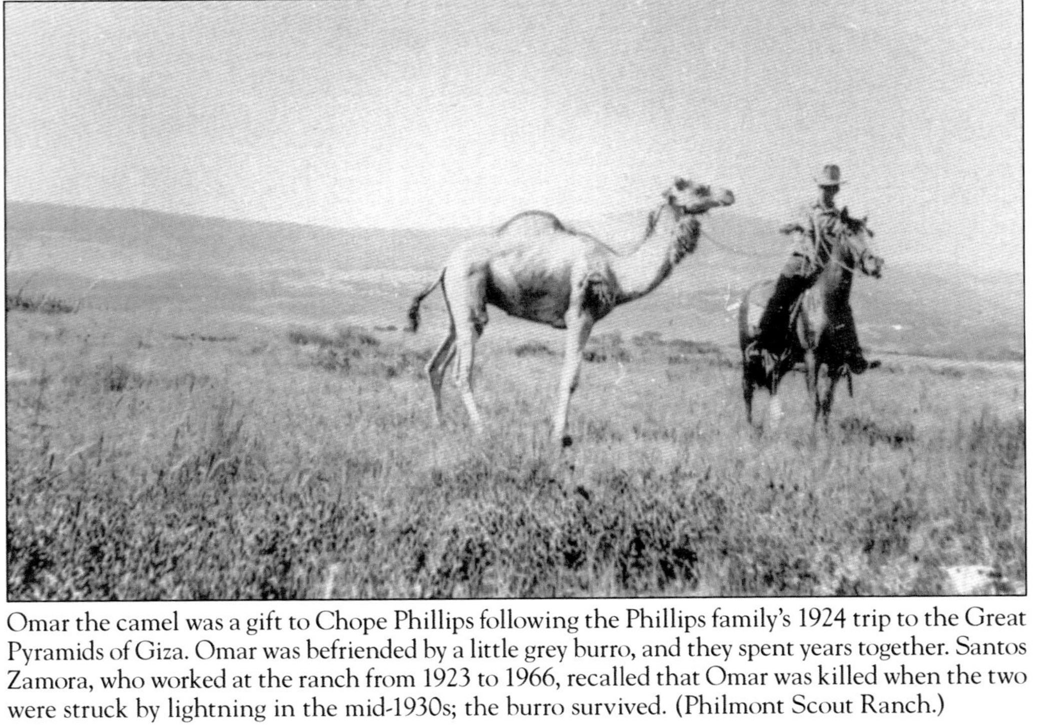

Omar the camel was a gift to Chope Phillips following the Phillips family's 1924 trip to the Great Pyramids of Giza. Omar was befriended by a little grey burro, and they spent years together. Santos Zamora, who worked at the ranch from 1923 to 1966, recalled that Omar was killed when the two were struck by lightning in the mid-1930s; the burro survived. (Philmont Scout Ranch.)

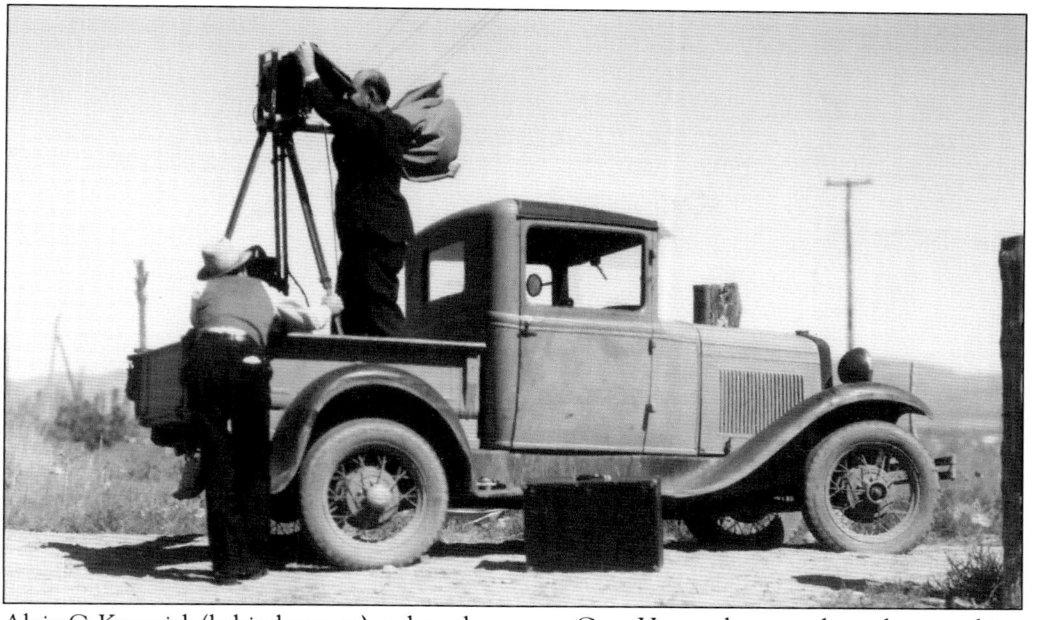

Alvin C. Krupnick (behind camera) and ranch manager Gene Hayward are seen here photographing ranch scenes for Waite Phillips. Krupnick was the Tulsa-based photographer whose images of the 1921 race riot there were seen by millions, and he was commissioned to take photographs of Philmont. Hayward was one of Phillips's most trusted assistants, having visited Cimarron for Phillips in advance of the ranch purchase. (Philmont Scout Ranch.)

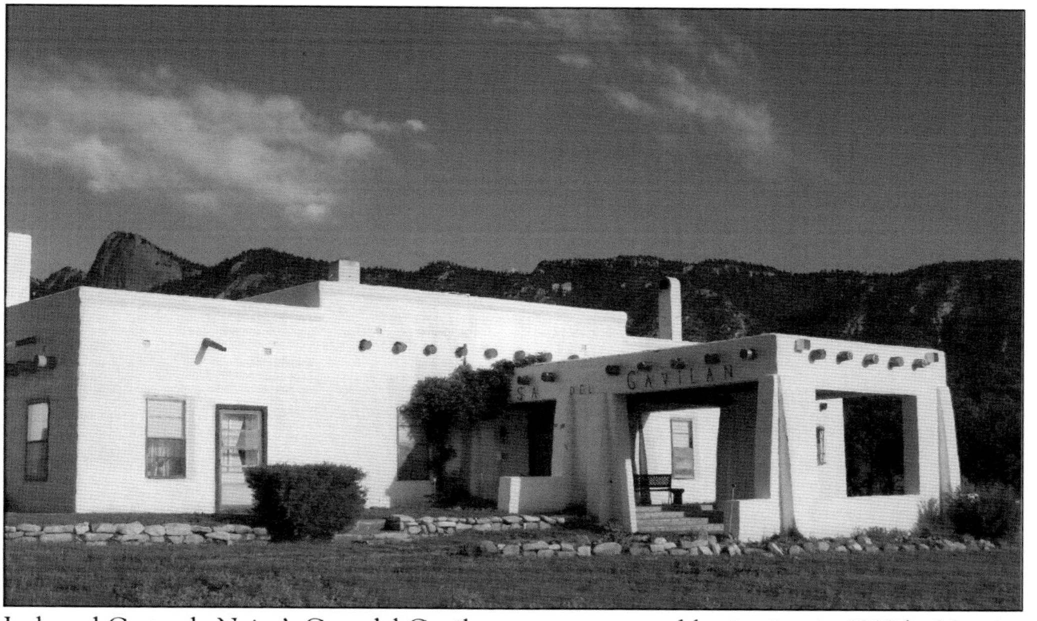

Jack and Gertrude Nairn's Casa del Gavilan was constructed beginning in 1910 by Narciso Federici. Local craftsman Ed Sitzberger Sr. constructed the fireplace mantels and doors. After 1941, the estate was purchase by Waite Phillips as headquarters for the UU Bar Ranch, and the home remained property of the UU Bar when the ranch was sold. It is presently owned by a group of former Philmont staff members. (Authors' collection.)

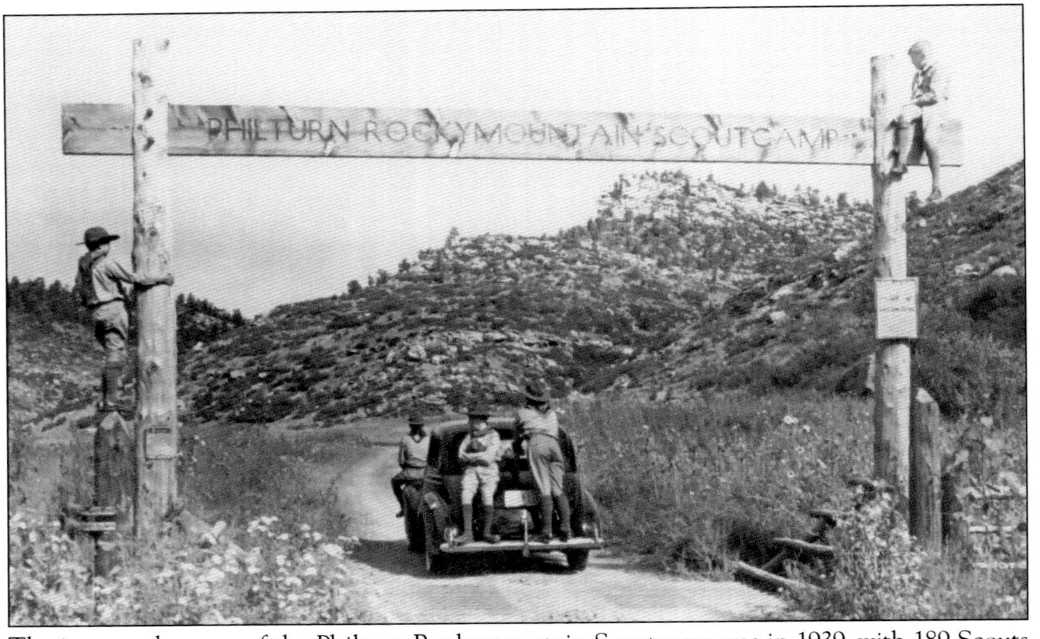

The inaugural season of the Philturn Rockymountain Scoutcamp was in 1939, with 189 Scouts from Kansas, Louisiana, Oklahoma, and Texas attending a high-adventure experience up to 12 days in length. Fees were $1.00 per week per person, and the camp director was B.B. Dawson. A year later, these Scouts from the Quivira Council in Wichita, Kansas, are embarking upon their own adventure. (Philmont Scout Ranch.)

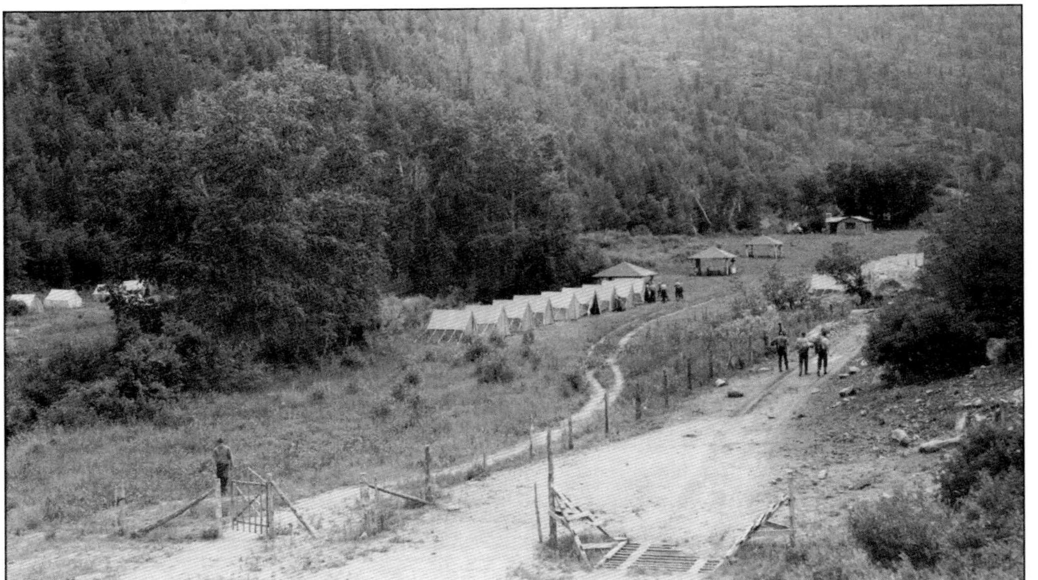

Following the Phillipses' second gift to the Boy Scouts of America, the ranch infrastructure was further developed and the central and southern sections of present-day Philmont were accessible to Scouts. This view of the Lovers Leap Meadow camp dates from the 1940s. Phillips took an active interest and was known to visit with Scouts or observe them, enjoying the program from afar. (Philmont Scout Ranch.)

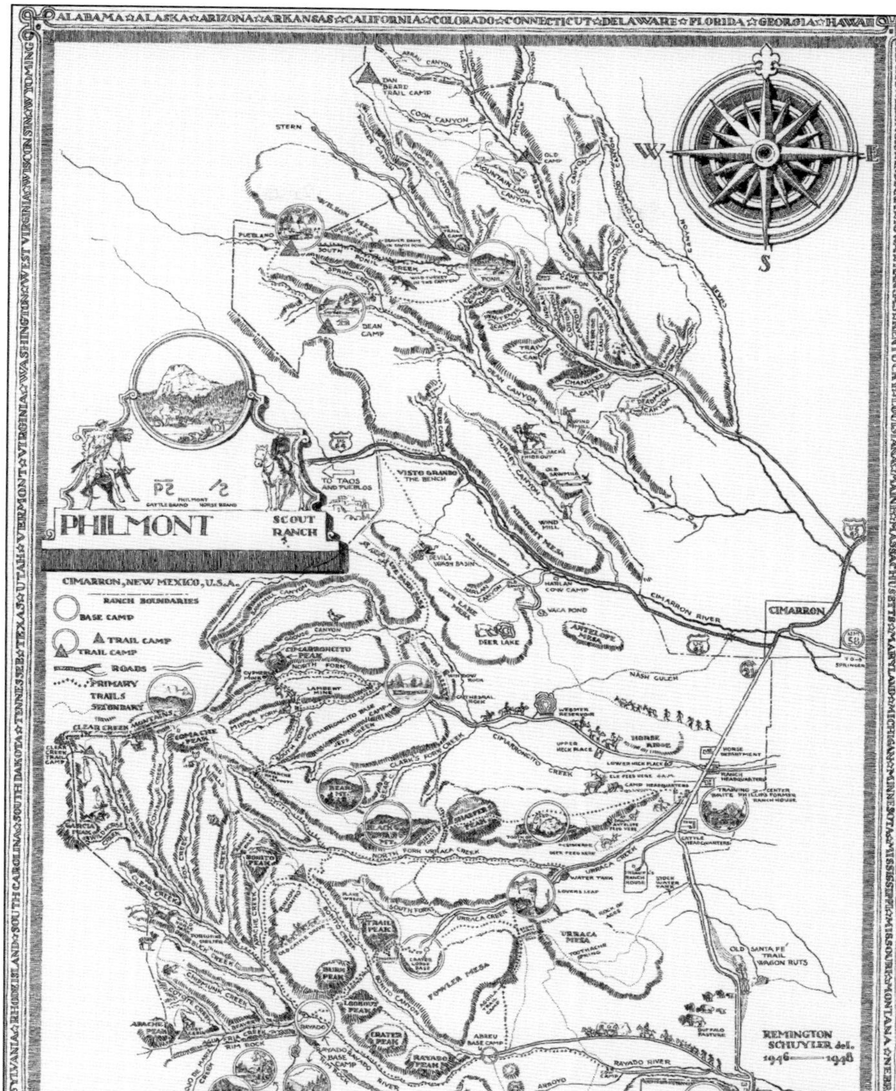

Illustrator and author Remington Schuyler (1884–1955) was a contemporary and friend of artist Norman Rockwell. While living near Rockwell in New Rochelle, New York, Schuyler served as a Scouting volunteer; and between 1934 and 1949, as a Boy Scouts of America (BSA) staff artist, he created hundreds of illustrations for the BSA. A selection of his original works was exhibited at the Philmont Museum in *The Scouting Art of Remington Schuyler* in 1996. Schuyler's interest and skill in the portrayal of Western themes is evident in his decorative 1946–1948 Philmont map. His map delineated the location of major land forms, base camps, trail camps, and trails, and noted where wild turkey, deer, antelope, and elk could be observed. In 1949, the BSA consolidated most Senior Scout programs into the new Explorer Scout program, and by 1950 the *Philmont Guide Book* addressed participants as if they were all Explorers, reporting that "Boy Scouts of America decided that Philmont was to be a National Explorer Camp." Philmont was known principally during the 1960s and 1970s as Philmont Scout Ranch and Explorer Base. (Authors' collection.)

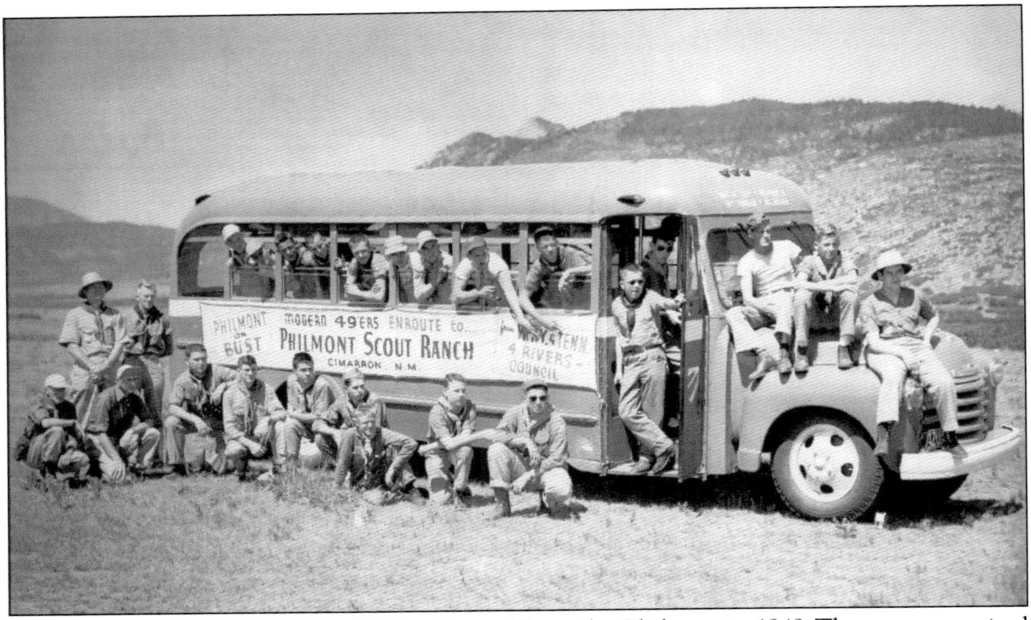

These "Modern 49ers" represent the Four Rivers Council at Philmont in 1949. They were organized by contingent leaders Elbert Johns Sr. and Phil Wehman, a 1944 Eagle Scout from Union City, Tennessee. Their nine-day trek extended from Crater Lake, to Carson-Maxwell (Rayado), (Old) Abreu, Rayado (Fish Camp), Cimarroncito, and back to base camp. They each received the leather Indianhead Nature Observation Award patch. (Charles Philip Wehman.)

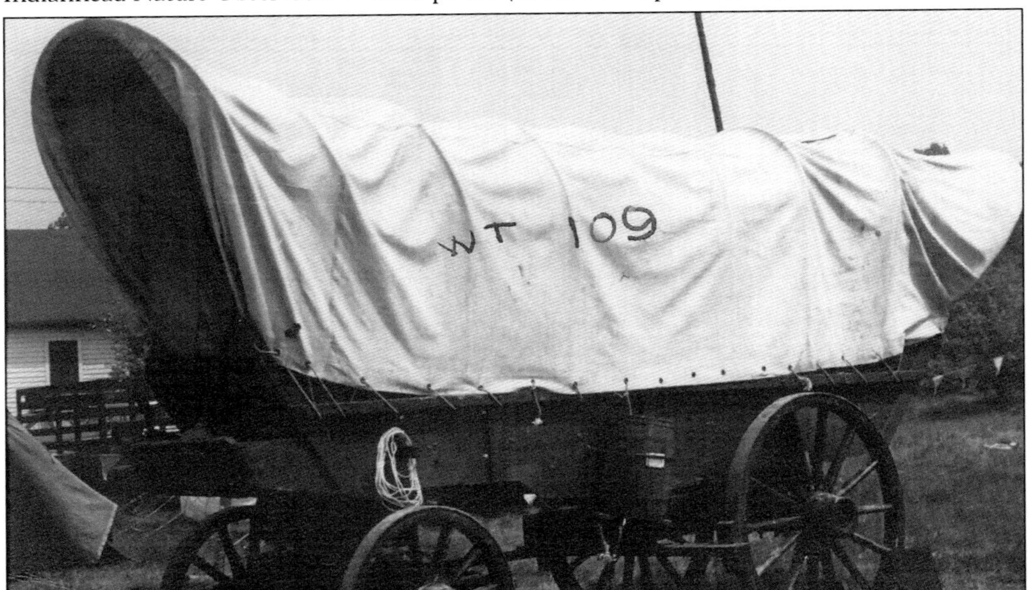

Beginning in 1947, camping director George Bullock developed a series of backcountry expeditions designed to emphasize Southwestern themes. The 21-day Wagon Train treks exemplified the best Philmont had to offer: Scouts rode horseback, hiked, fished, packed burros, and examined artifacts at the Indian Writings site. Shown here is Wagon Train (WT) 109, from 1949, in an image saved by Jim Ritter for his family in Elmhurst, Illinois. (Authors' collection.)

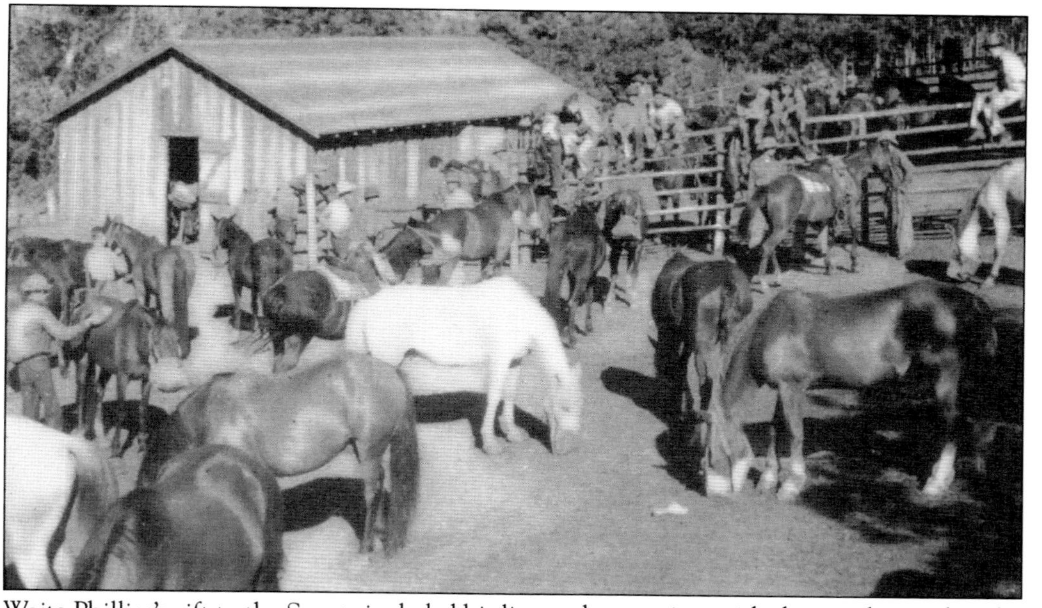

Waite Phillips's gift to the Scouts included his livestock operation, with the stipulation that the property remain a working ranch. Program participants—including those from the Philmont Training Center—still learn about the care and handling of horses and ride in the high country. The ranch department also cares for 250 cattle, 100 American bison (buffalo), and 100 burros. This corral was at Cimarroncito in 1952; horse camps include Beaubien, Clark's Fork, and Ponil. (Authors' collection.)

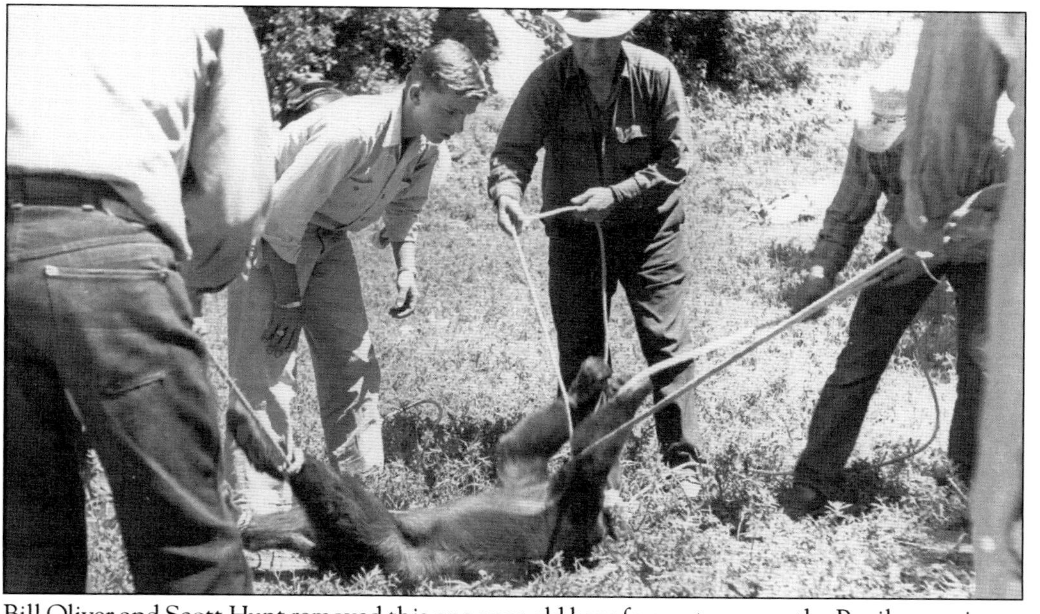

Bill Oliver and Scott Hunt removed this one-year-old bear from a tree near the Ponil commissary in June 1949. Close encounters with bears, deer, elk, and antelope are not uncommon at Philmont, and the summer staff includes two bear researchers who keep tabs on over 200 black bears that roam the ranch. Campers use the "Bearmuda Triangle" concept to promote human safety. (Philmont Scout Ranch.)

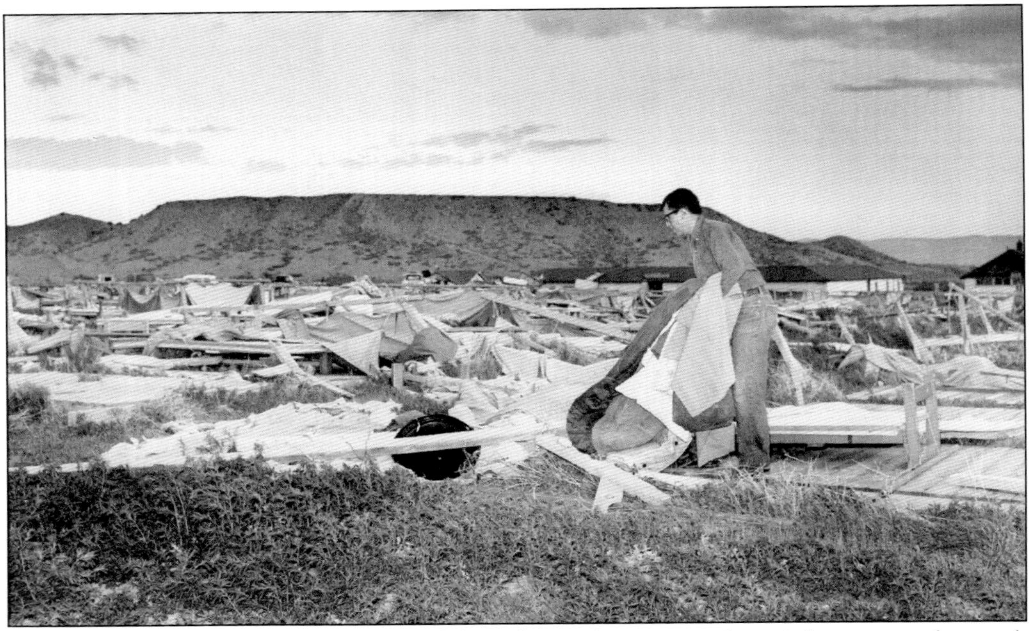

Cimarron and Philmont have withstood their share of severe weather. A fierce tornado struck base camp on June 25, 1960, leveling camper tent city and a chapel before depositing camping gear over the Tooth of Time Ridge. Ranger Ned Gold is among those picking through the scattered debris field. A July 1996 tornado struck Cimarron, destroying the post office and damaging other buildings. (Philmont Scout Ranch.)

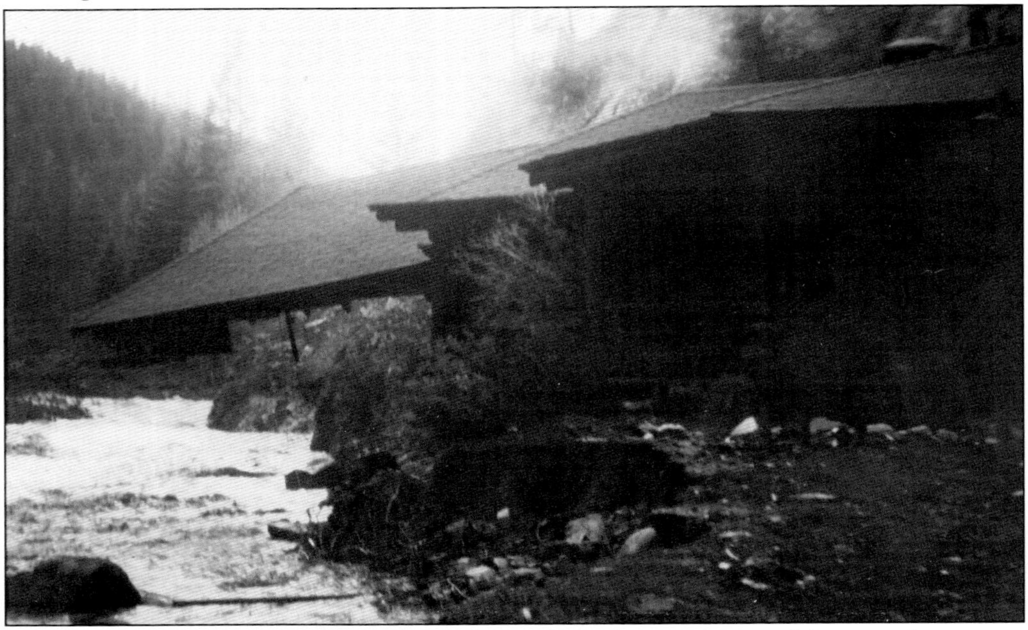

The kitchen end of Waite Phillips's beloved Rayado Lodge was destroyed during a devastating flash flood that raced down the Agua Fria and Rayado canyons on June 17, 1965. Staff member Philip L. Yunker recalled in 1990 that the water level had dropped two or three feet by the next morning when he took this and several other photographs. (Philmont Scout Ranch.)

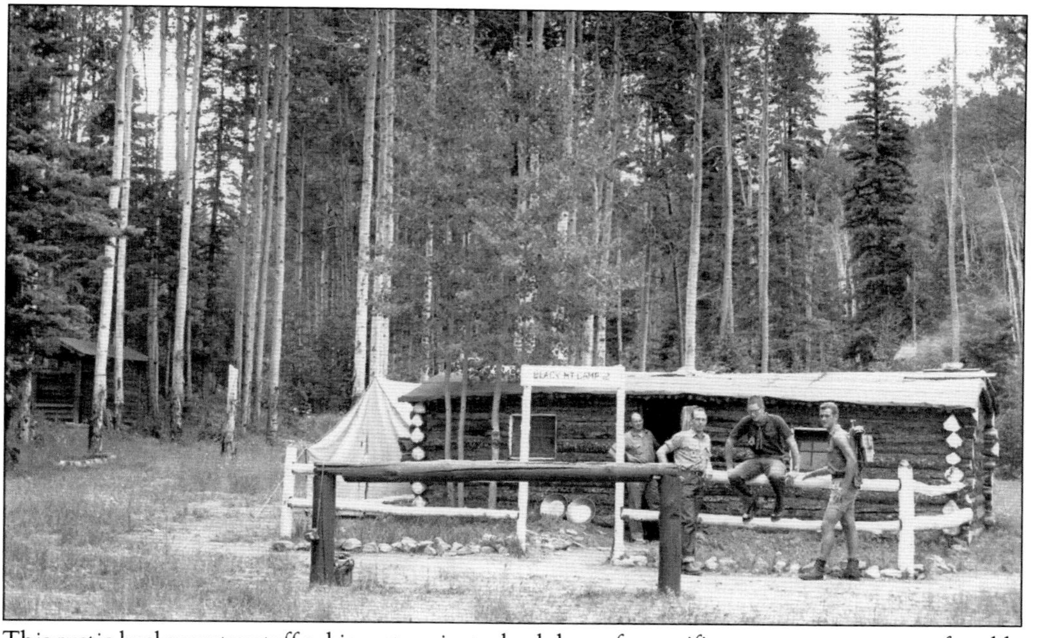

This rustic backcountry staff cabin, set against a backdrop of magnificent aspens, was a comfortable summer home for the early 1960s staff at remote south country Black Mountain camp. Sleeping quarters—a dependable canvas wall tent—were close at hand. The camp presently features a post–Civil War interpretive program with black powder rifle shooting and blacksmithing. (Philmont Scout Ranch.)

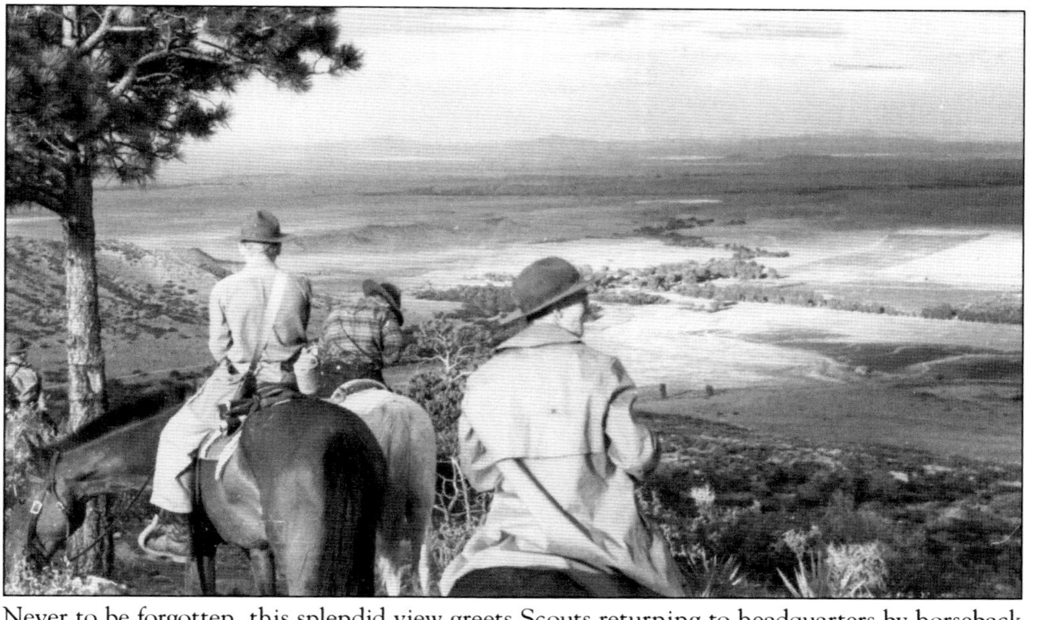

Never to be forgotten, this splendid view greets Scouts returning to headquarters by horseback during the 1940s. Today, the Philmont Cavalcade program is designed for crews of 10 to 15 participants who complete eight-day expeditions by horseback accompanied by seasonal staff wranglers. The week concludes with an equestrian gymkhana, where the young men and women demonstrate newly-acquired skills. (Philmont Scout Ranch.)

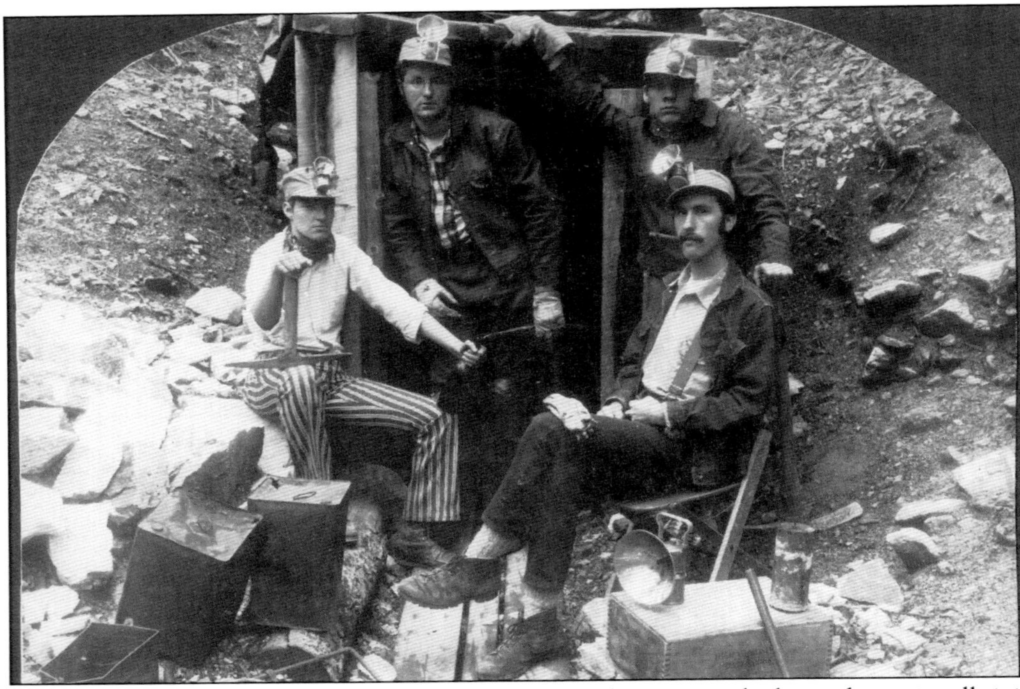

Interpretive staff are trained to immerse themselves in authentic period roles, and occasionally it is difficult to distinguish history from interpretive history. These 1971 Cypher's Mine staff members could easily be mistaken for miners from the early 1900s. They include, from left to right, Greg Hughes, Roger Manley, Mark Catlin, and Berne Holman (seated). The original photograph is entitled "Cyphers Mine Company, New Year's Day 1902." (Philmont Scout Ranch.)

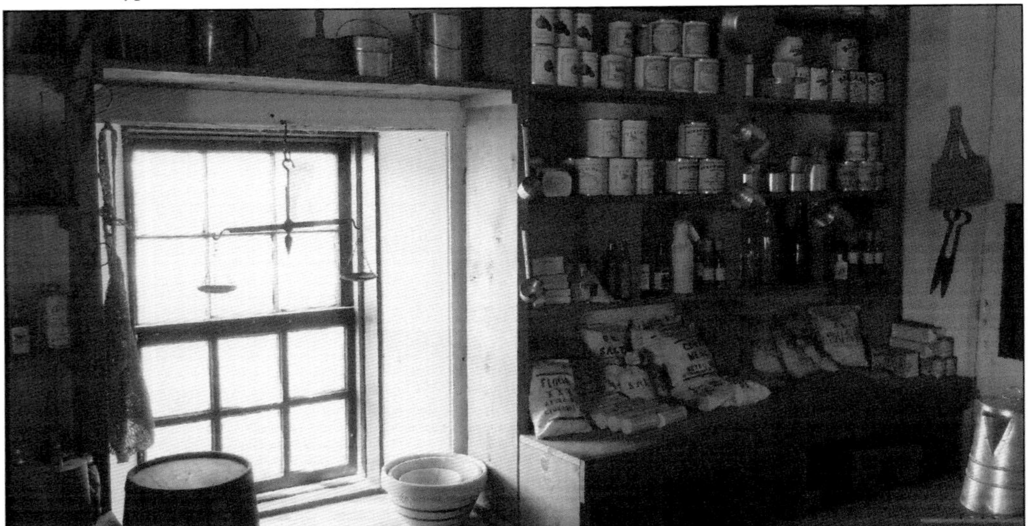

The interpretive camps at Philmont are designed to be authentic representations of specific periods and places in area history. Staff receive training from accomplished practitioners of historical interpretation, are given dossiers detailing their camp's place within the wilderness program, and are expected to remain in character while interacting with participants. Structures such as La Poste at Rayado are likewise authentically stocked. (Photograph by Steve Hentzelman.)

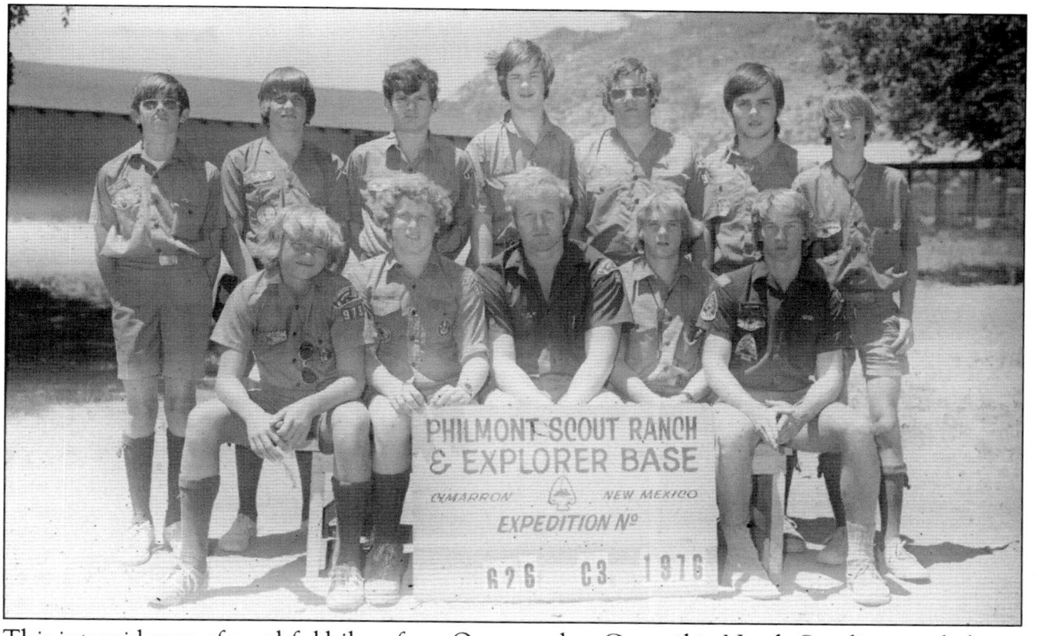

This intrepid crew of youthful hikers from Occoneechee Council in North Carolina was led into the backcountry by Ranger Greg Yeaton (seated, far right) in June 1976. Their itinerary took them past Ute Gulch through the north country to Miranda, Baldy Town and Baldy Mountain, French Henry, Ponil for a Bicentennial campfire, Indian Writings, and back to base camp. (News and Photo Services, Philmont Scout Ranch.)

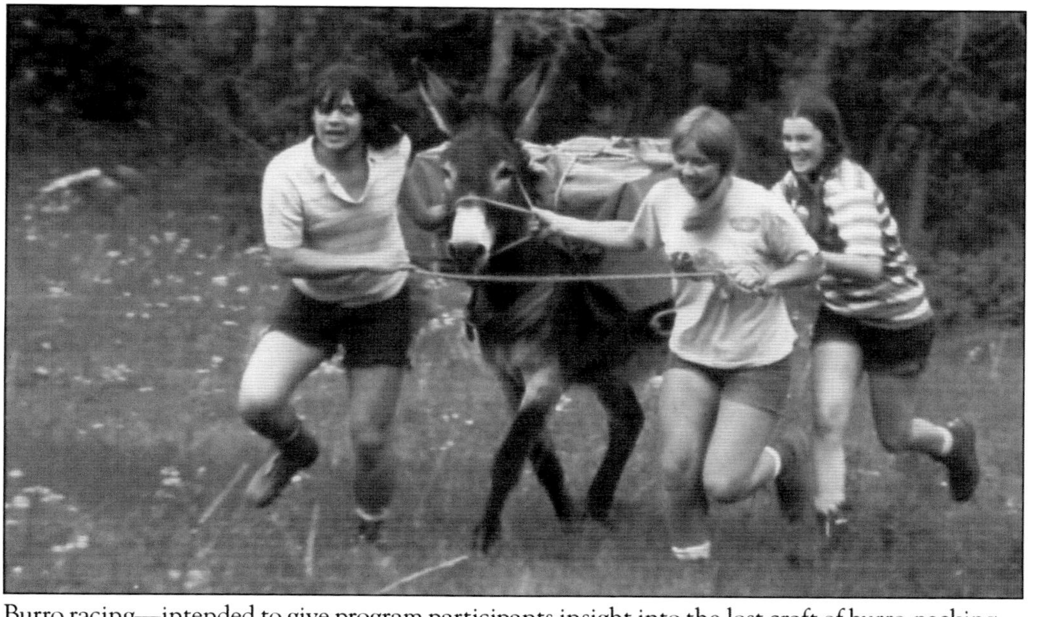

Burro racing—intended to give program participants insight into the lost craft of burro-packing—has a rich history at Philmont. Especially during the 1940s when the Philmont herd numbered 200, pack-trains of five or six burros carried gear for 15 to 18 Scouts and adult leaders during the longest treks. These noble creatures were lauded in Frank Brookshier's 1967 book *The Philmont Pack-Jacks*. Viva el burro! (Authors' collection.)

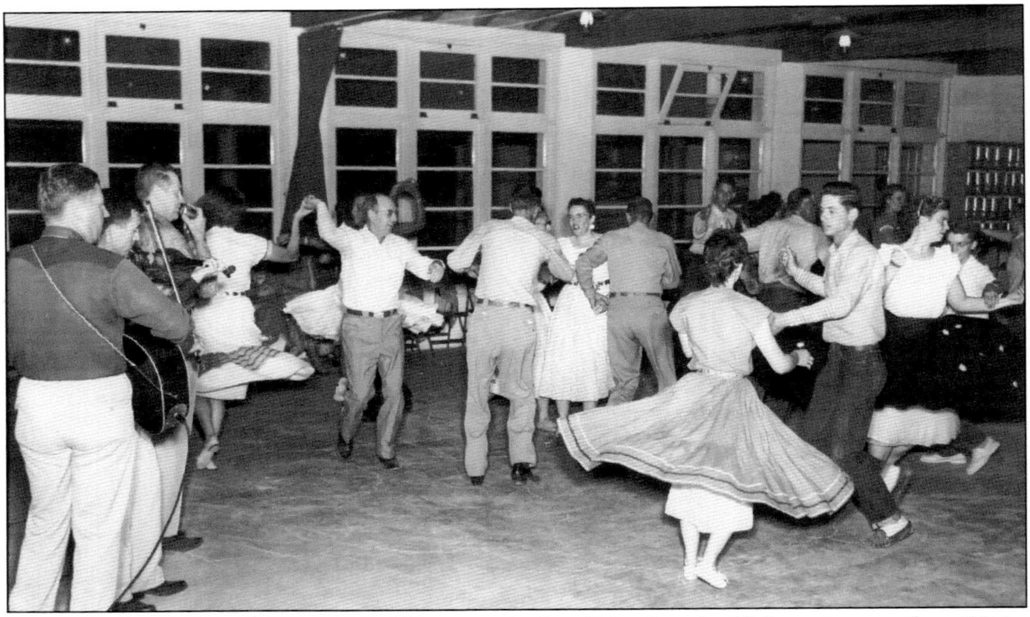

Under the leadership of Chief Scout Executive Arthur Schuck and with keen interest from Waite Phillips, the Philmont Training Center (PTC) was established around the Villa Philmonte in 1950. Tent cities opened in 1951 and 1957, and permanent facilities were built to provide an outstanding venue for Scouters and their families. Western night has been a staple of the PTC experience since the early 1950s. (Philmont Scout Ranch.)

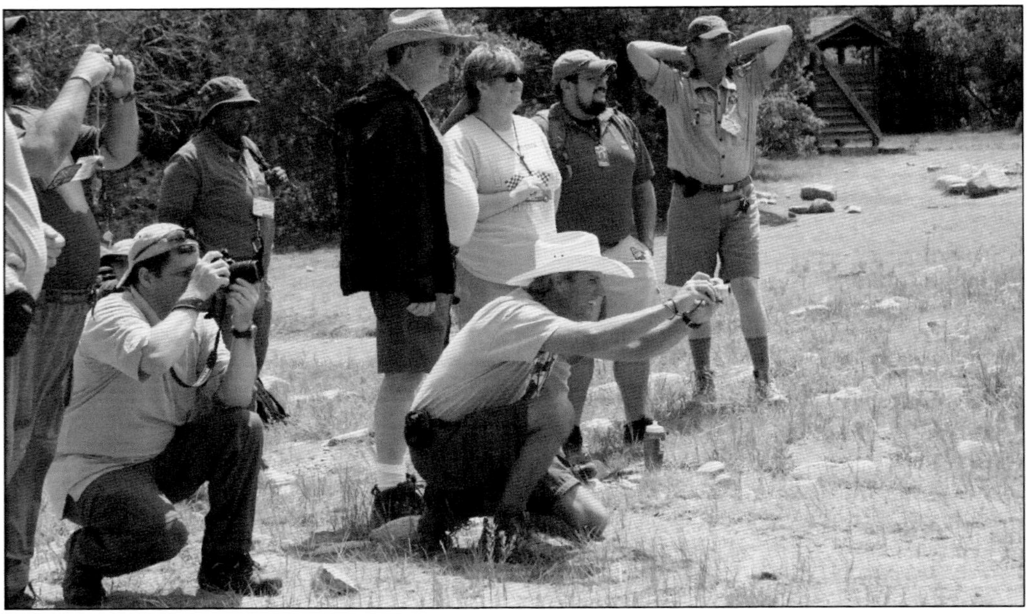

PTC instruction these days is as likely to occur outside of the classroom as within. This group of Scouters pauses for photographs near the Rocky Mountain Scout Camp below the Tooth of Time during a conference on geocaching and Scouting. Two of the faculty, Mary (not shown) and Brad Stevens (center, kneeling) were instrumental in bring geocaching to Scouting on a national level and helped shape the Philmont Leadership Challenge. (Authors' collection.)

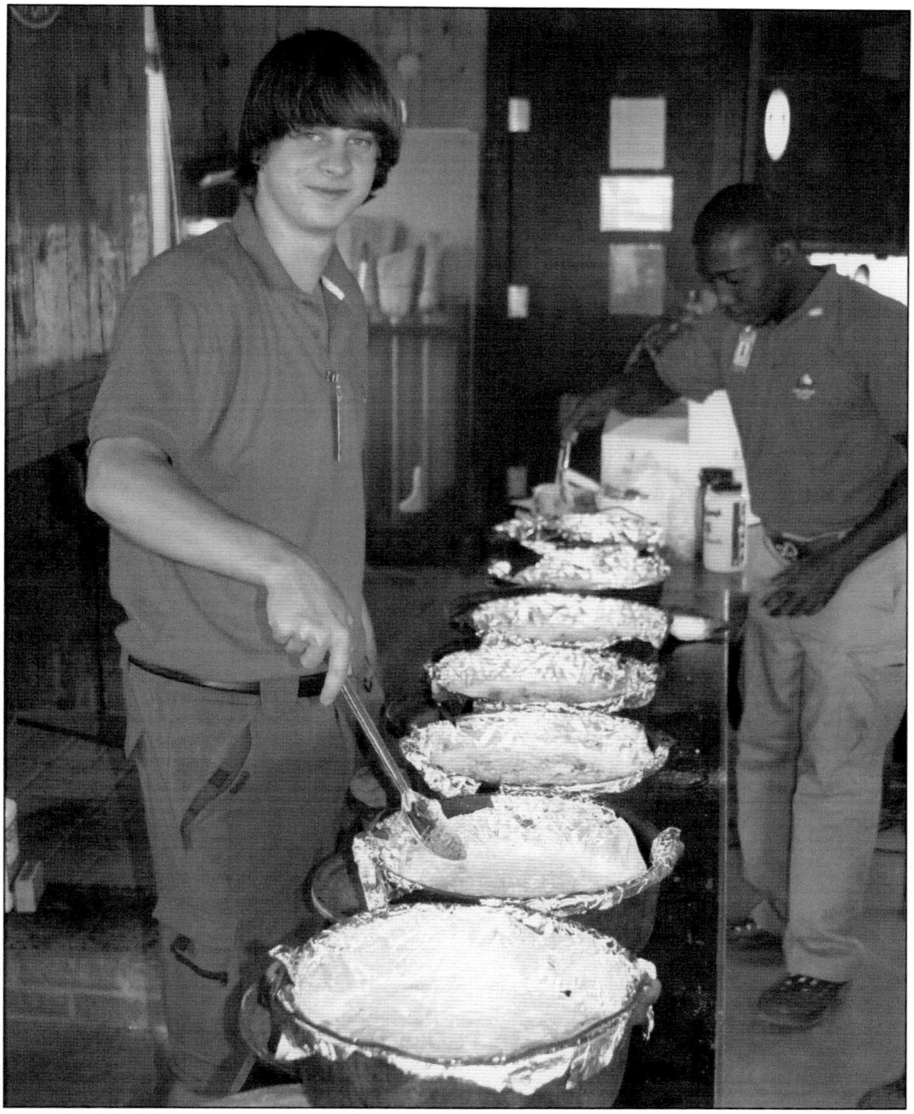

Staff members Aaron Smith (left) and Reginald Saintilus prepare flavorful Dutch oven–cooked cobbler for scores of Philmont Training Center participants one languid summer eve, while nearby, the PTC Wanna-Be Band provides sing-along entertainment. Each summer, Philmont Scout Ranch employs more than 1,000 superbly trained seasonal staff members to administer the exceptional wilderness and educational programs for which Philmont is known and admired. Philmont staff have diverse responsibilities. They serve in interpretive, program, or service-backcountry camps; as part of the ranger staff responsible for leading crews into the backcountry to begin hiking treks; in the dining halls; as wranglers; in logistical, support, administrative, and other roles at Camping Headquarters (CHQ), or at the Philmont Training Center. Thousands of staff and participants have also been affected by people they will never meet, such as Carlos and Valentina Gutierrez of Springer. As owners of the Springer Tribune Press for more than 40 years, Carlos and Valentina have printed Philmont promotional literature and books. They, too, have a Philmont story to tell, through their work and that of their daughters Lorraine and Nancy, who served on staff. (Authors' collection.)

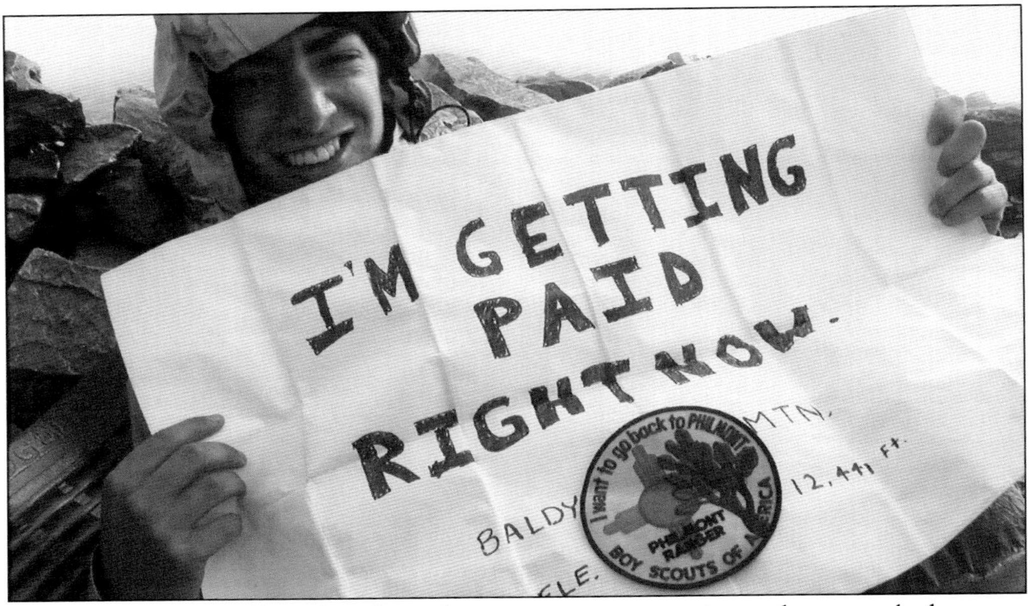

Philmont seasonal staff members have the opportunity to experience phenomenal adventures in the backcountry and throughout northeastern New Mexico. They are also well rewarded for their hard work, develop transferable leadership skills, and form enduring friendships. Ranger Alex Klausing sums things up well in this view atop Baldy Mountain, where he proudly displays his ranger staff patch after scaling Philmont's highest peak. (Alex Klausing.)

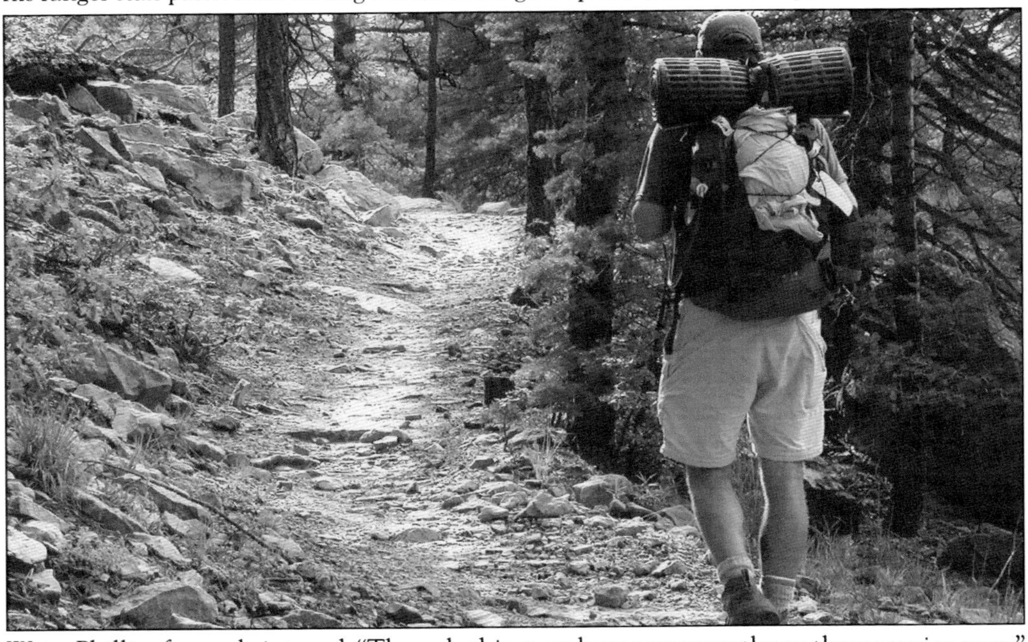

Waite Phillips famously intoned, "The only things we keep permanently are those we give away." Nearly one million have hiked the winding paths of Philmont; have received youth or adult Scout leadership training at the Philmont Training Center, Zastrow, or Rayado; or have otherwise benefited from the remarkable magnanimity of the Phillips family. Their generosity has infused lives and enriched souls, and for that, they should be thanked. (Alex Klausing.)

Bibliography

Armstrong, Ruth W. *The Chases of Cimarron: Birth of the Cattle Industry in Cimarron Country, 1867–1900.* Albuquerque: New Mexico Stockman, 1981.

Caffey, David L. *Frank Springer and New Mexico: From the Colfax County War to the Emergence of Modern Santa Fe.* College Station: Texas A&M University Press, 2007.

Cimarron Elementary Fourth Grade Students. *Where the Mountains Meet the Plains: The Cimarron Country Past and Present.* Cimarron: Cimarron Municipal School District, 2003.

The Cimarron News and Cimarron Citizen, *Cimarron News and Press*, and *Cimarron News-Citizen*. Various dates.

Murphy, Lawrence R. *Lucien Bonaparte Maxwell: The Napoleon of the Southwest.* Norman: University of Oklahoma Press, 1983.

———. *Philmont: a History of New Mexico's Cimarron Country.* Albuquerque: University of New Mexico Press, 1972.

Paisley, David P. *Miner's Park: A Climber's Guide.* Self-published, 1984.

Pearson, Jim Berry. *The Maxwell Land Grant.* Norman: University of Oklahoma Press, 1961.

Price, L. Greer, ed. *The Geology of Northern New Mexico's Parks, Monuments, and Public Lands.* Socorro: New Mexico Bureau of Geology and Mineral Resources, 2010.

Stanley, F. *The Grant that Maxwell Bought.* Denver: World Press, 1952.

———. *One Half Mile from Heaven: Or, the Cimarron Story.* Denver: World Press, 1949.

Taylor, Morris F. *O. P. McMains and the Maxwell Land Grant Conflict.* Tucson: University of Arizona Press, 1979.

Thomas, Alfred B. *After Coronado.* Norman: University of Oklahoma Press, 1966.

Wilson, Delphine Dawson. *John Barkley Dawson: Pioneer, Cattleman, Rancher.* Self-published, 1997.

Zimmer, Stephen. *For Good or Bad: People of the Cimarron Country.* Santa Fe: Sunstone Press, 1999.